STUDIES IN IMPERIALISM

general editor John M. MacKenzie

Established in the belief that imperialism as a cultural phenomenon had as significant an effect on the dominant as on the subordinate societies, Studies in Imperialism seeks to develop the new socio-cultural approach which has emerged through cross-disciplinary work on popular culture, media studies, art history, the study of education and religion, sports history and children's literature. The cultural emphasis embraces studies of migration and race, while the older political and constitutional, economic and military concerns are never far away. It incorporates comparative work on European and American empire-building, with the chronological focus primarily, though not exclusively, on the nineteenth and twentieth centuries, when these cultural exchanges were most powerfully at work.

Cultural identities and the aesthetics of Britishness

Published in our
centenary year
~ 2004 ~
MANCHESTER
UNIVERSITY
PRESS

Cultural identities and the aesthetics of Britishness

edited by Dana Arnold

MANCHESTER
UNIVERSITY PRESS
Manchester and New York

Distributed exclusively in the USA
by PALGRAVE

Published by MANCHESTER UNIVERSITY PRESS
OXFORD ROAD, MANCHESTER M13 9NR, UK
and ROOM 400, 175 FIFTH AVENUE, NEW YORK, NY 10010, USA
www.manchesteruniversitypress.co.uk

Distributed exclusively in the USA by
PALGRAVE, 175 FIFTH AVENUE, NEW YORK, NY 10010, USA

Distributed exclusively in Canada by
UBC PRESS, UNIVERSITY OF BRITISH COLUMBIA,
2029 WEST MALL, VANCOUVER, BC, CANADA V6T 1Z2

British Library Cataloguing-in-Publication Data
A catalogue record for this book is available from the British Library

Library of Congress Cataloging-in-Publication Data applied for

ISBN   0 7190 6768 5   hardback
       0 7190 6769 3   paperback

First published 2004

13 12 11 10 09 08 07 06 05 04   10 9 8 7 6 5 4 3 2 1

Typeset in Trump Medieval
by SNP Best-set Typesetter Ltd., Hong Kong
Printed in Great Britain
by Biddles Ltd, Guildford and King's Lynn

CONTENTS

ILLUSTRATIONS

GENERAL EDITOR'S INTRODUCTION

Let us imagine a historical conceit. We are set down, unexpectedly and without any briefing, in some part of the nineteenth- and early twentieth-century 'British world', in Ireland, in India, or some other part of the Empire, in an exhibition pavilion in Europe or overseas, in an art exhibition in an imperial city or town, even in a public park. We do not have the benefit of language and are only able to use our eyes and our aesthetic sense. Would we know immediately that the character of spatial arrangement, of architecture, artistic sensibility or selection, statuary, even the human 'formation' of landscape, pointed to this being part of that British imperial world, in however exotic a location, distinguishable from equivalents emerging from the French, German, Dutch or Italian empires?

It is the argument of this book that the answer, generally, would be 'yes', that a British aesthetic, however modified and manipulated in different contexts, can be identified as emerging over the past 200 or so years. It is an aesthetic that can be distinguished in a whole range of cultural forms, media and contexts (including the textual), emerging and extending over a period of almost 200 years. Moreover, we can read into it not only adaptation to locale, but also aspects of gender, of projected and perceived identities (personal, group and national), and notions of the patriotic, of a polity defined by royalty, even of cultural hegemony and incorporation.

This fundamental and striking contention may well be extendable to almost all aspects of an imperial culture throughout the world. Indeed the applications are almost limitless. This anglobal aesthetic can be found in the architectural presentation of technology, as in the railway station, in the 'furniture' of parks and botanical gardens, in distinctive approaches to 'orientalist' forms and in the extraordinary phenomenon of international exhibitions and expositions. It appears in the presentation of power through the 'government house', the law courts, military barracks, statues and monuments in squares, maidans and padangs; in the announcement of cultural influence in the mission station, the cathedral, church, cemetery, or the museum and art gallery; in the proclamation of economic assimilation through the plantation, the warehouse, the port, or the transport infrastructure; and in the assertion of racial and social superiority in the mansion, the club, the hotel, the school and the sportsground. All of these make statements about the (ultimately doomed) attempt of imperial peoples to create worldwide power systems and communities, about specific identities, and modes of political, cultural, military and economic power.

In other words, this book marks a path-breaking moment in the discussion of such a distinctive aesthetic. Its ideas and concepts can be developed, modified and applied in many other contexts and periods. It presents essays which are thought-provoking exactly because the reader will immediately make extra connections and applications.

It is thus, genuinely, a work which should stimulate additional research and debate. It is much to be hoped that many other publications will flow from it.

John M. MacKenzie

NOTES ON CONTRIBUTORS

DANA ARNOLD is Professor of Architectural History at the University of Southampton and Director of the Centre for Studies in Architecture and Urbanism. Her recent publications include: *A Very Short Introduction to Art History*, Oxford University Press, 2003; *Reading Architectural History*, Routledge, 2002; *Re-presenting the Metropolis: Architecture, Urban Experience and Social Life in London*, Ashgate, 2000; and the edited volumes (with Margaret Iversen) *Art and Thought*, Blackwell, 2003, and *The Metropolis and its Image: Constructing Identities for London c.1750–1950*, Blackwell, 1999. She is the series editor of New Interventions in Art History and general editor of two further series: Companions to Art History and Anthologies in Art History, all published by Blackwell. An anthology of her writings on London will be published by Manchester University Press in 2004.

ANDREW BALLANTYNE is Professor of Architecture at the University of Newcastle upon Tyne and Director of the Centre for Tectonic Cultures. His books include: *Architecture, Landscape and Liberty: Richard Payne Knight and the Picturesque*, Cambridge University Press, 1997; *What Is Architecture?* Routledge, 2001, and *Architecture: A Very Short Introduction*, Oxford University Press, 2002. He is the editor of: *Architectures: Modernism and After*, in the Blackwell series New Interventions in Art History; *Architecture Theory*, Continuum; and (with Dana Arnold) *Architecture as Experience*, published by Routledge.

FREDERICK N. BOHRER is Associate Professor of Art at Hood College in Frederick, Maryland (USA). He is the author of *Orientalism and Visual Culture: Imagining Mesopotamia in 19th Century Europe*, Cambridge University Press, 2003, and the editor of *Antoin Sevruguin and the Persian Image: Photographs from Iran 1870–1930*, Smithsonian Institution and University of Washington Press, 1999.

JULIE F. CODELL is Professor of Art History at Arizona State University. She has received six National Endowment for the Humanities' fellowships and grants and a fellowship from the Yale British Art Center. Her articles on Victorian art and culture have appeared in many scholarly journals, anthologies of collected essays and encyclopaedias. She wrote *Lives of the Artists: Artists' Lifewritings in Britain, c.1870–1910*, Cambridge University Press, 2002, and co-edited *Orientalism Transposed: The Impact of the Colonies on British Culture*, Ashgate, 1998. She is currently preparing a book entitled *'Nothing but the Sight': Visuality, Culture, and Imperial Identities in the Delhi Coronation Durbars and their Exhibitions of Indian Art, 1877–1910*, to be published in 2003.

CONTRIBUTORS

MARK CRINSON is Senior Lecturer at the University of Manchester, where he is also Head of the School of Art History and Archaeology. His books include: *Architecture – Art or Profession? 300 Years of Architectural Education* (with Jules Lubbock), Manchester University Press, 1994; *Empire Building: Orientalism and Victorian Architecture*, Routledge, 1996; and *Modern Architecture and the End of Empire*, Ashgate, 2002.

SOPHIA CROSS was born in Northern Ireland. She holds an MA in Country House Studies from Leeds University and is currently undertaking a part-time PhD at Southampton University entitled 'The Irish Country House 1790–1840: an exploration of identities and meanings'.

FINTAN CULLEN is Head of the Department of Art History and the author of *Visual Politics. The Representation of Ireland 1750–1930*, 1997, and *Sources in Irish Art: A Reader*, 2000, both published by Cork University Press. His contribution to this volume forms part of a forthcoming study on the politics of display in colonial Ireland. He has recently completed a book on Irish portraiture for the National Portrait Gallery, London.

JOCELYN HACKFORTH-JONES is Professor of Art History and Provost at Richmond, the American International University, London. She has published extensively on landscape painting and colonialism, as well as intercultural education and the visual arts. Her most recent book is *(Re)Forming Identities: Intercultural Education and the Visual Arts*. She is currently working on an exhibition for the National Portrait Gallery, London, titled 'London's Complexions. The Visual Representation of Non-Europeans in London, *c.*1750–1850' scheduled for 2006.

CYNTHIA E. ROMAN assumed the position of Curator of Prints, Drawings, and Paintings at the Lewis Walpole Library, Yale University in May 2003. Prior to that she was Associate Curator of European Art at the Wadsworth Atheneum Museum of Art, Hartford, Connecticut and Acting Director of the Watson Art Gallery, Wheaton College. Dr. Roman received her PhD from Brown University in 1997 writing her dissertation on Robert Bowyer's Historic Galley. She has taught courses in the history of art at Saint Joseph College, the University of Hartford, and Trinity College, Hartford. She was curator and catalogue author for the exhibition *From Canaletto to Constable: Paintings of Town and Country from the Yale Center for British Art* for venues in Hartford (1998) and Ferrara, Italy (2001) and has organized many exhibitions from the permanent collection of prints and drawings at the Wadsworth Atheneum.

SAM SMILES lectures in art history at Plymouth University. He has written widely on British art *c.*1750–1940. His books include *The Image of Antiquity: Ancient Britain and the Romantic Imagination*, Yale University Press, 1994, as well as studies on Turner and aspects of pictorial representation in the eighteenth and nineteenth centuries.

Introduction

Dana Arnold

The need for a single public culture – the creation of an authentic identity – is fundamental to our understanding of nationalism and nationhood. How are these manufactured cultural identities expressed? This book considers those questions in relation to the ways in which the aesthetics of national identities promoted the idea of *nation* that encompassed the doctrine of popular freedom and liberty from external constraint. Particular attention is paid to the political and social contexts of national identities within the British Isles; the export, adoption and creation of new identities in the British colonial world; and the role of gender in the forging of those identities. These elements combine to show that nationhood and nationalism are self-consciously defined tools to focus loyalty and are part of the larger process of making cultural identities. The focus of this study is the national, imperial and colonial aesthetic – how the aesthetics of architecture, landscape, painting, sculpture and literature were used, appropriated and re-appropriated in the furtherance of particular social and political aims. In this way aesthetic culture reinforced the culture of the dominant political and social ideologies; and it re-presented and reconstructed the notion of a national identity.

Each of the chapters of this volume provides a discrete investigation into these issues with particular reference to the interaction of indigenous cultural identity and empire, and how this impacted on the making of 'Britishness' in all its complexities. In this way the chapters provide stepping-stones across this complicated terrain which allow the reader to map important moments in the self-conscious evolution of the idea of *nation* against the broad cultural and historical frameworks of the book. The predominant themes that help form this narrative thread across the chapters include the landscape, together with picturesque and sublime systems of viewing it; the relationship between the past – history – and modernity in the making of national identity; the role of women; and, not least, the politics and ideology of exhibitions and display. In all the chapters a dialectical relationship between some or all of these themes emerges as an internal dynamic within the case study itself and as part of a larger discourse within the book as a whole.

Over the last twenty years the subject of colonialism has received much attention from scholars across a range of interconnected fields.[1] It is not the intention here to rehearse such arguments, nor to apply them to the specifics of *Britishness*. Instead, this volume examines the idea of empire from the point of view of the 'old colony', Anglo-Saxon, subject–object. To that end the period covered by the essays finishes at the eve of the Second World War – after which the entire structure of the British empire and British national identity changes. The concerns of post-colonial discourses tend to focus on the effects and consequences of colonization on the colonized. For instance in *The Location of Culture* Homi Bhabha[2] explores how the experience of empire and the end of empire have shaped and been shaped by culture. In the essay 'The postcolonial and the postmodern', Bhabha writes: 'a range of contemporary critical theories suggest that it is from those who have suffered the sentence of history – subjugation, domination, diaspora, displacement – that we learn our most enduring lessons for living and thinking'. In the light of Bhabha's ideas the wide range of voices from former new colonies, the Indian subcontinent or South America could shed a comparative, if not a more contentious, light on the aesthetics of Britishness. Although the aesthetics of Britishness as such is beyond our present concerns, one of the aims of this study is to highlight further areas of research into the visual culture of Britishness and its aesthetic consequences.

The Western viewpoint of this book does not attempt to negate these 'other' voices or arguments, nor does it ignore the post-colonial frames through which empire and colonialism have been viewed in the last two decades. Indeed, some chapters are clearly informed by these paradigms, while others, through their interests in indigenous constructions of Britishness, stand outside them. But the collective interests of the contributors point the way to a kind of 'unlearning' of the discourses of post-colonialism as a means of revisiting the cultural formulations behind the making of Britishness.[3]

Whose empire?

The importance of text and verbalized imagery to the creation of an imperial frame of mind – the cultural representation of Britain – is the subject of much post-colonial discourse. This aspect of the 'cultures of empire' is ably discussed by Catherine Hall in the Introduction to her volume of the same name, and does not warrant repetition here.[4] Suffice to say in this context that the *visual* rather than the verbal aesthetic have remained on the margins of the literature concerning the cultures of colonialism. But the idea that 'nation' can be 'imagined' or aestheticized opens up the possibilities for discourse around the different constructions of cultural identity. Edward Said first explored the idea of a cultural identity and its relationship to colonialism in his now canonical work *Orientalism*,[5] but the focus remains on textual discourses and the narratives of the formation of imperial and anti-imperial attitudes. Some of these issues are taken up in Said's later work *Culture and Imperialism*[6] in which his discussion of how 'the Orient' was constructed by Westerners as an explanation of the nature of the West shows how it became a reflective tool with which to articulate the existence and justify the behaviour of the 'Occidental' colonial powers. The extraordinary reach of Western imperialism in the nineteenth and early twentieth centuries is a predominant aspect of geopolitical history. Rome, Byzantium and Spain at the height of their glory did not come close to the imperial scope of France, the United States of America and, in particular, Great Britain in those years. Said argues that the justification for empire-building was inescapably embedded in the Western cultural imagination during the 'age of empire', and the imperial legacy remains influential on relations between the West and the formerly colonized world at every level of political, ideological and social practice. Said concentrates on literature, and not the visual arts, using a broad range of canonical works – including Jane Austen's *Mansfield Park*, Joseph Conrad's *Heart of Darkness* and Albert Camus' *L'Etranger* as his evidence. Through these examples he shows how culture and politics co-operated, knowingly and unknowingly, to produce a system of domination that involved more than military might – to produce a Western sovereignty that extended over forms and images, and the very imaginations of both the dominators and the dominated. The result was a 'consolidated vision' that affirmed not only the Europeans' right to rule but also their obligation to do so.

By contrast with Said's concerns, this book's interest is in the mechanisms involved in the creation of this 'consolidated vision'. The process of unpacking this vision, as it is worked through in each of the chapters, reveals complex and diverse results and possibilities. The broad time span of this volume and the cross-disciplinary subject matter are indicative of the possibility that the aesthetics of Britishness have varied in the purpose, expression and display between colonial situations, climates and periods. And it is part of the aim of the volume to highlight this potentially fruitful area of research. Whereas post-colonial study establishes the Western hegemony that is a necessary part of its discourse, this volume attempts to fracture that colonial monolith to examine the strategies used in the telling of the various narratives of nationalism and cultural identity. Moreover, the discussion is focused specifically on Britain – both the construction of a British national identity in colonial circumstances as well as at home, rather than the broader arena of European or Western imperialism.

Constructions of nation

The broader world stage is also the concern of Benedict Anderson's enduring and hugely influential *Imagined Communities: Reflections on the Origin and Spread of Nationalism*.[7] Anderson argues that national identity and national institutions are highly specific historical products. To that end he emphasizes the importance of print technologies in the process of nation-making and delineates the process by which the nation came to be at once imagined, modelled, adopted and transformed. He shows how the European processes of inventing nationalism were transported to the developing world through colonialism and adapted by subject races in Latin America and Asia, suggesting that nationalism was created in the eighteenth century as an 'imagined community' or a 'cultural artefact'.[8] For Anderson, the development of nationalism stems from the convergence of capitalism and print technology on human language, which is primarily responsible for the emotional attachment to nationalism. The global historical and present-day concerns of Anderson's study, which appeared almost a generation ago, are here focused in on Britain. Nationalism as a self-consciously constructed cultural artefact or imagined community – as expressed through different modes of visual rather than literary formulae, albeit that these formulae may have a literary or linguistic basis – becomes the route through which these kinds of national identities can be interrogated. Anderson's argument that print culture was central to the creation of an 'imagined' nation' is concerned principally with the act of reading, situating culture within a verbalized tradition. Homi Bhabha echoes this analysis of the construction of cultural identity, and his *Nation and Narration* explores the emergence of the novel and a growing sense of national identity.[9] These models for analysis can, however, be used in relation to the visual, and this is made evident by the chapters of this volume.

[4]

The problem of culture

The expression of Britishness through a visual cultural identity is a central concern of this volume. With that in mind, Raymond Williams's observation in *Keywords*[10] that 'culture' is one of the two or three most complex words in the English language indicates the complexity of locating specific cultural identities in relationship to Britishness. Williams observes that the notion of 'culture' is derived from 'husbandry, the tending of natural growth'. From the sixteenth century on this was extended to a process of human development: in Bacon's words, 'the culture and manurance of minds'. Williams identifies Herder's *Ideas of the Philosophy of the History of Mankind*[11] as a key moment in the evolution of the term. Herder argued the necessity of speaking of 'cultures', in the plural, attacking the assumption of the universal histories that 'civilization' or 'culture' – the historical self-development of humanity – was what we would now call a unilinear process, leading to the high and dominant point of eighteenth-century European culture. But this idea of culture places emphasis on national and traditional cultures, and brings to the fore the problematical relationship between the notions of 'culture' and 'civilization'. And it is the 'civilizing' aesthetic of Britishness that emerges as a potent theme in this volume. In recent years there has been a certain fashionable populism in the discourses of culture. In his recent study *The Idea of Culture*, Terry Eagleton considers why 'culture' has achieved its predominant position in our own period, and provocatively proposes, while acknowledging its significance, that it is time to put 'culture' back in its place.[12] Eagleton suggests that the denotation of 'culture' is perhaps 'both too broad and too narrow to be greatly useful'. But the word, precisely by virtue of its protean meanings, opens up a space in which the narratives around the construction of cultural identities in a colonial world can become part of the broader discourse that untells these stories.

The aesthetic

The aesthetic of the 'imagined political community' is discussed by Terry Eagleton in *The Ideology of the Aesthetic*. He sees the bourgeois subject as an essential agent in the establishing of a 'republic of taste' in which is encapsulated the range of values from good to evil, virtue to vice. But for Eagleton the whole of social life is aestheticized, and this signifies an inherently cohesive social order. By contrast, this volume sees aesthetic identities as more complex: while accepting Eagleton's proposed connection between aestheticization and nation –

which admits political and economic circumstances into the discourse – attention remains focused on the aesthetic consequences of those identities. The contributors to this book confront the internal discourses of notions of display, or art practice, in its broadest constituencies, whether it be issues of the picturesque or the sublime; classical versus Gothic architecture. As a consequence, these discourses are externalized to allow an examination of the practices and technologies of power expressed through the aesthetic to formulate a cultural identity that represents 'Britishness'.

The opening chapters focus on the eighteenth-century notion of a national school of art, architecture or landscape design, where the notion that aesthetic characteristics portray cultural characteristics is most firmly established. The opening chapter is Cynthia E. Roman's consideration of how a nation views itself and how this frame of viewing is revised and reviewed in response to broader cultural concerns. Roman's argument centres on Robert Bowyer's Historic Gallery – a series of prints of nationalistic subjects and the use of women in those images. During the late eighteenth century in Britain, the middle classes, empowered by commercial wealth, struggled for increased social and political power in the nation, in part by appropriating the authority of cultural expression. Guided by an tacit republicanism, Robert Bowyer's Historic Gallery and the accompanying illustrated edition of David Hume's *History of England* (1792–1806) challenged prevailing notions of British national identity that privileged the civic virtues and actions of the aristocratic male. The heroes in the historical pictures that Bowyer commissioned and published generally engage in some exemplary instance of feminized social behaviour. Many compositions directly feature female protagonists and the incidents of female subjects increased with the chronological advance of history and an espoused corresponding refinement of civilization. By assigning increasing importance to heroines, and thereby to feminine sentiment, Bowyer constructed an alternative national identity that reached beyond the civic virtue of the privileged to include members of the commercial classes, both male and female. In other words, ideal social behaviour was to some degree feminized and woman displaced man to become the primary site or model of domestic bonds that could be transferred to broader social models such as nationhood.

The theme of the resonance between literary and visual representations of *nation* continues in Jocelyn Hackforth-Jones's discussion of landscape in Wales and New South Wales from the late eighteenth to the mid-nineteenth century in relation to the creation of cultural identities. Her chapter introduces the aesthetics of the picturesque and the Burkean sublime as systems for viewing colonial landscapes, which remain important themes throughout the volume, Here, the sublime elevates the meaning of mountainous terrain to a representation of liberty and shows how, when used as a technique to represent the unfamiliar Australian landscape, the latter became familiar as it began to look like that of Wales. Hackforth-Jones considers why a colonial framework may be appropriate in relation to both 'new' and 'old' worlds, when comparing paintings of landscapes in Wales and New South Wales (given that the discourse of colonialism generally relates to Australia, Africa and the Americas during this period) and why such a comparison is useful for attempts to unpack different constructs of national identity. The parallels in the visual and literary views of Snowdonia (Wales) and the Blue Mountains (New South Wales) demonstrate how the views of each mountain range can be read in terms of forming and re-forming different national identities: Welsh, British, English and Australian. By demonstrating that landscape painting is not a fixed and stable aesthetic practice, Hackforth-Jones picks up on the notion introduced by Roman that history and liberty could combine to subvert traditionalizing forces in the construction of cultural identities.

Sophia Cross's chapter offers an aesthetic reading of the country house in Ireland in the opening decades of the nineteenth century, presenting it as a meeting-point between history and national identity where the re-ordering of its landscape and its architectural design both subvert and endorse political control. In an evocative analogy Cross argues that the Irish country house is comparable to the flags that colour the streets of present-day Northern Ireland – both are assertions of social, political and religious beliefs. In a country where land has been so ruthlessly broken up and distributed, insecurity is commonplace in the minds of the people of Ireland, and the juxtaposition of different political and religious beliefs problematizes the concept of 'the nation'. The turbulent history of Northern Ireland has shaped the design of many of its country houses – and has destroyed them as well, leaving them to stand derelict and desolate. Even in their ruined state, they remain a forceful presence; reminding us that people once lived there. In this way architecture, like illustrations and literature, becomes another form of propaganda and a tool in the creation of a national image and its political symbols. Here, Cross argues for the similarity of a flag, which might be construed as a more direct way of portraying cultural beliefs, and a country house, which is just as powerful in illustrating allegiance. On one level they fulfil an aesthetic function, but on another their appreciation requires and understanding of the culture from which they were created and which they are intended to represent.

The questioning of cultural characteristics and a national aesthetic continues in the editor's own essay on the Phoenix Park, Dublin, in the context of the making of an Anglo-Irish identity. The park was both a symbol of the city and of the British colonial presence. The improvement work in the Phoenix Park carried out between 1832 and 1849 is comparable to that carried out in the royal parks in London earlier in the century. As such it is argued that the Phoenix Park becomes a countersite – a Foucauldian heterotopia – of the capital of Britain and empire. The work in the royal parks in London has been shown to be one way in which the State tried to shape that urban experience and social interaction through the design of specific environments. This can also be identified as one of the motives behind the improvements to the Phoenix Park as many of the key figures involved in the project had also worked in the royal parks in London. This chapter constructs a contextualizing framework for the improvement of the park, examining its social, historical and cultural significance against the backdrop of important political change – not least the 1829 Act of Catholic Emancipation and the 1832 Reform Act. In this way the redesigning of the Phoenix Park becomes both a barometer of Anglo-Irish relations at that time and a means of exploring how the increasingly politically important Protestant urban bourgeoisie found an aesthetic identity in this colonial context.

The complex relationship between mainland Britain and its geographically closest colony continues in Andrew Ballantyne's chapter. Here again aesthetic theory, in the form of picturesque systems of viewing and the Burkean sublime, is used to examine literary and architectural constructions of national identity and the role of women as embodiments of national virtue. Continuing the debates of Dana Arnold's chapter, Ballantyne examines the politics of land-ownership as played out within the arena of the oppositional forces of the Irish Catholics and the Anglo-Irish Protestant ascendancy. Ballantyne's discussion, which considers two novels, opens with the Irish patriot Sydney Owenson, later Lady Morgan, who drew heavily on the theory of the picturesque in *The Wild Irish Girl* (1806), her third novel but her first major success. The discussion of the ways of viewing the landscape in her novel continue the debates about systems of viewing as a means of making the unfamiliar familiar raised by Hackforth-Jones in the context of Wales and New South Wales. Morgan's novel is paired with Benjamin Disraeli's *Sybil, or The Two Nations* (1845), which made strong associations between the heroine and the Gothic Revival, making the architectural style of the new Palace of Westminster emblematic of the one-nation toryism of the pre-Reformation aristocracy. Ballantyne argues that the two novels belong together because they share many characteristics. In each a female figure is made to embody the admirable qualities of an ancient autochthonous aristocracy which has been supplanted and is alienated from power and influence. In each the female figure is linked with a fashionable aesthetic which associates her with ruined places. And each novel's final resolution is achieved by means of a marriage across a sectarian divide. While Morgan uses this to emphasize the social and political divisions in Ireland, Disraeli is trying to invent a new national identity around and for the increasingly important urban middle class – a project not dissimilar to the remodelling of the Phoenix Park.

The particular concern of the chapter, however, is to draw attention to the way in which each novel brings architecture – in each case ancient buildings in ruins – into play in establishing the sense of national identity, and in each case the sense of national identity is called upon in the hope that it will be able to bring about practical political change. In each case the appeal is for people to listen not to those who currently wield power but to an older and more legitimate authority. In this way the use of the past identified by Ballantyne recalls the moralizing of Bowyer and Hume, while at the same time it strengthens the important role played by architectural aesthetics in the making of national identities, both core themes in the volume.

In Frederick N. Bohrer's essay attention turns again to Britain and the formation of British national identity. Bohrer argues that the reception of Austen Henry Layard's Mesopotamian discoveries in early Victorian England marks a unique moment in both the uniform enforcement and varied inflection of English national identity during a period of social cleavage and conflict. His close examination of the rhetoric of nationalism in a few specimens of commentary and imagery in the early coverage of Layard's finds reveals a situation in which the Mesopotamian 'other' (both ancient and modern) is narrowly defined and fixed across a wide social spectrum of British media. Indeed, Bohrer suggests this fixity contrasts sharply with the varied and even contradictory representations of Britain and its population overtly at play in many of the same media. There is a contrast here between interpretations of ancient Assyrian artefacts and the pattern of their aesthetic evaluations (both positive and negative). The dynamic between Mesopotamian fixity and British complexity is shown to have roots in the prevailing structures of knowledge and power of the time, and to offer important material for the defining of conceptions of national identity. Bohrer works through this material using theoretical models devised by Homi Bhabha and Benedict Anderson. In this way the chapter explores further the dependence obtaining between the two positions in the making of cultural identities. This dialectical relationship defines a principle at work in an entire range of enunciated nationalisms, another of the central concerns of this volume.

Bohrer focuses on the multiple workings of a concept of *nation* which underlay, at key points, the overwhelmingly positive response to the ancient Assyrian discoveries made by Layard in the 1840s and enshrined in the British Museum in the years around 1850. His consideration of the public sponsorship and reception of a major archaeological project is, at the same time, a study of the varieties and motivations of nationhood behind the very project, and which demanded in various ways its assimilation into the museum the very name of which evoked the unified body of Britain: the British Museum, which paradoxically was a museum of antiquities (and few of them British). Here, the anxious, uneasy dialectic of modernity and tradition, each both supporting and undermining the other, built into the very structure of the modern nation is brought to the fore. And the modern nation's near-obsession with the distant past fulfils a number of different needs. Moreover, examining the process of fixing nationhood through temporal projections, like those triggered by Assyria, magnifies, and makes even more evident, the discontinuities upon which the nation itself is constructed.

Fintan Cullen's chapter explores a different kind of nationalist aesthetic, albeit once again in the context of nineteenth-century Ireland. The display of British art in Dublin and Belfast became part of the popular culture of imperialism. The Irish became the consumers and agents of British imperial triumphs, where Irish troops made up part of the British forces, as seen in the success of the paintings that depicted those victories as public attractions. Here the Foucauldian idea of the 'sovereign gaze' replaces the picturesque or the Burkean sublime as a system for viewing, where the colonized becomes the colonizer. Cullen focuses on 'imperialist' images and the extensive display of 'British' art throughout the period. He examines the visual sources that attracted public attention during the period and offers a definition of the art of the union. To that end Cullen uses the work of Ashis Nandy and others as a means of analysing the 'cultural damage' inflicted by colonialism on the internal cultures of Britain and Ireland. Representations of imperial success as well as royal portraits were common in Irish exhibitions throughout the century. Cullen's discussion focuses on the exhibition in Ireland of two paintings. The first is a huge imperialist panorama by Robert Ker Porter, shown in 1801, celebrating the defeat of the Tipú Sultán in India. The popularity of this image is matched, some sixty years later, in the display of T. J. Barker's painting *The Secret of England's Greatness, or Queen Victoria Pre-*

[10]

senting a Bible to an African Chief. Cullen argues that in these two paintings union and display became one in the history of nineteenth-century access to the visual arts.

Julie F. Codell's chapter shifts the focus to the construction of a modern British imperial identity as seen in the 1903 durbar exhibition of Indian art. Codell uses Clifford Geertz's idea of the exhibition of Indian art as a 'thick' cultural experience to explore its multiple and contradictory representations of British imperial identity within the framework of gentlemanly capitalism.[13] The extensive catalogue of the durbar exhibition revealed permeable margins that undermined superficially imposed distinct boundaries between Indian and British cultural identities, giving the exhibition multiple 'webs of significance', even among the British. This catalogue is contextualized within the existing art knowledge–power base, the British art schools in India and their organ, the *Journal of Indian Art*, which, Codell asserts, might be called the cultural arm of the Raj. Out of these institutional forces and conflicts between stated ideals and actual practices – the ethnography of the exhibition – emerged unintended meanings for this dual display of Indian culture and Raj management. Furthermore, the combination of the notion of gentlemanly capitalism with the exhibition's purpose – to exonerate Britain of complicity in the decline of Indian art production – made it impossible to seal off Indian culture from global market demands and modern technologies. Codell examines the Indian press's reception of the exhibition which recognized inherent contradictions within the constructions of an ideal Raj administration of empire and of an essentialized 'Indianness', both inscribed by global markets which the exhibition was required to satisfy in demonstrating the well-intentioned paternalism and efficiency of British imperial management. Indian nationalists chose the exhibition as a flashpoint for their own political programme, and even for their own competing exhibitions, further thickening the exhibition's meanings.

In Sam Smiles's chapter attention returns to the resonance of text and image in the making of a cultural identity in later nineteenth-century Britain and the revival of the imagery of the distant past as means of doing this. Smiles examines the place of Arthurian myth in aspects of British culture, focusing on the late nineteenth-century Arthurian subject paintings of Edward Burne-Jones. He carries through the discussion of the interest in this myth – or, as it became known, the Matter of Britain – into the early twentieth century as seen in the work of the writers David Jones (*In Parenthesis*, 1937) and Charles Williams (*Taliessin Through Logres*, 1938). Smiles does not offer new iconographic interpretations of images; instead, he establishes an appreciation of such work within the broader framework of the place of myth in modern Britain and its refurbishing for modern usage. The Britain that emerges from this discussion hovers between an imaginary and a historicist identity. The meaning and character of a country are to be found as much in its myths and ancient history as in its contemporary social, economic and political formation. Although we might want to characterize such beliefs as implicitly anti-modern, if the experience of modernity is defined as a sense of a break with the past, their presence in the mature work of some significant artists and writers working in the modern period points to an understanding of British national identity which is inherently opposed to any straightforward notion of historical progress.

Mark Crinson's chapter continues the discussion of cultural identities and the aesthetics of Britishness in the twentieth century, introduced by Smiles. As with the chapters by Cullen and Codell, the making of an identity within the context of an exhibition – albeit this time with an international audience – here provides the case study. Crinson examines the use of architecture as a means of national projection as represented by the British Government Pavilions erected for international exhibitions between the two world wars. His principal focus is the British Pavilion at the 1937 Paris International Exhibition, an event usually discussed in terms of the ideological clash of 'worlds on exhibition' embodied by the German and Soviet Pavilions. But it is argued that the British Pavilion can be seen as a much more ambivalent and controversial response to the prestige and politically charged polemics of the moment. Was it and its displays 'comely, pleasant . . . a liberal conspectus of our English life', or was there 'nothing distinctly British about it', a building which 'might be anything – riding school, an aerodrome, or a factory on or off the Great West Road'?

At the heart of this dispute, Crinson argues, lay the various and apparently irreconcilable interests invested in the characterization of British national identity between the wars. Indeed, these differences demonstrate the continuation of the oppositional forces that exist in this definition, which is a potent theme of the volume as a whole. On the one side were those concerned with the durability of the weld between nation and empire, and on the other those that felt a new alliance might be made between national projection and the emerging forms of modernism. The debates surrounding the 1937 pavilion were, Crinson concludes, a constant, if differently resolved, issue in other earlier inter-war British Government Pavilions: at Wembley (1924), Paris (1925), Antwerp (1930) and Johannesberg (1936). Crinson provides a stimulating contrast to the workings of an exhibition that was for colonial audiences (both colonizer and colonized) as discussed by Cullen and Codell. Moreover, Crinson's consideration of the problematical relationship between capitalism, modernity and the aesthetic picks up on Codell's observations. The volume ends, then, at a moment when national identities were beginning to shift and change on the eve of the Second World War, after which the establishing of the Commonwealth completely transforms the relationship between colonizer and colonized and the kinds of cultural identities expressed by visual means.

This book appears in the 'Studies in Imperialism' series, which now has a long-standing reputation for innovative modes of enquiry into all forms of imperial culture. The series has brought to the fore important material on expressions of empire through a vast range of cultural outputs, including juvenile literature, music, film and exhibitions. There is no doubt that the audience for these kinds of manifestations of empire was and remains broad and diverse. What this volume attempts to bring to these investigations into popular culture is a contrasting survey of the 'high culture' – the rarified cultural outputs – that represented empire and national identity for the social elite. It is not always possible to gauge what the broader reception of these visual expressions was – although this is addressed in some of the essays, including the editor's own and Mark Crinson's. But it is still necessary to explore these more *recherché* displays of empire: such exploration enables the aim of both the volume and the series to fracture the canonical monolith of colonial culture as high art to reveal the various narrative strategies involved in its creation. The beginning and end points of this survey – the connection between British art, national projection and the emergence of a coherent cultural identity – create an appropriate frame for a volume that considers this phenomenon across a broad time-span and through a range of examples.

Notes

1 These include Stuart Hall, Gayatri Spivak, Edward Said, Benedict Anderson, Catherine Hall, Terry Eagleton and Homi Bhabha, as well as a range of French theorists from Lacan and Fanon to Foucault and Derrida.
2 Homi K. Bhabha, *The Location of Culture*, London and New York, Routledge, 1994.
3 Here I am following the Derridean idea of unlearning where one has to be of a skill or process in order to not be of it. See J. Derrida, 'To unsense the subjectile', in J. Derrida and Paule Théverin, *The Secret of Antonin Artaud*, trans. Mary Ann Caws, Cambridge, MA, MIT Press, 1998.
4 Catherine Hall, *Cultures of Empire; Colonizers in Britain and the Empire in the Nineteenth and Twentieth Centuries*, Manchester, Manchester University Press, 2000.
5 Edward W. Said, *Orientalism*, New York, Pantheon Books; London, Routledge & Kegan Paul; Toronto, Random House, 1978.
6 Edward W. Said, *Culture and Imperialism*, New York, Knopf, 1993.
7 Benedict Anderson, *Imagined Communities: Reflections on the Origin and Spread of Nationalism*, London, Verso, 1983.

8 For Anderson, the strength of this idea is evident in the way in which it has spread even to socialist states whose Marxist doctrine rejects it and intersocialist wars such as those between revolutionary Marxist regimes – Vietnam, Cambodia and China.

9 Homi K. Bhabha (ed), *Nation and Narration*, London and New York, Routledge, 1990.

10 Raymond Williams, *Keywords: A Vocabulary of Culture and Society*, London, Fontana, 1976, p. 87.

11 Johann Gottfried von Herder, *Ideas for the Philosophy of History of Mankind, 1784–91*, in *J. G. Herder on Social and Political Culture*, trans. and ed. F. M. Bernard, Cambridge, Cambridge University Press, 1969.

12 Terry Eagleton, *The Idea of Culture* Oxford, Blackwell, 2000.

13 Clifford Geertz, *The Interpretation of Culture* New York, Basic Books, 1973.

CHAPTER ONE

Robert Bowyer's Historic Gallery and the feminization of the 'nation'

Cynthia E. Roman

During the late eighteenth and early nineteenth centuries in Britain, the middle classes, empowered by commercial wealth, struggled for increased social and political power, in part, by appropriating the authority of cultural expression to re-represent the British nation. Exploding the idea of a single monolithic public, this emphatically middle-class revolution mobilized the arts against the vestiges of aristocratic and courtly culture.[1] To this end, tacitly republican sectors within print culture played a significant role in the transformation of epic history painting, informed as it was by civic humanism, into a sentimental genre informed by moral sympathy and emphasizing the domestic and the feminine. Under the publishing auspices of dissenting Baptist Robert Bowyer, the Historic Gallery (1792–1806) and its accompanying illustrated edition of David Hume's *History of England* usurped the 'privileges' of high art and forged a new British nation by engaging the commercial classes of private individuals, both men and women, in the consumption of feminized historical prints as 'public art.' Marking a critical moment in the rise of a national school of British art and responding to great social and political upheaval during the late eighteenth and early nineteenth centuries, the Historic Gallery simultaneously reformulated history painting and redefined the 'nation' to include new constituents from among culturally and politically disenfranchised counter-publics.[2]

This essay introduces the impact of Bowyer's project on the evolution of history painting through his re-representation of English history in a way that defined new counter-publics by constructing alternative identities for a moral British society through feminized historical images. Exhibiting a particular emphasis on the domestic, and assigning to the virtue and treatment of women a central position in imaginings of an ideal moral society, these paintings, commissioned from leading history painters of the day, depict the actions and attachments of private men and women, who, according to Bowyer's view, comprised the new nation and defined its character.

In keeping with his agenda to re-represent the British nation as a body of moral private individuals, Bowyer introduced his project between 1792 and 1806 in the private space of his own commercial gallery at No. 87 Pall Mall. Here he exhibited the original compositions that served as models for reproductive engravers who illustrated his publication. But the actual, most effective rhetorical space for Bowyer's project was located in the printed and illustrated pages of his book. John Francis Rigaud's *The Collector of the Poll Tax Murdered by Wat Tyler* (Figure 1) painted 1792, was one of the first pictures to be completed for the illustrated *History* and exhibited at Bowyer's Historic Gallery. Appearing in the inaugural exhibition of April 1793, Rigaud's *Wat Tyler* helped to introduce Bowyer's patrons and subscribers, as well as other members of the art-viewing public, to the tenor of his particular construction of British national history.

Bowyer's challenge to established systems of patronage for public art demanded that his illustrators engage with the dictates of history painting, the highest fine arts genre traditionally associated with public function. Like all the major historical illustrations from Bowyer's *History*, John Hall's full-page engraving of Rigaud's painting, published in 1798, proclaims the self-conscious ambition of high art. As reproduced by the engraving format, the composition maintains its unique integrity. The circumscribing black line frames the printed image on the page like a painting on a wall. The chosen reproductive print medium of line engraving was for many contemporaries the only appropriate technique for historical subjects. These persistent references to the high ambitions of history painting assert Bowyer's agenda to appropriate and reformulate that genre for audiences of prints and illustrated books.

The tale of Wat Tyler takes place in the reign of Richard II. As the story goes, in order to raise money for war with France, Parliament levied a tax on all individuals over the age of 15. This tax, falling disproportionately on the poor, goaded the oppressed. When the tax-collector came to call at the shop of Wat Tyler, the blacksmith testified that his daughter was not of age and therefore he was not liable to pay the tax for her. The collector grabbed the girl and offered to provide, in Hume's words, an indecent proof to the contrary. The blacksmith avenged this assault on his daughter by bludgeoning him to death with his forging hammer.

Hume's *History*, written in the 1750s, summarily records the blacksmith's act of murder merely as an incidental catalyst to subsequent popular insurrections against royal oppression. He clearly does not

THE COLLECTOR OF THE POLL-TAX
MURDER'D BY WAT TYLER.

1   John Hall after John Francis Rigaud, *The Collector of the Poll Tax Murdered by Wat Tyler* (September 1798), engraving from David Hume's *History of England from the Invasion of Julius Ceasar to the Revolution in 1688*, vol. 2, part 1, London; printed by T. Bensley for Robert Bowyer, 1806

deem the blacksmith heroic or even particularly interesting. In fact, Hume does not even identify the blacksmith by name. From Hume's perspective, rebel leaders of the insurrection against Richard II were audacious criminals rather than popular heroes. However, when Bowyer published his edition of Hume's *History*, he chose to attach Tyler's name to the anecdote, and Rigaud's illustration boldly identifies the blacksmith as 'Wat Tyler' in the title caption. The identification of the assassin of a royal tax-collector as Wat Tyler, the leader of popular insurrection, gives the illustration a decidedly political thrust in line with the views of the Historic Gallery's advisor David Williams, a dissenting minister to a moralist congregation in London and a well-known republican sympathizer with the revolutionaries in France where he accepted citizenship in 1793.[3]

In addition to the title, Bowyer provided viewers of his exhibition with a passage from Hume's text to further describe the narrative content of his pictures. The passage selected for Rigaud's picture in effect fundamentally transforms Hume's opinion to reflect Bowyer's own republican sympathies. Relating details of the unfair assessment of taxes by Richard II and the guilt of the tax collector that inspired Wat Tyler's action, the quoted passage finishes with the by-standers applauding the murder and exclaiming that it was full time for the people to take vengeance on their tyrants and to vindicate their native liberty. Ending with this rousing approval of popular insurrection, Bowyer does not indicate that Hume considered the subsequent uprisings unjustified and he omits the historian's disapproving judgement that 'the lowest populace rose against their rulers, committed the most cruel ravages upon them, and took vengeance for all former oppressions'.

Departing from the tenor of Hume's text, Bowyer and his illustrator Rigaud clearly found expressive potential in the scene of the blacksmith murdering the tax-collector with which to represent their partisan view of the nation's history. The artist depicted the most dramatic and critical moment of the narrative. The figure of the blacksmith looms large, poised for attack. He occupies the centre of the composition and his actions are the focus of the story. Rigaud makes clear the just reason for the father's aggression. His attack on the tax-collector is simultaneous with his attempt to shield and protect his daughter. Tyler's humble, even oppressed, circumstances and plebian station are indicated by the artist's careful description of the modest shop and the smith's tattered garments and coarse features. His powerful figure threatens an extent of physical violence to which the much slighter figure of the collector of royal taxes can offer little resistance, and he cowers behind the girl. There is no doubt that the blacksmith will vanquish his oppressor. In addition, the artist forecasts Tyler's role as a leader of popular insurrection: in the right background, the local populace has begun to gather at the shop door to rally behind Tyler's cause.

By the 1790s, the story of the blacksmith and his rebellion carried considerable force as a symbol of political radicalism, in some circles signalling the dangers of republicanism. Rigaud's interpretation, however, betrays a clear sympathy for this republican insurgent and a topical protest against royal oppression. Most significantly, Rigaud has tempered his representation of Wat Tyler with paternal emotion. His image focuses on sentimental affection as much as it does on violence. The pivotal act of the blacksmith's aggression represents only part of the meaning. The gesture of the father's outstretched arm grasping to shield his daughter from harm carries visual impact equal to that of the blacksmith's raised arm brandishing the hammer with which he threatens the tax-collector.

This element of sentiment was crucial in Bowyer's view and figured prominently in his defence of the image against the cautions of the eminent botanist Sir Joseph Banks concerning the radical tenor of Rigaud's representation. Acting as an unofficial advisor to the Historic Gallery project, Banks questioned the wisdom of Bowyer's selection of 'a peasant beating a king's officer' as one of the first plates in a work dedicated to royalty.[4] The publisher responded that the proprietors believed the tale to be 'expressive of the regard and affection naturally to be expected from a father to his daughter & conceived by them on that Account as a proper subject'. Representing Britain as 'eminently the nation of domestic sentiment', Bowyer explained that elsewhere it 'may occasionally burst out with momentary rapture; or strike the eye, with force indeed, but in solitary instances. Here it pervades a whole people, and burns with a durable flame.'[5] An ideal of considerable cultural currency during the British Enlightenment, the private family played a crucial role in social and political debates about what would constitute a new moral community and national polity.[6] For Bowyer, as for Hume, social sentiment, represented most effectively by the domestic, was an integral and celebrated component of English national identity; and, in consequence, it became a defining trait of Englishness in constructing aspiring counter-publics.

Rigaud's *Wat Tyler* significantly is at once a republican and a sentimental hero, a radical insurgent and a father who admirably protects his daughter. This sentimental aspect of Rigaud's picture in effect legitimizes the aspirations of the middle-class audiences of Bowyer's prints to usurp power and claim active inclusion in the British 'nation'. Shifting the burden of moral behaviour from reason to emotion, emotionalist or sentimentalist theories of eighteenth-century British moral philosophy positioned the surest groundwork for social cohesiveness within the natural stirrings of individual sentiment. The writings of David Hume and his Scottish compatriot Adam Smith thus allowed social sentiment to become the means by which the reality of private interests and passions among middle-class individuals could be communicated to a national community.[7] Thus Bowyer's defence of Rigaud's *Wat Tyler* on the basis of paternal or domestic affection did not in fact neutralize the radical content identified in Banks's indictment; rather, the infusion of sentiment enhanced the construction of republican sympathy represented in militant aspects of Rigaud's chosen subject. In this way, print culture appropriated historical representation to express the national identity of classes formerly excluded from the rhetorical space of high art.

Bowyer's decision to illustrate a national history of his own country in itself signalled a political agenda guided by republican convictions. Historians Linda Colley and Gerald Newman have shown that for many *nouveau riche* and bourgeois elements in Georgian Britain, patriotic activism provided an opportunity to assert their parity or even superiority to the landed classes. Patriotic vocabulary provided a means for those excluded from active citizenship to describe and legitimize their own endeavours to claim wider civic recognition.[8] Bowyer's selection of Rigaud's *Wat Tyler* in the act of violently attacking a collector of royal taxes as an appropriate subject for his English history demonstrates that Bowyer's nationalism betrayed an underlying aspiration to usurp power and authority from the old guard. His insistence on the domestic aspect of Rigaud's image signals Bowyer's mediation between the radical or republican and the domestic. Bowyer oriented his representations of domesticity to mobilize a public hitherto marginalized from established forms of political expression, even in the face of pervasive conservative representations of Jacobin politics as a threat to the integrity of domestic space and as an aspersion on the moral virtue of radical women such as Mary Wollstonecraft.[9] An ideology of great currency, sentimental conventions of the domestic, in fact, were evoked by figures as politically diverse as Edmund Burke and John Thelwall, testifying to the centrality of sentimentality in wide-ranging political discourses at the end of the eighteenth century.[10]

Amidst increasing middle-class challenges to artistocratic privilege, republican and radical political activity, and revolution in France, different sections of society attempted to validate their own interests by constructing diverse counter-publics. While very few women, even among the most privileged, held any real power in the public sphere, contemporary discourse concerning the role of women and feminine behaviour in civilized society pervaded cultural expressions of national history. Despite limitations on or exclusions of actual women, many male communities imagined counter-publics in which virtuous females provided ideal models of social morality.[11] Domestic affection within the conjugal family offered a model of the social capacity of private men and women of the middling classes that was capable of challenging the civic privilege of ruling classes. The discourse of sentiment that informs Bowyer's view of the nation positioned both women and men as active participants in a civil society in a way that civic humanism did not, and thus allowed the middle classes to contribute a civilizing social benefit to the nation.

Among the Historic Gallery's pictures, representations of domesticity and virtuous heroines, depicting the embodiment of feminine sentiment, were given a central role in the aesthetic production of moral sympathy. Like many novelists of the day, Bowyer's illustrators recognized the dramatic power of scenes of domestic love and filial affection, and many such scenes are included in the work.[12] Among the most effective portrayals of domestic sentiment in Bowyer's Historic Gallery project is John Opie's *Lady Elizabeth Gray Entreating Edward IV to Protect Her Children* (Figure 2), engraved by William Bromley in 1800 as a full-page illustration. In 1796, the printmaker James Fittler, originally also a proprietor of the Historic Gallery, engraved another scene based on the same tale, Henry Tresham's *Edward IV Declaring His Attachment to Lady Elizabeth Grey*, as a vignette for chapter XXII, on Edward IV. The story of the romance and subsequent marriage between Lady Elizabeth Grey and Edward IV is the only tale within the entire span of Hume's *History* that is represented twice in the repertoire of Bowyer's illustrations. Clearly the double effort of his illustrators on this particular anecdote suggests that the tale was identified as a powerful site of meaning for Bowyer's agenda to re-represent the nation's history. The narrative and pictorial content of these two engravings highlight the concepts of social passions and virtue constructed by Bowyer on the model of domestic sentiment. The woman with her family is the agent of social attachment. The evident pathos of the tragic group conveys the cause of Edward's passion and is equally calculated to engage the sympathy of the viewer.

The text of Hume's *History* explains that the marriage of Edward IV to Elizabeth Grey ensued when 'so libertine a prince' sacrificed so much to a romantic passion. Thus the episode is a clear example of the Humean notion that passion, in contrast to disinterested virtue, determined the course of human history: namely, that the union led

LADY ELIZ. GRAY INTREATING EDW. IV. TO PROTECT HER CHILDREN.

2 William Bromley after John Opie, *Lady Elizabeth Gray Entreating Edward the Fourth to Protect Her Children* (May 1800), engraving from David Hume's *History of England from the Invasion of Julius Ceasar to the Revolution in 1688*, vol. 2, part 2, London; printed by T. Bensley for Robert Bowyer, 1806

to political strife between the king and the powerful earl of Warwick. Once again Bowyer's reinterpretation of Hume's narrative transforms the meaning. Despite the important political fallout of the marriage identified by Hume, the illustrations of the subject by Opie and Tresham neglect the public realm of politics. The passages from Hume quoted in Bowyer's catalogue of the illustrations make no reference to any unfortunate consequences of the marriage. Instead, the narrative focuses solely on the stirrings of passion in Edward and the feminine virtue of Elizabeth that inspired it. This occasion of sentiment and virtue represented in Opie's picture is described by an excerpt from Hume's account:

> The king came accidentally to the house of her father, after a hunting party, in order to pay a visit to the duchess of Bedford; and as the occasion seemed favourable for obtaining some grace from this gallant monarch, the young widow flung herself at his feet, and with many tears, entreated him to take pity on her impoverished and distressed children.

The text used to describe Tresham's picture follows on immediately from the preceding narrative:

> The sight of so much beauty in affliction strongly affected Edward; love stole insensibly into his heart under the guise of compassion; and her sorrow, so becoming a virtuous matron, made his esteem and regard quickly rise to affection. He raised her from the ground with assurance of favour; he found his passion increase with every moment, by the conversation of the amiable object, and he was soon reduced, in this turn, to the posture and stile of a supplicant at the feet of Elizabeth. But the lady, either adverse to dishonourable love, or perceiving that the impression, which she had made was so deep as to give her hopes of obtaining the highest elevation, obstinately refused to gratify his passion, and all the endearments and importunities of the young amiable Edward proved fruitless against her rigid and inflexible virtue. His passion, irritated by opposition, and increased by his veneration for such honourable sentiments, carried him at last beyond all bounds of reason; and he offered to share his throne as well as his heart with the woman, whose beauty of person, dignity of character, seemed so well to entitle her to both. The marriage was privately celebrated at Grafton.

Having little first-hand testimony to the precise state of mind and feelings of these historical persons, the historian deliberately fabricated and fashioned the description of feelings and motives in order to promote the philosophy of moral sentiment. In the text, the focus on individual passions and virtue privileges the domestic life over matters of state and the feminine over the masculine.

[23]

The illustrations, like the narrative excerpts chosen by Bowyer, focus solely on the emotional dynamics of the story and the moral virtue of the female protagonist. In Opie's picture, Lady Elizabeth Grey and her two sons occupy the front and centre of the pictorial stage. The figures take up almost the entire composition. The setting is merely an empty stage draped with heavy swags above. The three main figures are described with the greatest clarity and are further emphasized by bright illumination. They are the focus of both the narrative and the sentimental meaning. Facial expression and gesture communicate the emotions: the sorrowful eyes of all three are directed at the compassion of the prince standing before them. The lady, kneeling with her children before the prince, pleads her case with arms extended to either side of the younger son who cowers close to her maternal shelter.

Edward's reaction is as marginal in the picture as is his position to the far edge of the canvas. Clearly, Opie has intended that not only Edward be moved by the plight of Lady Elizabeth and her family. The composition is calculated to engage the sympathy of the spectator as well as to explicate the motives of the historical narrative. The placement of Edward to the side allows the spectator to experience the pathos of the lady and her sons. The group of mother and sons is presented to the viewer's sentiment as much as to Edward's compassion. Opie's picture fulfils the conviction expressed in his lectures to the Royal Academy that the proper basis of all subjects peculiarly adapted to painting is 'striking situation, palpable sentiment, decided passion, beautiful forms and energetic action'.[13]

Tresham's *Edward IV Declaring His Attachment to Lady Elizabeth Grey* is more decorative than Opie's full-page composition. Gracefully curving figures are arranged in a frieze across the picture plane. While the expression of passion is less forceful in Tresham's work, the expressivity of the narrative is nonetheless evident. Elizabeth kneels with head bowed towards her younger child, here a mere infant who is cradled in her lap. (The discrepancy between the ages of the children in the two pictures further attests to the valuation of sentimentality over historical accuracy.) The infant reaches up to the prince. The monarch, standing in an elegant serpentine pose, bows his head and extends his hand to the lady. The second child, seated behind on the stone floor playing with two dogs, watches the tender scene. The narrative emphasis again is the moment of awakening passion and sentimental attachment formed between the king and the lady, acting for the protection of her family.

Recognized for its sentimental potential, the story of Lady Elizabeth Grey gained enormous popularity as a subject for history painting, reproductive engraving and book illustration among English audiences in the latter part of the eighteenth century. As early as 1778, the Society of Arts announced that the subject for that year's competition for premiums would be 'Lady Elizabeth Grey, petitioning Edward the Fourth'. Richard Westall in 1793 exhibited a version – *Lady Elizabeth Grey, Imploring Edward IV the Restitution of Her Husband's Lands* – at the Royal Academy to the acclaim of one critic who lauded it as 'a most beautiful picture', in which the manly figure of Edward IV is a fine contrast to the beautiful form of Lady Grey. Noting that the artist portrayed the story with great simplicity and taste, critics concentrated on the heroine's feminine grace and virtue, which were given as the basis of the king's passion.[14] More modest engravings, by Thomas Stothard and Mr Conde, are significant as they were among the many representations of the subject clearly intended for less wealthy audiences among the middle classes. Conde's print sold for a mere seven shillings.[15]

The endorsement of women as exemplar agents of social virtue and maternal protectors of children, so apparent in the representations of Lady Elizabeth Grey, also found expression in contemporary literature. In her work *Desire and Domestic Fiction*, Nancy Armstrong has shown, that, beginning in the eighteenth century, the cultural construct of the domestic woman established a hold over British culture. Eighteenth-century moralizing novels by English authors, male and female, share a focus on the heroine as the instrument of social virtue, commonly with moral didactic intent. The rise and dissemination of this new female ideal, to which theories of sentimentality attributed great social authority, empowered the middle classes in their aspirations to greater political and social inclusion.[16] The novel *Adeline Mowbray* by Amelia Opie, who was married to John Opie, the painter of Bowyer's *Lady Elizabeth Gray*, relates, conversely, the downfall of a privileged young woman due to some socially ill-advised actions. Amelia Opie's exploration of masculine and feminine codes of conduct chronicles the struggle of the virtuous Adeline to resolve an apparent discord between her convictions, based purely on intellectual reason, and the demands of established social customs. The author assigns much responsibility for the failures of such challenges to the neglect of Adeline's mother, who encouraged her daughter to pursue radical social ideas but failed to provide the requisite example of domestic virtue, familial attachment and social guidance. Adeline's misguided, though well-intended, decision to cohabit with Frederic Glenmurray, the young philosopher and author whose treatises are the source of her opinions, results in much suffering. She is disowned by her mother, excluded from virtuous female community and condemned to a life of repentance, before receiving maternal forgiveness just prior to her death.

Sentimental heroines, such as Fanny Burney's *Evelina* or Samuel Richardson's *Pamela*, likewise provide models of social virtue that are faithful to the particular formulation of moral sentiment set forward by Hume and Smith and appropriated by Bowyer's illustrations. *Pamela*, for example, operates through sentiment and advocates meritocracy in keeping with the aspirations of commercial classes seeking political and social privilege. Pamela, a servant girl, earns her place among squirearchy and aristocracy, despite adversity, through her moral virtue. The reader is compelled to find the heroine worthy of elevation through empathy with her feelings, which are so vividly expressed in her personal letters composing Richardson's novel.

In his visual re-representation of national history, Bowyer invested much in the power of the fine arts to contribute to the cultural production of moral sentiment among private individuals for the common good of society.[17] In addition to informing a viewer's reason or intellect, the visual arts have a special capacity to engage a viewer's sympathy. In Bowyer's estimation, subjects that 'interest' the viewer function as a correction to the regrettable circumstances that, 'in modern times, Historic Painting has been employed on detached subjects'.[18] The pictures produced for Bowyer's project were calculated to 'enliven' history and inspire feeling in the viewer, thereby promoting social improvement. In a prospectus for his project, Bowyer elucidated the social mission of his illustrated history:

> To hunt after knowledge would be frivolous, were the pursuit not to influence our actions;– a collection of pictures forming a complete series of English story holds out to the patriotic mind, an infinite display of delight and instruction; the liberal Arts contribute greatly to refine the affections, here they tend to fortify the judgment and to improve understanding . . . In short, many flattering ideas will arise in the breast of the feeling observer, when he reflects on the advantages resulting from an Historic Gallery, which when complete, is to become a National Monument of taste and splendour.[19]

The use of key words and phrases such as 'affection', 'feeling' and 'breast of the feeling observer' signal the currency of sentiment as a force in social philosophy and undoubtedly reference the social thought of Adam Smith and David Hume. Bowyer's certain intention that the illustrated *History* would play a role in the moral refinement of his commercial audiences is evident in his characterization of his potential patrons as those 'who had the taste to feel'.[20] Clearly operating within a general theoretical currency that assigned the visual arts value as a civilizing social force that could communicate emotional and moral impressions to a viewer, Bowyer envisioned his illustrations enhancing the written narrative of the English story as a construction of commercial ideology aimed at the improvement of the audiences of his Historic Gallery or the readers of his illustrated folio volumes. Convinced of the sentimental impact of viewing his pictures of national history, Bowyer thus identified the special contribution of the visual artist in assisting the prose historian.

> The historian traces the secret springs of a great event, pursues it through its progressive circumstances and develops its future consequences. He pleases and he instructs. But in many of those events, which strongly arrest the attention, there is some striking moment, the effect of which is unavoidably weakened by the mode of relating the tale. The deed of an instant is not told in the same space of time: and the exertion made by the mind, to figure herself ideas from the words that describe them, renders her perception of them less vivid. Here is the painter's advantage. What is done in an instant, his pencil as instantaneously tells. All the faculties of the mind are employed in contemplating the scene without any exertion on her part: the impression is indelible.[21]

Bowyer's use of the feminine pronoun to describe his imagined viewer betrays a gendered definition of the Historic Gallery's audience. Clearly he links the emotional experience of viewing a painting, as opposed to the more demanding intellectual exertion necessary for reading history, with the female viewer, the visual representation providing a striking and immediate impact in keeping with the feminine.

Although Bowyer's subscription list is unlocated, one can reasonably surmise that women would have been among the subscribers, or at least were valued and targeted as such. The inclusion of fifteen women in the subscription list to George Raymond's *History of England*, published in 1790, testifies that women, independent of male family members, patronized his illustrated publication at a date just prior to Bowyer's first proposals. In this regard, it is interesting to note that, under each letter of the alphabetical listing, the names of women subscribers are printed following and apart from the names of male subscribers. Although this segregation tends to emphasize women subscribers, it is unclear whether this effect was intended.

The ranks of women among visitors to the Historic Gallery, however, clearly did not go unnoticed. Their attendance at Bowyer's establishment apparently sparked the interest of the proprietor in his efforts to promote the exhibition. Bowyer fully exploited the potential correlation of female audiences and morally sympathetic viewing. A newspaper announcement for de Loutherbourg's *Earl Howe's Victory*,

[27]

which was exhibited on the first floor of the Historic Gallery, opened with the following remark:

> The ladies of fashion have made the picture . . . their favorite resort; and for the numerous visitors who daily frequent the admired Exhibition, it is become a mourning Ranelagh to all those who are celebrated for their taste, rank, and beauty, and who take a delight in surveying that glorious object of national honour, so admirably represented.[22]

Furthermore, the same advertisement closed with a list of 'ladies of rank' for whom it was the 'reigning fashion' to become subscribers to the engraving after de Loutherbourg's picture of Lord Howe; the names of no men are mentioned. Such announcements suggest that Bowyer perceived some promotional advantage in a respectable female audience for the viewing experience he intended. Similarly advertisements for de Loutherbourg's *Attack on Valenciennes* suggest that that picture 'affords also one of the most pleasing proofs of the attention of our fair country-women to the perils and dangers to which so many of our bravest men are exposed in the service and defense of their king and country, the object of every true Englishmen's veneration and pride'.[23] Female visitors were an important aspect of audience-building also at the Royal Academy exhibitions. Kay Dian Kriz has recently shown that British commentators on the fine arts likewise identified respectable women as crucial constituents of a Royal Academy 'public' that was capable of legitimizing the artistic and moral ascendancy of England as a civilized commercial nation.[24]

This seems to extend Hume's own notion that history is particularly effective in instilling moral sentiment. In his essay "Of the study of history" Hume positioned history not only as a valuable part of knowledge, but also as a means of extending the experience of moral virtue. History, Hume explained, interests readers in characters and events sufficiently to evoke a lively sense of sentiment of blame or praise.[25] He devotes considerable ink to women as readers of history, noting that 'there is nothing which I would recommend more earnestly to my female readers than the study of history, as an occupation, of all others, the best suited to their sex and education'. The particular benefits and attractions to women readers are enumerated. History, Hume notes, is "[m]uch more instructive than their ordinary foods of amusement, and more entertaining than those serious compositions, which are usually to be found in their closets'. Hume proceeds to point out the many advantages resulting from the study of history, showing how well suited it is to everyone, but 'particularly to those who are debarred the severer studies, by the tenderness of their education'. The advantages found in history, Hume concludes, seem to be of three kinds, as it amuses the fancy, improves the understanding and strengthens virtue.[26]

Following the special value of history in the education of women identified by writers like Hume, many women, of wide ranging political convictions, addressed their own work to the improvement of their sex. The radical feminist Mary Hays thus directed her *Female Biography; or Memoirs of Illustrious and Celebrated Women, of All Ages and Countries* to women, who 'unsophisticated by the pedantry of the schools read not for dry information, to load their memories with uninteresting facts, or to make a display of vein erudition . . . they require pleasure to be mingled with instruction, lively images, the graces of sentiment'. Hays further explained that 'their understandings are principally accessible through their affections'.[27] Others composed histories expressly for women. The author of *The Female Aegis; or, the Duties of Women from Childhood to Old Age* (1798) pointed to the importance of the female character in the national history, stating that 'mankind owe so much to the influence of the female character for the degree of refinement to which we are at this moment arrived . . .".[28] The more conservative Mrs Pilkington calculated her *A Mirror for the Female Sex* for 'amusing their fancies, informing their understandings and bettering their hearts'. She likewise argued that history

> expands the intellects by anticipating the sources of experience; corrects and moderates our passions, by exemplifying the various excesses and obliquities to which they are liable; and lays a foundation for culture and exercise of every noble virtue and honourable pursuit, by a series of moral painting in perfect unison with the original.[29]

This focus on female audiences and the advantages of the study of history in the acquisition of moral sympathy among women connects closely with Bowyer's notion of the historical evolution of the British nation. Bowyer mobilized a prevalent eighteenth-century discourse that identified the feminine character of virtuous women and their treatment and position as a measure of the civilization achieved by a particular society. According to the philosophy of moral sentiment, as adopted from the writings of David Hume and a host of others, the moral sensibility of women was a matter of historical progress, and one that increased with the other refinements of civilization, particularly as a result of the rise of the middle and commercial classes. In that connection, the ideal women undertook new and significant roles as practitioners of sociability and models of virtue. According to a number of recent studies, many among late eighteenth-century literary circles, including some women, were keenly aware of the connections between the home and the political arena, and often sought to redefine the domestic realm and the roles that women play in society.[30] The domestic became intimately linked with the political and the private family was central to social and political thought about the public good. As Bowyer's above-cited newspaper reports, connecting the spectatorship of honourable women with patriotism, make apparent, preserving female virtue became a highly political act: it was a way of upholding British pride and valour.[31]

Bowyer's Historic Gallery likewise created positive and strong female models imagining an identity for women as active agents in the middle-class social structure. Among the illustrations, there are many instances in which women are positioned as primary protagonists in acts of sympathy and moral virtue. Robert Smirke's *Burghers of Calais* (Figure 3), engraved by Anker Smith in 1796, represents a potentially heroic event involving noble sacrifice and royal pardon, as a sympathetic scene of feminine intercession.

Following his victory at Crécy, Edward III laid siege to Calais. When Calais surrendered in 1347, the English king agreed to spare its inhabitants if six of the most esteemed citizens were sent to him for execution, bare-headed, bare-footed, with ropes around their necks and carrying the keys to the city. Edward III relented, yielding to the intercession of his queen, Philippa. West's portrayal of the event is grand in scope and populated with numerous figures. The burghers are rendered with a dignity equal to that of the king and his queen: their noble sacrifice is given as much attention in the representation of the narrative as is the king's ultimate pardon at the intercession of the queen. Philippa does not plead or beg: she implores the king to act with humanity through an eloquent, yet restrained, gesture. One hand is held to her heart; the other is upturned in favour of the burghers.[32]

The potential of this subject to be interpreted as 'a precisely defined event of crucial moral decision' is apparent in the 1789 painting by Benjamin West, president of the Royal Academy and historical painter to George III. West's *Burghers of Calais* was one of the series of paintings depicting the life of Edward III, commissioned by the king, in which the painter presented his 'career, described by Hume as a series of aggressive military campaigns, as the progress of royal valour, justice and magnanimity'.[33] By contrast, Robert Smirke's scene is far less heroic. Rejecting West's conception of the story of the burghers of Calais as a grand occasion of civic action and heroic virtue, Smirke imagines a feminized sentimental tale of moral sympathy. His attention is given almost exclusively to the exchange between King Edward III and Queen Philippa. The queen, as the moral agent of humanity, is a primary protagonist. Smirke depicts her pleading on her knees at the feet of a seemingly unrelenting king. Edward only glances in the

THE SURRENDER OF CALAIS.

3   Anker Smith after Robert Smirke, *The Surrender of Calais* (August 1796), engraving from David Hume's *History of England from the Invasion of Julius Ceasar to the Revolution in 1688*, vol. 2, part 1, London; printed by T. Bensley for Robert Bowyer, 1806

[31]

direction of the burghers. His posture, turned away with cloak tightly wrapped about his body, suggests that he was unreceptive to the plight of his prisoners. The emotional distress of the queen is reiterated by the three women immediately behind her at the opening of the tent: one weeps with her head in her hands; another crosses her hands over her chest; and the third holds her hand to her face in anxious antici- pation. The valour of the burghers is of negligible significance in Smirke's narrative. Their presence is literally marginalized, suggested only by the city keys at Edward's feet and the minimal inclusion of the bowed heads of two prisoners at the far left.

Smirke's illustration of the queen, pleading on her knees, relies more closely than West's on the events described in the fourteenth- century *Chronicles* of Jean Froissart. Hume repeated Froissart's account with reservations, for he remarked that 'it is surprising that so generous a prince should ever have entertained such a barbarous purpose against such men; and still more that he should seriously persist in the resolution of executing it'.[34] In fact, Hume devoted a lengthy note to questioning the truth of the story.[35] This rejection of the legendary tales was in fact pervasive in Bowyer's day. In her brief biographical sketch of Philippa's military accomplishments, Mary Hays quotes Hume's dismissal of the queen's sentimental intercession.[36]

Bowyer's persistence with the discounted legendary tale, and par- ticularly his choice of Smirke's representation, therefore clearly signals a commitment to a feminized national history in which female pas- sions and sympathy inform a moral society. Robert Smirke, well known for his intimate illustrations for sentimental novels and comic plays, was the largest contributor to the Historic Gallery. His procliv- ity for humorous and sentimental subjects, in the tradition of that most English of painters William Hogarth, operated compatibly with the conception of audience mapped out by Bowyer's project. Smirke's manner both accommodated the requirements of an extant con- stituency – those spectators already sensitized to moral sentiment – and also served well to construct another audience, one which con- ceived of itself in especially Humean terms and in keeping with Smirke's own well-known openly republican proclivities.[37] Female protagonists prevail in the majority of his pictures. Furthermore, he generally delineated his leading women by a delicate figure and a demeanour consistent with the graceful serpentine pose in which they are normally portrayed. Passions displayed are soft, expressive gestures are gentle.

In conclusion, grappling with an ideology of significant currency, Bowyer's feminized historical illustrations assign primacy to social passions and moral virtue, thereby privileging the private or domestic over public matters of state and the feminine over the masculine. Ideal social behaviour was to some degree feminized and woman displaced man to become the primary site or model of domestic bonds. With the transfer of these alternative norms to broader social models, such as nationhood, the commercial-class audiences of Bowyer's prints appropriated historical representation to express a new national identity and to claim active inclusion in the British 'nation'.

Notes

1   For a study of the ways in which publics and counter-publics were imagined, represented and constructed in the literary sphere during the 1790s, see Andrew McCann, *Cultural Politics in the 1790s. Literature, Radicalism, and the Public Sphere*, St. Martin's Press, New York, 1999. McCann's study, however, does not include the visual arts.
2   For a full study of Robert Bowyer's Historic Gallery, see the author's dissertation, 'Pictures for private purses: Robert Bowyer's Historic Gallery and illustrated edition of David Hume's *History of England*', Department of the History of Art and Architecture at Brown University, Providence, RI, 1997, and Richard Wetherill Hutton, 'Robert Bowyer and the Historic Gallery: a study of the creation of a magnificent work to promote the arts in England', dissertation, University of Chicago, 1992.
3   Stephen Francis Dutilh Rigaud, 'Facts and recollection of the XVIIIth century in a memoir of John Francis Rigaud Esq., R.A.', ed. William Pressly, in *The Walpole Society*, vol. 50, 1984, pp. 1–33.
4   Interestingly, in keeping with Bowyer's republican sympathies, the work includes, in addition to a dedication to the king, a second dedication to the legislature. This is atypical of historical works of this date. Robert Bowyer, Letter to Joseph Banks, November 1792, Correspondence of Joseph Banks, (Manuscript) Library, Royal Botanical Gardens, Kew, fo. 85.
5   *Elucidation of Mr. Bowyer's Plan for a Magnificent Edition of Hume's History of England, with a Continuation by G. Gregory*, London, T. Bensley, 1812, pp. 9–10.
6   Eve Taylor Bannet, *The Domestic Revolution. Enlightenment Feminisms and the Novel*, Baltimore, MD, and London, Johns Hopkins University Press, 2000; and McCann, *Cultural Politics in the 1790s*.
7   Terry Eagleton, *The Ideology of Aesthetic*, Oxford, Blackwell, 1990; John Mullan, *Sentiment and Sociability. The Language of Feeling in the Eighteenth Century*, Oxford, Clarendon Press, 1988.
8   Linda Colley, *Britons: Forging the Nation, 1707–1837*, New Haven, CT, and London, Yale University Press, 1992; Gerald Newman, *The Rise of English Nationalism: A Cultural History, 1740–1830*, New York, St. Martins, 1987.
9   McCann, *Cultural Politics in the 1790s*, p. 23; for representations of females as morally corrupt, see chapter 4, 'Disreputable women (1782–1792)', of Ellen D'Oench's '*Copper into Gold': The Prints of John Raphael Smith*, New Haven, CT, and London, Yale University Press, 1999; and Eleanor Ty, *Empowering the Feminine: The Narratives of Mary Robinson, Jane West, and Amelia Opie, 1796–1812*, Toronto, Buffalo, NY, and London, University of Toronto Press, 1998.
10 Ty, *Empowering the Feminine*, p. 19. Ty analyses the ideologies of femininity in the writings of Mary Robinson, Jane West and Amelia Opie whose narratives explore the role of women in society.
11 McCann, *Cultural Politics in the 1790s*.
12 Ty, *Empowering the Feminine*, p. 139.
13 John Opie, 'Lectures on painting', in Ralph Wornum (ed.) *Lectures on Painting by the Royal Academicians*, London, Henry G. Bohn, 1848, p. 273.

14 Courtauld Institute of Art, London, Press Cuttings, vol. 1, p. 148; Academy review by 'Florian' and Courtauld Press Cuttings, May 1793, vol. 1, p. 149.
15 A reproduction of Stothards's print is in the Photo Archives of the Paul Mellon Centre, British Museum (Belmanno Collection 2, 1050). Conde's stipple engraving was advertised in the *Morning Chronicle*, 30 May 1794, p. 1.
16 Armstrong considers sexual relations the site for changing power relations between classes and cultures. Nancy Armstrong, *Desire and Domestic Fiction: A Political History of the Novel*, New York and Oxford, Oxford University Press, 1987.
17 David Solkin has shown that painters played a vital part in creating a symbolic repertoire which affirmed the moral character of the privatized commercial social order in the first part of the eighteenth century: David Solkin, *Painting for Money: The Visual Arts and the Public Sphere in Eighteenth-Century England*, New Haven, CT, Yale University Press, 1993.
18 *Prospectus of the General Design and Conditions for a Complete History of England from the Invasion of Julius Caesar to the Revolution in 1688 by David Hume; from the Revolution to the Present Time by David Williams*, London, 1792, p. 2. Published also in *Mr. Bowyer's Address to the Patrons of the Fine Arts Respecting His Splendid National Undertaking of the History of England*, 1793. This passage is, however, not original to Robert Bowyer, but is borrowed closely from Richardson's *Theory of Painting* in *The Works of Jonathan Richardson*, London, 1792.
19 *Morning Chronicle*, April 1793.
20 *Mr. Bowyer's Address*, n.p.
21 *Mr. Bowyer's Elucidation*, pp. 7–8.
22 Victoria and Albert Museum, Press Clippings, vol. 3, p. 712.
23 Victoria and Albert Museum, Press Clippings, vol. 3, p. 680.
24 K. Dian Kriz, '"Stare cases": engendering the public's two bodies at the Royal Academy of Arts', in David H. Solkin (ed.) *Art on the Line. The Royal Academy Exhibitions at Somerset House 1780–1836*, New Haven, CT, and London, Yale University Press, 2001.
25 'Of the study of history', in David Hume, *The Philosophical Works of David Hume*, Edinburgh, Adam Black & William Tait, and London, Charles Tait, 1826, vol. 4, pp. 531–2.
26 Hume, *Philosophical Works*, vol. 4, pp. 529ff.
27 Mary Hays, *Female Biography; or Memoirs of Illustrious and Celebrated Women, of All Ages and Countries, Alphabetically Arranged*, 3 vols, Philadelphia, PA, 1807, Preface to vol. 1, p. iii.
28 *The Female Aegis; or, the Duties of Women from Childhood to Old Age, and in Most Situations of Life*, London, J. Granger, 1798, p. 2.
29 Mrs Pilkington, *A Mirror for the Female Sex. Historical Beauties for Young Ladies Intended to Lead the Female Mind to the Love and Practice of Moral Goodness*, London, Vernon & Hood, 1799.
30 See Ty, *Empowering the Feminine*, and Bannet, *The Domestic Revolution*.
31 Ty, *Empowering the Feminine*, p. 104.
32 Helmut von Erffa and Allen Staley, *The Paintings of Benjamin West*, New Haven, CT, and London, Yale University Press, 1986, pp. 197–9.
33 Wendy Geenhouse, 'Benjamin West and Edward III: a neoclassical painter and medieval history', *Art History*, vol. 8, June 1985, pp. 178–91.
34 David Hume, *The History of England from the Invasion of Julius Caesar to the Abdication of James the Second, 1688, A new edition*, 6 vols (first published in its entirety 1763), Philadelphia, PA, Porter & Coates, 187[?], vol. 2, p. 233.
35 Hume, *History of England*, vol. 2, p. 520, note G.
36 Hays, *Female Biography*, vol. 3, p. 281.
37 According to the testimony of Joseph Farington, Smirke's election as keeper of the Royal Academy Library in 1804 was rejected by King George III due to the artist's revolutionary principles and his open expression of satisfaction at events in France: Joseph Farington, *The Diary of Joseph Farington*, ed. Kenneth Garlick and Angus McIntyre, New Haven, CT, and London, Yale University Press, 1978.

CHAPTER TWO

Re-visioning landscape in Wales and New South Wales, c.1760–1840

Jocelyn Hackforth-Jones

This chapter focuses on the representation of a stretch of new world terrain – the mountain range known as the Blue Mountains in New South Wales, Australia – and makes some comparisons with the representation of mountains in Snowdonia, Wales. Here Wales is used as a prompt, but not as a focus for discussion, in order to consider its antipodean counterpart in 'New Wales' and to chart some of the processes in the construction of the shifting identities of both.[1]

My starting point is *Wentworth Falls* (Figure 4) by Augustus Earle, c.1829.[2] This painting is a view of Wentworth Falls in the Blue Mountains, New South Wales. The foreground of the painting features a standing aboriginal figure looking out towards the viewer. In the centre the artist is apparently sketching something to our left. An aboriginal figure in the centre foreground points also to our left (although, as I show, there is considerable ambiguity in the representation both of the aboriginal figures and of the artist). To our right four individuals are attempting to scale the cliff face. There are a number of ways in which we might unpack this painting in relation both to landscape portrayal and to the representation of the individual figures. We could, for instance, engage in close formal analysis; or we could attempt a more penetrating excavation of the painting's meaning in relation to emergent 'Australian' identities. W. J. T. Mitchell may assist us in the latter process, since in *Landscape and Power* he argues for a more comprehensive model that would ask not just what landscape 'is' or 'means' but 'what it does, how it works as cultural practice', particularly in relation to colonial landscape.[3] One model which may be helpful in the attempt to unravel the complexities of identities and national identities in relation to landscape representations of Wales and New South Wales is the notion of *internal* and *external* colonialisms. Certainly, it is important to be mindful that a colonial frame may be appropriate when considering visual representation in both old and new

4 Augustus Earle, *Wentworth Falls* (1830)

worlds, although this at first might seem surprising – given that the discourse of colonialism is generally regarded as relating to countries such as the Americas, India and Africa. But if we briefly consider the colonial circumstances in Wales and New South Wales, similarities emerge.

Britain's relationship with Australia and New Zealand in the latter part of the eighteenth and the first half of the nineteenth century was broadly *external* in the sense that it was one between a major colonizing power and its colonized 'other'. The England–Wales colonial relationship, however, was *internal* in terms of the geographical proximity of the two countries and also in the processes of assimilation at work, which from the thirteenth century also ensured that Wales was considered – psychologically, politically and culturally – to be part of England. While the Welsh may have thought of themselves as nationally distinct, the English had a different view of them: until 1974, Wales was regarded as part of England.[4] In all acts of Parliament, Wales has been included as 'England and Wales'. For its parliamentary representation, and its administrative and legal system, Wales was until recently part of the English system.

The relationship of centre to periphery is germane to the construction of colonial identities, and this can be seen in the exploration of Wales alongside that of more remote territories. In his tour of south Wales in 1773, Sir Joseph Banks was accompanied by the artist Paul Sandby, who recorded the physiognomy of unfamiliar terrains, while the botanical specimens were recorded by the Swedish naturalist Daniel Solander.[5] Banks had already made a journey to the South Pacific prior to this Welsh trip, having sailed with Cook on the *Endeavour* in 1768, accompanied by a retinue of artists and scientists, which included Solander, to record 'new' sights. The circumstances surrounding this subsequent Welsh trip, and the way in which the land was mapped and recorded, remind us that as late as 1773 south Wales (a mere 200 miles from London) could be thought to have uncharted territory that was still appealing to explorers, artists, scientists and botanists. It also suggests that, in Banks's case, the very process of travelling farther afield had led to a (re)discovery and a (re)appraisal of unknown lands close to home.

From the middle of the eighteenth century, English artists and travellers were drawn to Wales for many of the same reasons that they were drawn to other British colonies in the Americas, Asia and the South Pacific. It is important to recognize that Wales readily lent itself to a fictionalized representation because of its colonial position *vis-à-vis* England. One example of the transformation of the Snowdonian landscape in Wales was Richard Wilson's reconfiguring of the raw mountain scenery in *Llyn Peris and Dolbadern Castle* (Melbourne, National Gallery of Victoria, 1762–64) into a gentle, civilized, arcadian site and (as David Solkin has posited) making a connection here between Wales and Italy in a manner that would have been attractive to his patron group, which included Anglo-Welsh aristocrats.

Solkin has argued that Wilson's view of Wales in paintings such as this represents a fictional and nostalgic view of 'Historic Britain' that would have satisfied the requirements of his Anglo-Welsh aristocratic patrons. He suggests that Wales lent itself to being depicted in this way because it was, as compared to England, economically and commercially deprived and because the vast majority of its people were much poorer than were England's.[6] Although the landowners and squirearchy were not necessarily wealthier than their English counterparts, they did have a great deal of authority, so that to the casual observer Wales appeared to be in an almost feudal state, peopled by primitive peasants and ruled over by powerful landlords.

How do we explain the (apparent) suddenness with which Wales became popular with artists from the late 1760s? David Solkin has stated that 'an artistic discovery of Wales' took place in and from 1766 (the year in which seven Welsh subjects were exhibited at the Royal Society of Artists).[7] Solkin considers that this so-called 'discovery' occurred because 'Wales had come to symbolise a particular social ideal which seemed critically threatened elsewhere'.[8] This is one significant reason for the particular attraction of Welsh landscape at that time, but it was a considerably more complex process than Solkin's account suggests and there were a number of other factors involved.[9] Along with the artistic discovery of Wales came that of other parts of Britain, like the Peak and Lake Districts.[10]

This was symptomatic of a more general interest in landscape which developed from the 1760s. From the middle of the eighteenth century onwards it is possible to identify an increasing group of people who were wealthy, leisured and interested in the arts.[11] They were also keen travellers. Their cultural aspirations were catered for (and in a sense indicated by) the publication of books that were concerned with analysing and explaining matters of taste (often using landscape exemplars) which appeared in the 1750s, 1760s and 1770s – J. G. Cooper and Edmund Burke's publications being cases in point.[12] The process of enclosure, which accelerated during the 1760s and 1770s (and again during the period of the Napoleonic Wars), made the landscape more orderly and accessible, since it was accompanied by better modes of transport and the building and improving of roads, canals and turnpikes. Anne Bermingham has considered the coincidence of this 'social transformation of the countryside with the rise of a cultural–aesthetic idealising of the countryside'.[13]

A more nationalistic interest in the British landscape and the remains of Britain's past can also be linked with the surge of patriotism around the time of George III's accession to the throne.[14] The identification of Wales as 'Historic Britain' ran together with other developments in the 1760s. The Celtic revival in the middle decades of the eighteenth century indicated both an English and a local resurgence of interest in Celtic culture. Thomas Gray's *The Bard*, published in 1757, is the best-known product of a movement which was partially generated by the notion that Britain had a past and a history to rival that of Greece or Italy; and, given that a number of Wilson's patrons were members of the Honourable Society of the Cymmrodorion, that was certainly one reason for the appeal of his paintings of Wales.[15] Yet it is difficult to explain the suddenness with which Wales became popular with artists from the late 1760s. The phenomenon would also appear to fit with that more general interest in landscape which developed around the 1760s. The representation of Wales as 'Historic

Britain' was but one of the perceptual interpretations of that country which manifested itself with such suddenness in the 1760s.

While there are a number of reasons for the attractiveness of Wales at this time, I would argue that it is crucial to situate the phenomenon within the context of *internal* colonialism. This colonial view regarded Wales as having an uncharted landscape inhabited by a 'primitive' and foreign people, with its own culture, language and mythology. The appealing difference, when one compares Wales with colonial sites farther afield, was that Wales was both 'foreign' in cultural terms but in geographical proximity to England, so that by the late eighteenth century the Principality had become one of the most popular touring sites in Britain. Paul Sandby's drawing of *Snowdon* (1779, National Library of Wales, Aberystwyth) emphasized both Snowdon's distinctive and easily identifiable peak and also the sense of cultural difference: the bard and other inhabitants featured in the foreground are there to typify Welsh culture and Wales's inhabitants, and to remind the viewer of their different and distinctive history, culture and mythology.

Throughout this period a number of different 'Waleses' came to be constructed in relation to Welsh identity and nationalism and to emerging British nationalism. The emergence of nationalism(s) in relation to Wales helped to increase the desirability of the Principality as a place to visit and to shape patterns for visiting and recording Wales in ways which parallel representations of more distant colonies. From the late eighteenth century we can chart the cultural creation of Snowdonia as British – more particularly as the British Alps (and the classification of Welsh mountains as British Alpine scenery was one popular way of further colonising the landscape and making connections with Europe). At the same time, there was the transformation of various sites in Wales from touring to tourist attractions – Rowlandson's watercolour of *Llanberis Lake and Dolbadarn Castle* (1797) being a visual case in point.[16] From the beginning of the nineteenth century the Principality gradually became a *tourist* rather than a *touring* site, meaning that from this time there were increasing numbers of people going to Wales (plus rising numbers of middle-class travellers), and that a whole industry was developing to cater for them, so that one can chart here the beginning of an era of commercial exploitation. There was, too, a marked change in the nature of the travel literature, which no longer had the feel of 'pioneer travel' evident in earlier publications. Snowdon had long been an attraction as the tallest mountain in Wales, but its associations were also important. For the English, Snowdonia was attractive as the 'Welsh Alps' and as the setting for a 'primitive' mountain people who were regarded as anthropological curiosities – a view which infuriated some contemporary Welsh writers.[17] For many Welsh people, on the other hand, Snowdon historically had been the refuge for besieged Welsh princes and the home of 'true sons of liberty'. It thus could also have subversive import.

By the end of the eighteenth century there was a spate of descriptions (both visual and literary) that invoked the Burkean sublime.[18] Burke's *Philosophical Enquiry into the Origin of Our Ideas of the Sublime and the Beautiful* was enormously influential. Its popularity may be most readily gauged from the fact that by the time of his death, in 1797, sixteen editions of the book had been published. Twenty-five years after its publication the book entered its ninth edition. While both the print runs and, therefore, the readership of these editions are difficult to determine, it must be remembered that the actual readership would have been several times the number of volumes sold, as the book would also have been passed around via circulating libraries. Often the literary accounts were somewhat repetitive – this may also have had something to do with the peculiarities of the site, as Snowdon is frequently obscured by mists and bad weather, which also made ascent difficult. Some resorted to quoting other writers: for instance, the Reverend William Gilpin quoted Thomas Pennant's description of the summit of Snowdon as a substitute experience. The Reverend Richard Warner must have had Burke in mind forty years later when he visited Snowdon in August 1797:

> Huge rocks, abrupt precipices, and profound hollows, exciting emotions of astonishment and awe in the mind, which the eye darting down an immense descent of vacuity and horror, conveyed to it under the dreadful image of inevitable destruction.[19]

John Warwick Smith had responded in similar Burkean fashion to Pont Aberglaslyn in his watercolour *The Thunderstorm* (National Library of Wales, Aberystwyth), painted in the summer of 1792. The watercolour depicts an incident, or – as described on the mount – an

> Actual Occurrence, on the steepest Ascent of the Mountain Road between Pont Aberglaslyn and Tan y Bwlch; during a most Violent Thunder Storm, which so terrified the Horses, that in consequence they have refused collar. Merionshire.

The view shows the phaeton on a mountain road, the driver desperately trying to control the terrified horses while another figure (the artist?) throws up his hands in a gesture of horror and amazement. It is dramatically lit by a flash of lightning, which, together with the inhospitably rocky landscape, adds to the drama of the event.

Furthermore, reactions to the event depicted could be categorized as 'stock' sublime. The viewpoint is distanced from the scene, the viewer situated above it, giving us a sense of control as we are not directly involved in it.

This 'standard' Burkean sublime continued into the nineteenth century as in De Loutherbourg's aquatints *Snowdon* and *Cataract on the Llugwy in Snowdonia*, both published in 1805. Although one wonders whether the latter view of mountain scenery might not, by 1805, have appeared a bit old-fashioned, that would, of course, have depended on its intended audience. De Loutherbourg must have been confident of its appeal – presumably to those familiar not only with Burke's treatise but with an appropriate pictorial language to communicate this most popular version of the sublime – which was still being discussed and debated, by Uvedale Price and Payne Knight, at the turn of the century. In each work, the staginess of the setting and the artificial nature of the lighting reinforce the impression of stock sublime in which the emotions are rationalised. In the view of the Snowdonian waterfall (Figure 5), the spectators respond with gestures

5 P. J. de Loutherbourg, *Cataract on the Llugwy in Snowdonia* (1805), aquatint

[41]

appropriate to Burkean rhetoric to signify awe and amazement at such wonders.

Certainly Burke's *Enquiry* paved the way for an aesthetic of mountain scenery. This is one of the many reasons why Snowdonia became a significant site and a powerful image during the period of the Napoleonic Wars. During that period, with Europe effectively out of bounds for the English, Wales was to become increasingly popular as an alternative site for artists and travellers, so in one sense Snowdonia could be said to have been reinforcing British nationalism during this period. Much of the travel literature on Snowdonia was employing what were, by then, conventional aesthetic frameworks of the sublime to promote a positive aesthetic of mountainous scenery which celebrated the scale and elevation of these mountains.[20] My point here, in these few visual examples, is to emphasize also (the perhaps obvious point) that by the second decade of the nineteenth century Wales and, in particular, Snowdonia could be and were represented in terms of elevation – the emphasis being on its distinctive peak. This is, as I show, in marked contrast to the so-called mountains of New South Wales.

We shift now from Wales to focus on New South Wales (NSW) and the representations of mountainous landscape there in relation both to external colonialism and the emerging notions of a local 'Australian' identity. Here, again, I focus on a journey across a particular locale, the tour over the Blue Mountains undertaken by Governor Macquarie in 1815 and his attempt to apply to this landscape, in his account of this journey, a domestic aesthetic model predicated on notions of the 'sublime', the 'beautiful' and the 'picturesque'. Not only does the landscape, by the very nature of its configuration, frequently appear to resist such attempts in visual representations, but what we find in the course of Macquarie's tour is an attempt to turn the so-called periphery into the centre and construct particular kinds of 'Australian' colonial identities so that the landscape is being shaped and reshaped, both aesthetically and in terms of colonial ideology, the two processes working side by side.

Macquarie, the road across the Blue Mountains and the naming of sites

The mountain range known as the Blue Mountains begin about 40 miles west of Sydney. Almost from the beginning of European settlement, in 1788, there was an expansionist drive to establish what lay beyond these mountains and an increasingly pressing concern to find land with potential to feed the population. The first governor of New

South Wales, Governor Philip, sighted this configuration on 13 February 1790 and called them the Carmarthan Hills, making an associative connection with the 'old' world – in this instance, Wales.[21] This practice was to become increasingly common. By 1804 Governor King had concluded from the accounts of a number of explorers that the mountains were impenetrable.[22] In May 1813 there was a literal and metaphorical breakthrough, when three men, Gregory Blaxland, William Lawson and William Charles Wentworth, negotiated a route through the ridges of the Blue Mountains before returning to Sydney. In July 1814 Governor Macquarie commissioned William Cox to supervise the making of a road over the mountains – astonishingly, all 126 miles of it was completed by convict labour in just over six months. In April and May 1815 Governor Macquarie and his party journeyed down that road and named the proposed new town of Bathurst.[23] This drive to expand westwards and the 'breaking down' of these natural impediments plus the process of traversing this difficult terrain all constituted a potent myth which was later to contribute to emergent notions of Australian white-settler nationhood: 'Here . . . was won the first major battle against the mighty bush. Here was the land first subdued and conquered.'[24]

Governor Macquarie's account was the first to be well publicized – his tour over the Western or Blue Mountains published in the *Sydney Gazette* on 10 June 1815 was extensively reprinted.[25] For Macquarie the benefit of the road over the Blue Mountains was that it constituted a crucial part of the colonizing process and of claiming the land. For here we see the creation of a civilized path and an affirming statement of the colonial presence. In discussing Governor Macquarie's progress over the Blue Mountains I consider in particular some of the literary and visual representations of the road, during both this first and later journeys, as well as visual and literary responses to and constructions of the landscape. Macquarie's party included gentlemen, officers, soldiers and the artist John Lewin. Lewin's watercolour *Cox's Pass* (Sydney, Mitchell Library) suggests a trajectory of travel further westwards: the road and the fencing constitute a veneer of civilization and an attempt to impose order on this wild and unruly landscape.

Augustus Earle's later watercolour *The Blue Mountains from the Emu Plains Road* (1826, Canberra, National Library of Australia) has the traveller with his swag over his shoulder starting off the journey from Emu Plains, the road snaking ahead and pointing the way through the landscape. By 1826 this road marks the presence of civilized Europeans. In the course of the journey, Macquarie engaged in naming the sites, views and landscape features he encountered – making associations with the familiar, that is, with the old world, as one would

[43]

expect. This worked in a number of ways – naming the views and making links literally back to the settlements closer to Sydney by means of reassuring English names, so that, for example, he commented on the fine prospects at King's Tableland and noted with pleasure that he could see the town of Windsor and Liverpool, 'and other objects within that part of the Colony now inhabited', thereby bringing the 'wilderness' of the Blue Mountains in contact with the recently created European 'civilisation', using these familiar proper nouns to create pathways for the mind to travel from the familiar to the unfamiliar.[26]

Macquarie then doubly civilized and made sense of the landscape he encountered, giving it names again redolent of the old world: King's Tableland, Prince Regent's Glen, Pitt's Amphitheatre, Mt York (in honour of the duke of York), the Vale of Clywd 'in consequence of the strong resemblance it bore to the vale of that name in North Wales'[27] and Sidmouth Valley, where he commended the improved pasturage and which John Lewin commemorated in the watercolour *Sidmouth Valley* (1815, Sydney, Mitchell Library), celebrating the verdant pasture and pastoral potential of the locale. At the same time Macquarie was ordering the landscape in visual terms and rendering it domestic via a conventional aesthetic of cultivation and fertility (as in the example of *Sidmouth Valley*), and, when appropriate, invoking an aesthetic of sublimity (see below), all the while looking for landscape that would demonstrate a potential for settlement and fine land. For Macquarie, the attraction of these plains was that 'mechanics and settlers, of whatever description, who may be . . . permitted to form permanent residences . . . will have the highly important advantages of a rich and fertile soil, with a beautiful river flowing through it for all the uses of man'.[28] He went on to mention its potential for both pastoral use and cultivation, suggesting that this scenery could improve and promote the lives of the inhabitants of NSW. The implication is that this would also remove the so-called 'stain' of convictism.

The same applies when we consider aesthetics of mountains in relation to Macquarie's project: for Macquarie also, paradoxically, one way of civilizing this foreign land was by focusing on the transformative potential of its mountainous scenery, more particularly with reference to the sublime. For Macquarie the contemplation of majestic and worthwhile mountain scenery presented the colony with an opportunity to transform itself from a penal colony to a free society. His was a political agenda, and he expressed the hope that 'New South Wales would one day emerge from the desolate landscape of convictism to something nobler, that the love of liberty and worthy sensibilities would be born in people who had worthwhile mountain scenery to contemplate'.[29] While Macquarie was able, in relation to New South Wales, to make the connection between a free (non-convict) settler society and the contemplation of 'worthwhile' mountain scenery, in Wales the situation was slightly different. Although in the literature the connection was made, once again, between mountains and liberty, it was in relation to Snowdon's integral associations with liberty and independence from England. This was obvious for the Welshman Thomas Pennant[30] who remarked that the mountains had been the natural fortifications of the Welsh princes and that individual mountains were linked specifically with past heroes. The ghosts of the past were so strong for Pennant that he fancied he could make out 'the beard of an ancient inhabitant, an arch-druid', when he looked up at Trevaen.[31] For the Welsh, Snowdon was both visually and conceptually an image of power. Some Welsh writers, such as William Williams of Llandegai, saw the mountains of Snowdon as natural bulwarks, and pointed out that it was the inaccessibility of these mountains that had contributed to the preservation of the Welsh language.[32] While there is no contemporary European account of Aboriginal people living in the ridges of the Blue Mountains, it is tempting to speculate that, as with Wales, the indigenous inhabitants of New South Wales also regarded the higher ridges of the Blue Mountains as hiding places with secret and sacred meanings.

From 1789 the Burkean sublime had been employed as a means of describing the inaccessibility of the Blue Mountains' terrain and its 'barren and forbidding aspects', and the scenery was described variously in terms of its 'horrible perpendicular mountains', 'wild inaccessible scenery' and 'inaccessible ravines'[33] (by William Dawes, William Paterson and George Bass, respectively). After the 1815 crossing and the making of the road, constructs of the sublime were used to civilize and lay claim to the mountains as this aesthetic became more familiar. It is clear that for some, however, such constructs were not always adequate to describe the unfamiliar landscape they encountered. During the tour, Macquarie's aide-de-camp Major Antill resorted to the standard language of the Burkean sublime as a convention for describing grand scenery such as King's Tableland. He also commented approvingly on the 'interesting' nature of the mountainous terrain and its aesthetic appeal. For example, of Pitt's Amphitheatre he wrote that

one of the grandest views that can be imagined was opened to our sight. In the foreground was a deep glen . . . and around it an immense amphitheatre of lofty hills crowned with rocks . . . In the distance were lofty mountains as far as the eye could reach, forming a grand circumference and background – the whole coup d'oeil *grand beyond the power of my pen to describe*.[34]

The watercolour *Pitt's Amphitheatre* by John Lewin could be regarded as a complementary visual record of Antill's narrative.[35] While the sheer scale and structure of the scene seems to have been beyond the descriptive power of Lewin's brush, as it was also for his literary companion, he does make a real (if clumsy) attempt to suggest the grandeur and circumference of the scene. This appears to have been the first watercolour to acknowledge that the Blue Mountains were not in fact mountains in the conventional sense. Lewin, however, lacked the pictorial repertoire to communicate the actuality of the scene. What we have in both instances is a suggestion of the landscape itself resisting attempts to categorize it. This is unusual, since for four decades after the first European literary descriptions of the Blue Mountains the physical features coincided with English conventions of mountain description.

Until about 1830 many travellers described the Blue Mountains as sublime (generally invoking the Burkean sublime) without necessarily explaining that their mountainous characterisitics were different from those of Europe, England, Wales and Scotland.[36] The site of Wentworth Falls demonstrates some of the difficulties and issues encountered in the representation of new and unusual terrain. Significantly, this site is also a graphic reminder that the Blue Mountains were represented largely as mountains when in fact they featured also a series of high ridges and canyons.[37] Wentworth Falls is the subject of Earle's only known oil painting of the Blue Mountains.[38] He visited the area in late 1826, and while the work is undated he probably painted it after his return to London in 1829.[39] Elizabeth Johns has reminded us that, as in British representations, 'the foreground figures in American and Australian images of waterfalls expressed emotions that in turn guided the contemporary viewer of the picture'.[40] Here a comparative case in point is De Loutherbourg's aquatint view of a waterfall in Snowdonia, *Cataract on the Llugwy*, (1805, Figure 5[41]). Here the guide guides the figures within the painting as well as guiding the contemporary viewer's focus on the sublime phenomena. Waterfalls, like other familiar landscape features, also assured tourists of the resemblance of the new worlds to the old.[42]

In the painting by Earle this process is a little more complex. His painting has the artist in the foreground with his back to the view, his discarded clothes a reminder of the effort exerted in the climb, seemingly preparing to sketch an Aborigine posed on the rock on the left. Behind the artist, another Aborigine makes eye contact with us while simultaneously pointing to the viewer's left, apparently to attract our attention both to the standing Aboriginal and to the waterfall, thus (as Andrew Sayers suggests) drawing the viewer's attention to what, by then, were for those versed in the picturesque and the sublime two conventional reference points – the figure of the black and the waterfall.[43] However, as Leonard Bell has indicated, the painting is a little more complex than first appearances would indicate.[44] A closer inspection reveals that the central Aboriginal figure is not gesturing towards the figure of the black and the waterfall. This standing Aboriginal figure is in fact on a plane further back, so that the central Aboriginal figure is gesturing towards something that is not in the picture, suggesting that much of this landscape is unseen and therefore not orchestrated or accessible via European conventions. This central Aboriginal figure is also somewhat enigmatic, functioning as a sublime type, as a mediating figure and as an individual who has knowledge of 'sights' that are not accessible to the viewer.[45] Similarly, the artist is not sketching the standing Aboriginal figure, as at first sight he appears to be doing, but is looking off to the viewer's left at an unseen landscape, thus picturing himself in an atypical fashion, not as possessor of all he surveys in the standard colonial mode, 'not looking in the usual way ... but rather as a kind of intermediary figure, on the threshold of a very different experience and knowledge of place, not yet acquired, and thus not represented'.[46]

Almost inevitably there is some artistic licence in this scene. The figure on the left is based on an earlier sketch by Earle – *Native of N. S. Wales* (Canberra, National Library of Australia) – in the Wellington Valley further to the west of these mountains. Also Earle has wildly exaggerated the 'torrent' issuing from the rock on the left of the painting, and in so doing he contradicts contemporary written descriptions which lamented the absence of rushing water. This general impression was perhaps best summed up in 1827:

> It lies about two miles off the road, at the Kings Table Land, which is nearly the highest point of the mountains, and for this reason can never, in the wettest weather, exhibit any large stream of water ... To call it a cataract is absurd; it would be easy to make as good a one with a tea-kettle; but the abyss is awful, into which the little stream falls down, and had it been called the Buller [Bouilloire or boiler] of the Blue Mountains for it is an immense caldron [*sic*], or chasm of unknown depth, perhaps two thousand feet perpendicular, the name would have been more appropriate.[47]

Indeed as the writer, Captain Dumaresq, described them, the 'falls' are in fact a thin stream of water dropping into a deep vertical ravine. The volume of water was considered meagre – mainly because visitors expected waterfalls to be broad and thundering in the manner of Niagara or of European waterfalls. Presumably Earle has the waterfall gushing down in order to appeal to a European audience, and hence to make the painting more saleable. Most contemporary artists did the same, such as E. B. de la Touanne who emphasized the torrent rushing over the top of the falls, and the sublime scale, in his view published as a lithograph in 1837, although the accompanying text also acknowledged the 'mean thread of water'.[48]

It is when we consider the representation of the other features in the painting – the remaining figures and the landscape (disjunction?) – that the work becomes harder to read. A nineteenth-century European audience may have had more difficulty in appreciating the aesthetic of the scene. The figures on the right remind us of the difficulties associated with exploring and crossing these mountains. One man is being helped to climb a rocky outcrop to a vantage point; two others are clinging to a ledge and looking down the cliff face to the sheer drop and damp vegetation below. As do these two figures in the painting, contemporary travellers found this drop remarkable, and it was graphically described in contemporary written accounts. The surrounding landscape, including the rocky cliff face supporting King's Tableland to the right of the waterfall, was also considered fascinating. In his earlier tour, in 1815, Antill had resorted to standard language of the Burkean sublime to make sense of the unfamiliar: 'The whole of the tableland next to the chasm appeared as if it had undergone a violent volcanic eruption, the stones seemed to have been in a state of fusion, forming all manner of shapes, and having the resemblance of melted sand in ironstone . . .'.[49]

Earle's painting is 'conventional' in its deployment of standard foreground structuring devices and in the focus on the waterfall. It becomes more interesting for us, and it less obviously reproduces European landscape conventions in the representation of King's Tableland and the drop of almost 3,000 feet to the valley below, although the scale is only suggested. Earle was skilled in adapting techniques to suit the demands of the site, but this emphasis on the waterfall may have been because the actual scale of the landscape overwhelmed him and challenged his notion of the sublime.

In 1837, a more famous visitor to the Blue Mountains – and, it would seem, a more perceptive one – came to terms with the actuality of the site. Charles Darwin's trip points to the real challenges posed by this terrain – that it could not be easily accommodated within standard European aesthetic frameworks. He asserted that the Blue Mountains were different from typical European mountainous scenery. He also hinted at the ways in which these mountains challenged European preconceptions of the sublime. If the local inns reminded

Darwin of north Wales and connected him in some way with 'home', the landscape evoked a different response:

[O]ne stands on the brink of a vast precipice, and below is the grand bay or gulf (*for I know not what other name to give it*), thickly covered with forest. The point of view is situated as if at the head of a bay, the line of cliff diverging on each side, and showing headland behind headland, as on a bold sea-coast. About five miles distant in front, another line of cliffs extends, which thus appears completely to encircle the valley; and hence the name of bay is justified, as applied to this grand amphitheatrical depression. If we imagine a winding harbour, with its deep water surrounded by bold cliff-like shores, laid dry, and a forest sprung up on its sandy bottom, we should then have the appearance and structure here exhibited. This kind of view was to me quite novel, and extremely magnificent.[50]

Darwin was, then, the first writer to recognize and extensively explore the wonder of the scene, not only its difference from European mountains; he also recognized the landscape in its own terms as being made up of a series of canyons. In order to effectively convey to the reader the appearance of the scene he invoked the language of association, presenting us with a composite yet fragmented picture of this wondrous whole. He reminds us that this landscape is 3,000 feet above sea-level and suggested that the only way for the reader to comprehend this 'novel' landscape was to think of it as a sea bed, the bay surrounded by high cliffs.

While Darwin managed to represent the 'non mountainous' nature of the site, that, as we have seen, proved to be more difficult for contemporary artists. After the advent of tourism and rail travel from Sydney to Wentworth Falls from 1867, contemporary viewers had experienced for themselves the reality of these 'tea-kettle' trickles, and artists such as J. H. Carse and Eugene von Guerard had to accommodate the experience of viewers in their paintings of Wentworth Falls. Both von Guerard (in 1866–68) and Carse (in 1873) represented the canyon-like nature of the Blue Mountains; but, as I have suggested, we see the beginnings of this process at work in some of the views by John Lewin and Augustus Earle.

This comparative discussion reminds us that the construction of national identity in relation to landscape painting was not, and is not, necessarily a fixed and stable practice. During this period the determining of national identities was an elusive process. As we have seen, the writings of both W. J. T. Mitchell and David Solkin are helpful in any attempt to unpack the complexities of landscape practice and viewing landscape in relation to constructs of national identity during this period. Mitchell has proposed that we consider how landscape works as cultural practice, particularly when deconstructing colonial landscape. David Solkin has provided a compelling model for the examination of Richard Wilson's views of Wales, arguing that in the 1760s Wales readily lent itself to this fictionalized representation as 'Historic Britain'.

While clearly the construction of nationalism(s) – Welsh, British and emergent Australian identities – helped to make both Wales and New South Wales places desirable to visit and to shape patterns for visiting and recording them, I have argued for a comparative framework in my discussion of the two places, via the notion of internal and external colonialisms. Here the relationship of centre to periphery is crucial to the construction of colonial identities, and this is evident in an examination of colonial landscapes. In both cases, landscape conventions have been employed for colonizing purposes. Thus in both the 'old' and 'new' worlds, constructs of the sublime, beautiful and picturesque, and an aesthetic of cultivation, have been used to both 'civilize' and lay claim to unfamiliar territories. During Governor Macquarie's tour of the Blue Mountains not only are such frameworks invoked, but the 'wilderness' is further controlled by the very process of naming it, both to make contact with the recently created European civilization and because Macquarie recognized that proper names redolent of the old world were one way of doubly civilizing and making sense of the landscape he encountered. While in both Wales and New South Wales there is evidence of the landscape appearing to resist categorization, that is particularly apparent in the Blue Mountains where there is a stronger sense that the landscape is not always assimilable via contemporary aesthetic codes and conventional modes of viewing. This is first evident in John Lewin's watercolour *Pitt's Amphitheatre*, and is echoed in the writings of his fellow-traveller Major Antill, who exclaimed that he was unable to describe the scale and grandeur of the scene.[51] In Augustus Earle's *Wentworth Falls* there is a stronger sense of this 'resistance' to colonizing strategies in the representation of landscape and in some of the individuals portrayed. Finally, Charles Darwin also recognized that this terrain could not be easily accommodated within standard European frameworks and was the first to come to terms with the actuality of the site.

Notes

1　I would like to thank Mary Roberts, Michele Cohen, Michael Hatt and Alastair Wright for their constructive comments and feedback on spoken versions of this paper. I would also like to acknowledge the support of the British Art Center at

Yale. Much of the research for Welsh part of this paper was undertaken in January 1998 when I was a visiting fellow there.

2   This painting is now in the Rex Nan Kivell Collection, National Library of Australia, Canberra.

3   W. J. T. Mitchell (ed.) *Landscape and Power*, Chicago, University of Chicago Press, 1994, Introduction, p. 1.

4   The shires created by the legislation of 1536–43 remained unchanged until 1974 when they were replaced by new counties.

5   In the summer of 1773 Banks made a tour of Wales with Paul Sandby, Daniel Solander and John Lightfoot. See Peter Hughes, 'Paul Sandy's tour of Wales with Joseph Banks', *Burlington Magazine*, vol. 117, 1975, pp. 452–7.

6   See David Solkin, *Richard Wilson*, Exhibition Catalogue, London, Tate Gallery, 1983, pp. 93ff.

7   Solkin, *Richard Wilson*, p. 102.

8   Solkin, *Richard Wilson*, p. 102.

9   See Jocelyn Hackforth-Jones, 'Views of Wales c.1770–1820', PhD thesis, University of Sydney, 1988, ch. 2: 'The pattern of travel to Wales: touring and tourism'.

10   And, like Wales, the Lake District was also conceived as arcadian in literary and pictorial representations. See John Murdoch, *The Discovery of the Lake District*, Exhibition Catalogue, London, Victoria and Albert Museum, 1984, p. 11.

11   See Michael Rosenthal, *British Landscape Painting*, London, Phaidon, 1983, p. 45.

12   See John Gilbert Cooper, *Essays on Taste*, London, 1755, and Edmund Burke, *Philosophical Enquiry into the Origin of Our Ideas of the Sublime and the Beautiful*, London, 1757.

13   Anne Bermingham, *Landscape and Ideology: The English Rustic Tradition 1740–1860*, London, Thames & Hudson, 1987, p. 9.

14   Rosenthal, *British Landscape Painting*, p. 48.

15   The Honourable Society of the Cymmrodorion was founded in London in 1751. Its membership from among the London Welsh was increasing and the society had the support of large numbers of the gentry in Wales. Its main aim was to hold social meetings, and it was also engaged in philanthropic activities, and in stimulating and furthering an interest in Welsh antiquity, language and literature, customs, natural philosophy and manufactures.

16   This watercolour is in the National Library of Wales, Aberystwyth.

17   Such as William Williams of Llandegai, author of *Observations on the Snowdon Mountains, with Some Account of the Customs and Manners of the Inhabitants.* London, 1802.

18   Edmund Burke first published his *Philosophical Enquiry into the Origin of Our Ideas of the Sublime and the Beautiful* in 1757.

19   Richard Warner, *A Walk Through Wales, in August 1797*, London, 1797, letter XIII.

20   An interesting example is Thomas Compton's aquatint *South View from the Summit of Snowdon* (1820) in the Victoria and Albert Museum.

21   *Historical Records of Australia*, Series 1: Governors' despatches to and from England, vol. 1, 1788–96, Library Committee of the Commonwealth Parliament, Canberra, 1914, pp. 155ff.

22   George Mackaness, *Fourteen Journeys Over the Blue Mountains of New South Wales 1813–1841*, Sydney, Horwitz–Grahame, 1965.

23   Named after Lord Bathurst, secretary of state for the colonies.

24   Chris Cunningham, *Blue Mountains Rediscovered. Beyond the Myths of Early Australian Exploration*, Kenthurst, Kangaroo Press, 1996, ch. 1.

25   See Julia Horne, 'Favourite resorts: aspects of tourist travel in 19th century New South Wales', PhD thesis, University of New South Wales, 1995, pp. 123ff. Macquarie's tour was reprinted in: *Naval Chronicle*, vol. 35, January–June 1816; *Colonial Journal*, vol. 1, January–July 1816; *New Monthly Magazine and Universal Register*, vol. 5, no. 25, 1 February 1816.

26   Lachlan Macquarie, 'Journal of a tour of a newly discovered country west of the B– M–. 25 April 1815–19 May 1815', Mitchell Library MS A779. p. 9.

27 Lachlan Macquarie, 'Tour over the Western or Blue Mountains, 1815', *Sydney Gazette*, 10 June 1815.
28 Macquarie, 'Tour over the Western or Blue Mountains'.
29 See Horne, 'Favourite resorts', p. 129.
30 Thomas Pennant, *Tours in Wales*, London, 1778–81, vol. 2, p. 135.
31 Pennant, *Tours in Wales*, p. 153.
32 See also Hackforth-Jones, 'Views of Wales *c.*1770–1820', pp. 197–202.
33 William Dawes (1791), William Patterson (1793) and George Bass (1796), respectively; quoted in Horne, 'Favourite resorts', pp. 107–8; see also Mackaness, *Fourteen Journeys*, Introduction.
34 Major Henry Antill, 'Opening of the road across the B– M–. An authentic copy of the diary of Governor Macquarie's journey across the New Road, and the foundation of the city of Bathurst kept by Major H. C. Antill ADC', Mitchell Library MS; italics added.
35 Antill made a second copy of his journal and the artist John Lewin made another copy of his watercolour drawings, and the two men later exchanged them.
36 Horne, 'Favourite resorts', p. 130.
37 I am grateful to Julia Horne for drawing my attention to this; see also Mary Mackay, 'The geological sublime: a new paradigm', PhD thesis, University of Sydney, 1990.
38 Originally named Campbell's Cataract by Macquarie, this waterfall was also known early on as Weatherboard Falls since it was close to the Weatherboard hut (later inn). It was named Bougainville Falls by Governor Brisbane after the French expedition of 1825. In 1869, it was renamed Wentworth Falls.
39 Augustus Earle (1793–1838) was an Anglo-American painter. He was the first freelance artist to tour the world, and spent three years travelling in Australia and New Zealand (1825–28); see also Jocelyn Hackforth-Jones, *Augustus Earle, Travel Artist*, Canberra, National Library of Australia, 1980.
40 Elizabeth Johns, Andrew Sayers, Elizabeth Mankin Kornhauser, *New Worlds from Old: 19th century Australian and American Landscapes*, Exhibition Catalogue, Canberra, National Gallery of Australia, and Hartford, Wadsworth Atheneum, 1998, p. 27.
41 Discussed earlier in relation to its invocation of the Burkean sublime.
42 Johns *et al.*, *New Worlds from Old*, p. 27.
43 Johns *et al.*, *New Worlds from Old*, pp. 56–7.
44 Leonard Bell, 'Colonial eyes transformed: looking at/in paintings. An exploratory essay', *Australian and New Zealand Journal of Art*, vol. 1, no. 1, 2000, pp. 47–9.
45 The whole question of indigenous agency is fascinating in relation to Earle's work. Leonard Bell ('Colonial eyes transformed', p. 48) has also made a convincing case for the Aboriginal figure on the left who seems to be adopting a pose suggestive of ownership or control of the land and which recalls English country house views in which the gentry are depicted in terms of property and ownership. Earle may be suggesting here that this land was far more accessible for its indigenous inhabitants than it was for European visitors – as is evidenced by the awkward efforts of the four men struggling up the rockface on the right.
46 Bell, 'Colonial eyes transformed', p. 49.
47 Captain William John Dumaresq, 'A ride to Bathurst, 1827', reprinted in Mackaness, *Fourteen Journeys*, pp. 176–7.
48 La Touanne had sketched the Wentworth Falls in 1825 when with the scientific expedition led by Commodore Hyacinthe de Bougainville, but his lithograph of the area was not produced until 1837.
49 Antill, 'Opening of the road across the B– M–'.
50 Charles Darwin, 'Journey across the Blue Mountains to Bathurst in January, 1836', in Mackaness, *Fourteen Journeys*, p. 232; italics added.
51 Antill, 'Opening of the road across the B– M–'.

CHAPTER THREE

The country house is just like a flag
Sophia Cross

This chapter is concerned with great country houses built or altered in Ulster during 1790–1840. This is a vital period for Irish history, with the formal transition of legislative power from Ireland to England through the Act of Union (1800).[1] The repercussions of the Ulster Plantation (1611), and the strong presence of Scottish, English and Irish in Ulster, make it an essential area of study in relation to colonialism and post-colonialism as discerned in the architecture of the Irish country house.

Recent and past critiques on Irish history and literature have provided a focus on issues of national identity, colonialism and post-colonialism.[2] In terms of this chapter these critiques inform the debates concerning the existence of an Irish cultural identity in the period 1790–1840. The country houses built or altered in Ulster at that time provide an appropriate vehicle for a discussion of the question of national identity. The discussion is complemented by the writings of Irish authors, such as Maria Edgeworth and Sydney Owenson,[3] who through the guise of literature could address current social and political trends in Ireland. Their observations could be read on different levels and would have been readily identified with by contemporary society in Ireland and England. Contemporary literature, like the country house, provides a further framework for an exploration of attitudes of the time towards cultural and national identity in Ireland.

I make analogical use of a flag (Figure 6). My aim is to illustrate that the Irish country house is no different from the flags that colour the streets of Northern Ireland today in asserting social, political and religious beliefs. A flag might be a more direct way of portraying such beliefs, but the image of the country house is just as powerful an illustration of allegiances. Both the country house and the flag can be interpreted on different levels. On one level they fulfil an aesthetic function; but on another level, with an understanding of the culture

6   A loyalist mural on the Donegall Pass, Belfast

from which they were created, they are potent symbols of the cultural values that they are intended to represent. In the context of this brief study my concerns are confined to the question of architectural style. This is at once the fundamental 'aesthetic' quality of the Irish country house and the route into a more complex reading of style in relation to the history of architecture.

Let us explore the country house–flag analogy further. The opening passage of Lucy Bryson and Clem McCartney's book *Clashing Symbols* clarifies the analogy:

Flags have practical uses, but their primary function has always been social communication. National flags in particular stimulate the viewer to feel and act in a calculated way. They represent or identify the

[54]

existence, presence, origin, authority, possession, loyalty, glory, beliefs, objectives, and status of an entire nation. They are employed to honour and dishonour, warn and encourage, threaten and promise, exalt and condemn, commemorate and deny.[4]

These remarks could refer equally to the country house, the sheer scale and presence of which indicates that it fulfils more than an aesthetic function. Regardless of when or where it was built, a country house is still an affirmation of ownership, territory and identity. An understanding of architecture or of the design of a flag depends on the individual viewer's interpretation and perception of the culture that each is supposed to represent.

Viewers' education and social environment also help determine their perception of the country houses built in Ulster between 1790–1840. As E. H. Carr writes in *What Is History?* an individual is a 'social phenomenon, both the product and the conscious or unconscious spokesman of the society to which he belongs'.[5] During the eighteenth and early nineteenth centuries the landed elite would have been familiar with current trends in fashion and taste. These trends were shaped not only by leading social and political figures but by aesthetic debates focusing around philosophical treatises, such as John Locke's *An Essay concerning Human Understanding* (1689) or the architectural philosophy of Abbé Marc-Antoine Laugier (1713–69[6]). For example, among that elite land was more than an economic asset, becoming embroiled in complex aesthetic debates. The manner in which a demesne, or garden, was landscaped held certain social and political associations. Andrew Ballantyne's research on Richard Payne Knight[7] and Stephen Bending's studies on late eighteenth-century landscape gardens[8] prove invaluable in understanding the complexity of those debates and what the landscape stood for in contemporary society. Their work illustrates how an agenda lay hidden behind the design of a landscape garden or a country house, just as it does the design of a flag, that goes beyond its visual appeal. The extent of people's appreciation of the country houses built at this time would have been dependent on their understanding of a distinct aesthetic vocabulary.[9] The building of a country house was a useful vehicle from which the landed elite could express their knowledge of this exclusive cultural vocabulary. In light of this it is worth considering how familiar the Irish landed elite were with this aesthetic vocabulary and whether they applied it to the country houses and estates they built in Ireland? In Ireland, as in England, the lower classes' appreciation of these country houses would have been less complicated, as for them these houses were symbols of power and a reminder of the persons to whom they owed allegiance. Not only did the individual's class influence his or her perspective on the country house but in Ireland that perception would have been influenced by his or her colonial identity.

By studying the architecture of the Irish country house and its estate in 1790–1840 the conflicting concepts of Irish nationhood become apparent. The idea of an Irish nation was problematical at that time (it still is in Ulster), and it is worth briefly looking at the circumstance which created this situation. It is more than just a juxtaposition of different political and religious beliefs in Ireland which makes the notion of a nation state so alien to contemporary society: it is the ruthless manner in which land was taken from the native Irish, broken up and then distributed among English settlers.

The plantation schemes implemented under Elizabeth I, James I and Oliver Cromwell, during the sixteenth and seventeenth centuries,[10] continued the trends of previous English monarchs who, beginning with Henry II in 1171, had set about colonizing Ireland. Through the power of such legislation as the Statute of Kilkenny (1366)[11] the English government tried to prevent an Irish culture from taking hold in the colonized areas. These laws did little to advance the aims of the British monarchy, as the first English settlers had through marriage gradually integrated with the native Irish, the Catholics; and, despite their loyalty to the English crown, these settlers perceived themselves to be Irish. The plantation schemes were another way in which the English government sought to impose its national identity on the Irish. The New English, the more recent planters, saw themselves as superior to both the native Irish and the Old English.[12] The subservient and inferior image of the native Irish, exemplified by English legislation, was advanced also through contemporary literature. The Irish were seen as wild, drunken and untrustworthy, as illustrated by Lady Morgan in *The Wild Irish Girl*, when the gentleman HM recounts in Letter I:

> But whatever may be the *cause*, I feel the strongest objection to becoming a resident in the remote part of a country which is still shaken by the convulsions of an anarchical spirit; where for a series of ages the olive of peace has not been suffered to shoot forth *one* sweet blossom of national concord, which the sword of dissension has not cropt almost in the germ; and the natural character of whose factious sons, as we are still taught to believe, is turbulent, faithless, intemperate, and cruel; formerly destitute of arts, letters or civilisation, and still but slowly submitting to their salutary and ennobling influence.[13]

In the plantation of Ulster (1609–13), the treatment of the native Irish and the manner in which land was distributed place little doubt on the English government's intentions. Chief undertakers were expected to settle English and Scottish families on their land, bear arms and build defences,[14] such as tower houses.

The Irish were further alienated from the English not only by the quantity and tenures of the land granted to them, but by the location and quality of that land. Such land was often located on coastal and more exposed areas. For example, in Donegal the Kilmacrenan barony, situated on the north-west corner of Donegal, was granted to Irish grantees and servitors, with the Irish grantees retaining 60 per cent of the land, though not always their original land.[15] In Ulster James Magrath was one of the few Irish grantees to retain his lands at Termon, Pettigoe. He built Termon Castle shortly after the re-grant of land in 1610. His father's conversion to Protestantism under Queen Elizabeth in 1567 would have helped convince the English monarchy of the family's loyalty to the crown and ensure the security of the family estates.

The English government had ensured through the settlement of land that the Irish and the English were seen as two separate nationalities. This, combined with the presence of Scottish settlers on the north coast of Ireland,[16] created a complex melée of cultures in Ulster. It was this mixture of cultural identities that would create so many problems over the coming centuries as different nationalities sought supremacy, especially in areas such as County Armagh. This turbulent past perhaps explains the need for loyalists and republicans today to cover their streets with flags, banners and murals.

The proximity of Ulster to England and Scotland created additional problems, with English and Scottish settlers able to return to their native homes if conditions became uneasy or unsettled, holding little loyalty to Ireland. This disjointed loyalty which the Anglo-Irish then held for Ireland, as distinct from that of the first settlers, can be contrasted with native Irish loyalty. This is evident, for instance, in the character of Lois in Elizabeth Bowen's *Last September*:

> It must be because of Ireland he was in such a hurry down from the mountains, making a short cut through their demesne. Here was something else that she could not share. She could not conceive of her country emotionally: it was a way of living, an abstract of several landscapes, or an oblique frayed island, moored at the north with an air of being detached and washed out and west from the British coast.[17]

This continual flow of people to and from Ireland made it even more difficult to create a unified Irish nation.

An additional consequence of Ireland's proximity to England was the problem of absenteeism among the landed elite, resulting in a substantial amount of money leaving Ireland in the form of rents, most notably during the eighteenth and early nineteenth centuries. Members of the aristocracy who owned estates in both Ireland and England often preferred to reside on their English estates, allowing the rents procured from their Irish estates to fund their lifestyles in England. The extent of this absenteeism and its consequences on the Irish economy can be illustrated in contemporary publications, including *A List of the Absentees of Ireland and the Yearly Value of Their Estates and Incomes Spent Abroad with Observations on the Present Trade and Condition of That Kingdom* (1730). In the *Minutes of Evidence taken before the House of Lords*, on 28 May 1824, John Lloyd, a sergeant-at-law, describes to the lord president in the chair how a declining economy is not the only consequence of absenteeism:

> In the south of Ireland, at least the parts with which I am acquainted the principal part of the gentry have deserted it; they have become absentees, and I am sure I am ought not to have omitted to enumerate that as a very principal cause of the disorderly state of the disturbed counties.

He goes on to discuss how the Act of Union was responsible for an increase in the number of absentees.

Both Maria Edgeworth's *The Absentee* (1812)[18] and *Castle Rackrent* (1800)[19] are powerful commentaries on the consequences of absenteeism. Absenteeism and a changing political and economic situation in Ireland led to the declining fortunes of some Irish landlords. The Irish country house and its estate in literature and art are not always portrayed as sites of wealth and colonial power: often they are associated with deterioration and neglect. Elizabeth Bowen's description of the destruction of three Irish houses during the 1920s is a poignant reminder of what the houses had represented for the Irish nationalists:

> For in February, before those leaves had visibly budded, the death – execution, rather – of the three houses, Danielstown, Castle Trent, Mount Isabel, occurred in the same night. A fearful scarlet ate up the hard spring darkness; indeed, it seemed that an extra day, unreckoned, had come to abortive birth that these things might happen. It seemed, looking from east to west at the sky tall with scarlet, that the country itself was burning; while to the north the neck of mountains before Mount Isabel was frightfully outlined.[20]

During the early 1920s many great houses throughout Ireland were attacked and burnt. For the nationalists these houses represented all that was oppressive about British and 'Ascendancy' rule. The image conveyed by the ruin of a once-proud edifice is often a powerful symbol of the loss of colonial cultural dominance.

Religion and nationality became synonymous after the introduction of the Penal Laws.[21] Furthermore religious and national identity became much more than cultural issues. Religion provided the pretext needed for a Protestant minority to ensure that it maintained its superior position in politics, society and land-ownership. The leniency with which William III, after the Battle of the Boyne (1690), treated the Catholics at the Treaty of Limerick (1691),[22] caused bitter resentment and resulted in the (predominantly Protestant) Irish Parliament passing a series of Penal Laws between 1695 and 1728 which penalised Catholics, the majority of the Irish population, in the Protestant elite's effort to retain wealth and power. Land-ownership, possibly the greatest concern of the Protestant elite, was addressed in the Penal Statute which prevented Catholics from buying land or leasing land for more than thirty-one years or passing on an estate to a single heir.[23] However, by converting to Protestantism or by bringing up their eldest sons as Protestants, some Catholic landowners did manage to hold on to their estates, as seen, for instance, when to preserve the family estates, John Savage of Portaferry, County Down, converted to Protestantism around 1725.[24] Moreover, by converting to Protestantism, Catholic landowners were also able to fight their cause within the Irish Parliament and hold seats in Westminster.[25] The Penal Laws ensured that Irish society was divided into two distinct groups, preventing any hope of a united national identity.

The eighteenth century saw the emergence of an Anglican minority, a Protestant landed elite who dominated politics and society and was to become identified as the Protestant Ascendancy.[26] With life centring around the Irish House of Commons, Dublin continued to be the elite's social base. The architectural activity in Dublin at that time reflected the importance of the city and the status of those who held power, for example the Parliament House, designed by Edward Lovett Pearce (1729). Some of the finest classical country houses in Ireland were built at the time, often located within the Pale, a 70-mile radius of Dublin, for example Castletown built for William Connolly, speaker of the House of Commons, by Edward Lovett Pearce, Richard Castles and Alessandro Gallilei (c.1719–22). As J. Genet suggests in *The Big House in Ireland in Reality and Representation*, these houses provided a 'power base through which the English government controlled the island'.[27]

The country houses built in Ulster during the late eighteenth and early nineteenth centuries incorporated a wide range of architectural styles, from Gothic to Greek Revivalist. In their book *The Houses of Ireland*, de Breffny and Ffolliott suggest that the architecture of the Irish country house was not as advanced as that of its English counterparts, for the reason that some members of the Protestant Ascendancy never visited England. Does this, as they suggest, imply an *Irish* style of architecture?[28] In parts of Ireland, as in some areas of England, there may have been a time-lag in the dissemination of architectural taste. As was the case in England, in Ireland not all members of the propertied elite could afford a known architect, and they instead relied on local craftsmen to carry out plans from pattern books. Even if some members of the Protestant Ascendancy did not visit England, most would have been familiar with Dublin, especially if they held seats in the Irish Parliament, and so could not have avoided the frantic architectural activity occurring there. The country houses surrounding, and the prominent buildings in, Dublin would have set a trend for architectural activity elsewhere in the country.

The late eighteenth century saw an increase in the number of British architects working in Ireland,[29] and they further disseminated English taste. But practical considerations come in to play here: for instance, did these English architects adapt their designs to suit the climate of the Irish country house? At Lissadell, County Sligo,[30] Francis Goodwin was forced to make accommodation to the Irish climate (Figure 7). Evidence for this can be seen in the heavy wooden gates enclosing the *porte corchere*. In his account of Lissadell in *Rural Architecture* Goodwin states that such gates were a necessity

> because the violence of the wind on the coast is at times so furious, that it was necessary to provide shelter against it; and it is accordingly intended, that whenever such is the case, one of the gates shall be closed, in order that visitors may alight without being annoyed by it.[31]

The *porte corchere* fulfilled an additional function, one of security. Goodwin would have been only too aware of the turbulent political situation in Ireland at the time. The locating of a spy-hole on the left of the front door and the placing of iron bars across the basement windows are further examples of the security measures that Goodwin incorporated into the design and planning of Lissadell.

During the late eighteenth and early nineteenth centuries, the Ascendancy's tenuous hold on the land and its growing concern over the rising Catholic middle class became more pronounced and can be seen in the country houses and estates that its members built. The Act of Union was partly responsible for this sudden surge of building. With many members of the Protestant elite losing their parliamentary seats as legislative power transferred from Dublin to Westminster, Dublin became for this social group less attractive as a centre. The compensation[32] paid for the loss of their seats provided landowners, for example Lady Downshire,[33] with the financial incentives they

[60]

7   South front of Lissadell, County Sligo

needed to return and resume a period of building and reorganization on their Irish estates and to pay off any substantial debts that they had incurred. The gradual growth of a prospering Catholic middle class must have added to the insecurity of these Protestant landlords, who were acutely aware of the manner in which they had acquired their estates. The country house, whatever its architectural style, became a medium through which they could impose their identity on the landscape and so create some semblance of permanence.[34] For some members of the Ascendancy a country house that reflected their political aspirations was equally important. Landowners, Sir Robert Gore-Booth, for example, who built Lissadell and Charles Brownlow, who built Brownlow House,[35] needed a house that would help establish them in their respective constituencies. They may have lost their seats through the Act of Union, but that did not quell their desire to regain them in the English Parliament.

Country houses became power bases from which the Protestant Ascendancy could rule, a position which its members would be unable to equal on their estates in England. English high society saw the Anglo-Irish elite as inferior, and Edgeworth's treatment of Lady Clonbrony in *The Absentee* is indicative of this.[36] The Anglo-Irish found themselves in the position of not quite belonging or being accepted in either England or Ireland. They had a shared identity which was neither Irish nor English, but an amalgamation of both. It was that identity to which Conor Cruise O'Brien refers with regard to Edmund Burke and Jonathan Swift in *The Suspecting Glance*: 'What they shared was not a national characteristic but a social experience of an underside, of a wilder and more dangerous world, and one in which assumptions current in the more comfortable society came up against limits.'[37] Was this shared identity also apparent in the architecture of the Irish country house, creating a distinct Irish style? Or were the houses simply adaptations of the English country house, with no distinctive features? For example, would Castle Coole, County Fermanagh, built (1790–97) by James Wyatt for the first earl of Belmore, have seemed out of place in the English landscape?[38]

In addition to comparison of the English with the Irish country house, a similar comparison could be made between the country houses built by Catholic landowners and those built by the Protestant Ascendancy in Ireland. In literature and art the native Irish were often depicted as living in mud cabins, the Catholic landowners in ramshackle castles, like the castle the prince of Inismore inhabits in Lady Morgan's *The Wild Irish Girl*.[39] This fitted with the English perception of the native Irish as uneducated, uncivilized and unruly, whereas members of the establishment were often depicted inhabiting country houses that were representative of current fashions and taste.

The Irish country house saw as its predecessors the castles and tower houses that dominated the Irish landscape from the twelfth century onwards. Tower houses and castles, established features of the Irish landscape, became even more embedded in 1429 when a statute was passed which gave £10 subsidies to English settlers who built small towers and castles to specific specifications.[40] As Alistair Rowan states, the great Norman castles, such as Carrickfergus Castle, built for John de Courcy (*c*.1185), were 'not Irish building but the architecture of international feudalism built as a demonstration of Norman superiority both to control and to intimidate the local population'.[41]

Walshestown Castle in the Lecale district of County Down is a fifteenth-century tower house with bawn, built by the Welshe Family. The Lecale was an area, similar to the Pale, bearing a strong English influence which had developed through close trading links with England. It is one of the few preserved castles in the area and would have been similar to Audley's and Jordan's Castle.[42] These tower houses were distinguished by their defensive qualities, strategically sited as they were: for instance, the siting of Walshestown Castle overlooking the approaches to the Quoile Estuary in Strangford Lough. The height of these castles aided visibility and communication, while also conveying an image of power and dominance to the surrounding population. With the threat of local rebellion and foreign invasion, defence considerations were of paramount importance to the design of the Irish country house. It was not until the latter part of the seventeenth century that Irish domestic architecture started to fulfil an aesthetic rather than a primarily functional role. Tower houses were often incorporated into the design of subsequent houses.

After 1800 castles became a popular form of domestic architecture among the Ascendancy. Following the ideals of the picturesque and writings such as *The Landscape* by Richard Payne Knight (1794), the castle conjured up a romantic and sublime image, free from the tyranny of political control. As Knight approved of the 'political and religious freedom'[43] of the ancient Greek civilization, so the Ascendancy seemed to recreate the architecture of an age that predated the plantations of Ireland. The asymmetry of the castle would have blended with the landscape, giving the impression of permanence, as if the structure had always been there, like the castles built by the first settlers and the Gaelic lords in Ireland. Such is the castle Lord Glenthorn describes, in Maria Edgeworth's *Ennui*:

> When I awoke, I thought that I was on a shipboard; for the first sound I heard was that of the sea booming against the castle walls. I arose, looked out of the window of my bedchamber, and saw the whole prospect bore an air of savage wildness. As I contemplated the scene, my imagination was seized with the idea of remoteness from civilised society: the melancholy feeling of solitary grandeur took possession of my soul.[44]

This dual sense of remoteness and permanence might explain the earl bishop of Derry's choice of the design and location for Downhill (*c.*1770–88), which overlooks the Atlantic ocean, on the north coast of Ulster, County Londonderry. Peter Rankin's account of Downhill in *Irish Building Ventures of the Earl Bishop of Derry* illustrates the earl's deep involvement with Michael Shanaghan, his architect, in drawing up the plans.[45] The dramatic scenery surrounding Downhill conforms naturally to the ideals of the picturesque without any human intervention. Downhill is of particular interest because of the two distinct architectural styles present. The north front overlooking the Atlantic ocean, which housed the offices and stables, was castellated and constructed in basalt. With its strategic location, imposing and defensive qualities, Downhill, as viewed from the sea, would not have been dissimilar to the Norman and plantation castles situated along the north coast, for example Dunluce Castle on the north Antrim coast. In contrast to the north front, which could be identified as Irish in character because of its adoption of certain features similar to those of the early Norman castles, the south front and block are classical and reflect a more refined taste. The inclusion of a gallery to house the earl bishop's collection of masterpieces is evidence of this. The south front, with its two projecting bays, rusticated basement and courtyard, is more akin to Italian Renaissance than to Norman architecture. The earl bishop had spent time on the continent, and continental influence, combined with his English ancestry (he was brother to the third earl of Bristol), might explain his educated choice of architecture.

In view of the juxtaposition of architectural styles, could Downhill stand as an example of the conflicting identities that faced the Anglo-Irish and to which Conor Cruise O'Brien referred. In 1770 as the earl bishop embarked on the building of Downhill, his English education must have jarred with his Roman Catholic sympathies. On the one front, Downhill could be seen to symbolize, as identified by Alistair Rowan, the 'Irishness of Irish architecture';[46] on the other, it typified the idea of 'Englishness', as discussed by Nikolaus Pevsner in *The Englishness of English Art*.[47]

Like their cultural environment, the country houses built in Ulster at the end of the eighteenth and the beginning of the nineteenth century appear to have an identity that is neither English nor Irish, but an amalgam of the two. The strong presence of Scottish settlers on the north coast adds a further dimension to this already complex melée of architectural styles. English governments, aware that they could not colonize the whole of Ireland, tried to colonize parts of it, as in Ulster. The result was that the native Irish lived adjacent to English and Scottish settlers, and their different cultures remained distinct from each other. What the country houses – like the flags that cover the streets – of Ulster show is a shared experience, one shaped by the environment and landscape but which is distinguished by the owner's own social background and sense of national identity.

Notes

1 For an understanding of the Act of Union (1800), see the entry in S. J. Connolly (ed.) *The Oxford Companion to Irish History*, Oxford, Oxford University Press, 1998, p. 565.
2 See S. Deane, *Strange Country: Modernity and Nationhood in Irish Writing Since 1790*, New York, Oxford University Press, 1996, for an example of such a critique.
3 Sydney Owenson went under the pen name 'Lady Morgan'.
4 L. Bryson and C. McCartney, *Clashing Symbols: A Report on the Use of Flags,*

Anthems and Other National Symbols in Northern Ireland, Belfast, Institute of Irish Studies, Queen's University, p. 8.

5 E. H. Carr, *What Is History?* Harmondsworth, Penguin, 1990, p. 35.
6 The architectural philosophy of Abbé Marc-Antoine Laugier can be seen in his two works *Essai sur l'architecture* (1753) and *Observations sur l'architecture* (1765).
7 A. Ballantyne, *Architecture, Landscape and Liberty: Richard Payne Knight and the Picturesque*, Cambridge, Cambridge University Press, 1998.
8 S. Bending, 'One among the many: popular aesthetics, polite culture and the country house landscape', in D. Arnold (ed.) *The Georgian Country House: Architecture, Landscape and Society*, Stroud, Sutton Publishing, 1998, pp. 61–78.
9 See Bending, 'One among the many', for a discussion of this aesthetic vocabulary with regard to the country house landscape.
10 For a fuller account of these plantation schemes, see R. F. Foster, *Modern Ireland 1600–1672*, Harmondsworth, Penguin, 1989, pp. 15–163.
11 For a fuller account of the Statute of Kilkenny (1366), see the entry in Connolly (ed.) *The Oxford Companion to Irish History*, pp. 286–7.
12 The Old English were the first English settlers who arrived under Henry II in 1171.
13 S. Owenson, 'Lady Morgan', *The Wild Irish Girl*, Oxford, Oxford University Press, 1999, p. 13.
14 See Foster, *Modern Ireland 1600–1972*, pp. 60–1.
15 For a fuller account of the Plantation Scheme in Donegal, see R. J. Hunter, 'Plantation in Donegal' and K. J. McKenny, 'British settler society in Donegal, *c*.1625–1685', in W. Nolan, L. Ronayne and M. Dunlevy (eds) *Donegal History and Society*, Belfast, School of Geography, Queen's University, 1995, pp. 283–356.
16 See J. C. Beckett, *The Making of Modern Ireland 1603–1923*, London, Faber & Faber, 1981, pp. 43–8.
17 E. Bowen, *The Last September*, London, Vintage, 1998, p. 34.
18 M. Edgeworth *The Absentee*, Oxford, Oxford University Press, 1988.
19 M. Edgeworth *Castle Rackrent*, Harmondsworth, Penguin, 1992.
20 Bowen, *The Last September*, p. 206.
21 For a fuller account of the Penal Laws, see the entry in Connolly (ed.) *The Oxford Companion to Irish History*, p. 438.
22 A fuller account of the Treaty of Limerick, 1691 can be found in the entry in Connolly (ed.) *The Oxford Companion to Irish History*, p. 316.
23 The Act to Prevent the further Growth of Popery (1704).
24 See C. Chenevix Trench, *Grace's Card Irish Catholic Landlords 1690–1800*, Dublin, Mercier Press, 1997, pp. 123–4.
25 For an example see S. Lynam, *Humanity Dick Martin, 'King of Connemara' 1754–1834*, Dublin, Lilliput Press, 1997, p. 5.
26 For a fuller understanding of the Ascendancy see Foster, *Modern Ireland 1600–1972*, pp. 167–94.
27 J. Genet, *The Big House in Ireland: Reality and Representation*, Cork, Brandon, 1991, p. 46.
28 B. de Breffny and R. Ffolliott, *The Houses of Ireland*, London, Thames & Hudson, 1992, p. 84.
29 For example, James Wyatt, William Playfair, Sir John Soane.
30 Lissadell, County Sligo, was built for Sir Robert Gore-Booth by the English architect Francis Goodwin between 1830 and 1833.
31 F. Goodwin, *Rural Architecture*, London, John Weale, 1835, Part II: 'Lissadell, the seat of Robert Gore-Booth Bart. Design No. 15', p. iii.
32 On average £15,000 was granted in compensation for every seat lost. See W. E. H. Lecky, *Ireland in the Eighteenth Century*, London, Longmans, Green & Co., 1892, vol.5, pp. 293–300.
33 W. A. Maguire, *The Downshire Estates in Ireland, 1801–1845: The Management of Irish Landed Estates in the Early Nineteenth Century*, Oxford, Clarendon Press, 1972, p. 9.

34 L. Proudfoot, 'Place and mentalité: The 'big house' and its locality in County Tyrone', in C. Dillon and H. A. Jefferies (eds) *Tyrone History and Society*, Dublin, Geography Publications, 2000, pp. 537–40. Proudfoot discusses the building intentions behind some of the 'big houses' in County Tyrone and the impact they had on the geography of the landscape.

35 Brownlow House, County Armagh, was built for Charles Brownlow by the Scottish architect William Playfair, c.1836.

36 Edgeworth, *The Absentee*, pp. 1–7.

37 C. Cruise O'Brien, *The Suspecting Glance*, London, Faber & Faber, 1972, p. 43.

38 Castle Coole was built by the English architect James Wyatt, in the neo-classical style using English materials. The Portland stone was imported at vast expense.

39 S. Owenson, Lady Morgan, *The Wild Irish Girl*, Oxford, Oxford University Press, 1999, pp. 44–5.

40 For a fuller account of tower houses, see M. Craig, *The Architecture of Ireland from the Earliest Times to 1880*, Dublin, Lambay Books, 1997, pp. 95–110.

41 A. Rowan, 'The Irishness of Irish architecture', *Architectural History. Journal of the Society of Architectural Historians of Great Britain*, vol. 40, 1997, p. 8.

42 Both Audley's Castle, Audleystown, and Jordan's Castle, Ardglass, are in the Lecale district.

43 A. Ballantyne, *Architecture, Landscape and Liberty: Richard Payne Knight and the Picturesque*, Cambridge, Cambridge University Press, 1998, p. 36. For a fuller account of Knight's approval of ancient Greek civilization, see pp. 28–60.

44 M. Edgeworth, *Ennui*, Harmondsworth, Penguin, 1992, p. 179.

45 P. Rankin, *Irish Building Ventures of the Earl Bishop of Derry 1730–1803*, Belfast, Ulster Architectural Heritage Society, 1972, pp. 12–26.

46 Rowan, 'The Irishness of Irish architecture'.

47 N. Pevsner, *The Englishness of English Art*, Harmondsworth, Penguin, 1993.

CHAPTER FOUR

Trans-planting national cultures: the Phoenix Park, Dublin (1832–49), an urban heterotopia?

Dana Arnold

The Phoenix Park lies to the north-west of the centre of Dublin, standing, in the nineteenth century, between the city and the countryside beyond. It represented both the city through the presence of the Phoenix Pillar – the symbol of Dublin – and the British colonial presence, as official governmental residences and army barracks were situated in the park. The scale and significance of the improvement works in the Phoenix Park carried out between 1832 and 1849 are comparable to those carried out in the royal parks in London earlier in the century.[1] By the mid-century the Phoenix Park had been transformed into an attractive landscaped space with public areas and private, though now visible, official residences. This transformation included a clear definition of the perimeter of the park, which was punctuated with new entrance gates and lodges. The landscape was drained, remodelled and replanted, and public pleasure grounds created. New directional axes through the park were established in the form of the Straight Avenue and other new roads, rides and walkways, and the Wellington Testamonial provided a monumental reminder of British military and imperial might. There is no doubt that the public open spaces of the urban parks in London and Dublin took on a new significance in the nineteenth century as those cities grew in size and political importance. The work in the royal parks in London has been shown to be one way in which the State tried to shape this urban experience and social interaction through the design of specific environments.[2] And this can also be identified as one of the motives behind the improvements to the Phoenix Park, as many of the key figures involved in the project had also worked in the royal parks in London.

This chapter constructs a contextualizing framework for the improvement that was made to the park, examining its social, historical and cultural significance against the backdrop of important political

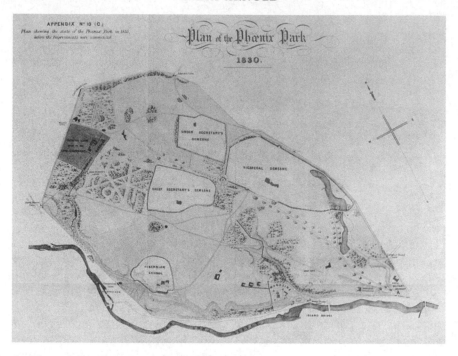

8   Plan of the Phoenix Park, Dublin, 1830

change – not least the Act of Catholic Emancipation (1829) and the Reform Act (1832). Indeed, the establishment of an urban bourgeois culture[3] in the first half of the nineteenth century affected the relationship between state and monarch and encouraged the promotion of a nationalistic cultural identity. This impacts on the bourgeois experience of the metropolis as seen in the new city plans and the development of the urban landscape. The public 'body politic' was an essential part of this identity, so in that way the redesigning of the Phoenix Park becomes a barometer of Anglo-Irish relations in the second quarter of the nineteenth century.

The relationship between Dublin and London – the first city of empire – can be read through the Foucauldian notion of a *heterotopia*, according to which the Phoenix Park may be seen as a space that reflects an inverted image of the royal parks in London.[4] As a heterotopia the Phoenix Park becomes an oppositional space, in terms of both its own internal dynamics between the public and the private and the cultural and the useful, as well as of its ability to refract the royal parks in London. Thinking about the Phoenix Park in this way enables

[68]

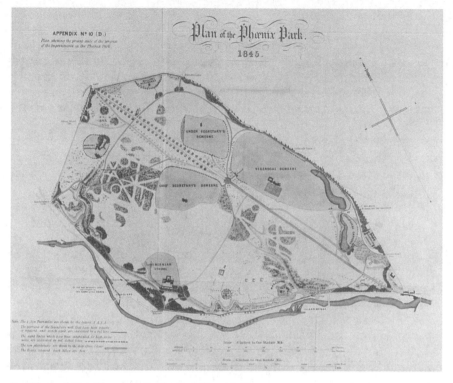

9   Plan of the Phoenix Park, Dublin, 1845

us to see the significance of urban landscapes in their space-time location through a kaleidoscopic image of spatial oppositions, political
readings, social rituals and cultural practices.

Transformations

The picture that emerges of the Phoenix Park prior to its improvement
is of an area with hilly aspects, boggy land, ramshackle buildings,
uncontrolled grazing which was subject to frequent trespass as a result
of the inadequate provision of a perimeter wall and insecure gateways
(Figure 8). Despite these somewhat inhospitable surroundings, the
Vice Regal Lodge – the official residence of the lord lieutenant of
Ireland – the Chief Secretary's and Under Secretary's Lodges were situated in the park, each within its own private demesne concealed from
public view by overgrown planting. Alongside them the Mountjoy
Barracks, the Hibernian Military School and the Magazine and Star

Forts were to be found within the Phoenix Park and, not least, the Phoenix Pillar, the symbol of the park and of Dublin itself. The transformation of the Phoenix Park into a smoothed and levelled landscape with a politically charged meaning is not unlike the large-scale landscaped gardening projects which had become so popular as socially desirable objects and visitor attractions in the eighteenth century (Figure 9). Indeed, the physical work involved in the re-imaging of the Phoenix Park rivalled the grand schemes of the landed elite, who embellished their land with an aesthetic dressing representative of their political power and aspirations, while deflecting attention from the more rugged appearance of the working land which underpinned their financial fortunes.

National landscapes

Despite the increasing importance of the metropolitan landscape in the social and cultural map of Britain in the opening years of the nineteenth century, the rural landscape was not forgotten. The latter provided both examples of how the landscape could be remodelled as well as guidelines for the viewing and consumption of these symbolic spaces. Home tourism had helped to impart nationalistic sentiment to the enjoyment of the British landscape. This was encouraged by writers like the Reverend William Gilpin who, in the 1780s, presented templates, or guides, to tourists on how to interpret views along picturesque lines, so making them evocative of freedom and nationhood. Gilpin's way of seeing remained influential and prepared the way for the reading of the urban parks as a complex narrative where the correlation of freedom and nature inherent in the iconography of English garden design, as well as the landscape, was brought into the city for political and nationalistic ends. The urban landscape became an important element in the creation of nationalist feeling and a sense of belonging within an established social framework, especially for the urban middle class.

The eighteenth-century country house and its garden were symbols of the new society – aristocratic, leisured, landed and rich. But in the nineteenth century the city became ever-more important and a home to an increasingly significant middle class where landscape remained a powerful element. Towards the end of the eighteenth century home tourism had developed to include the appreciation of the landscape in general, rather than just landscaped gardens, and here advice was on hand as to how to view it.[5] The political significance of the landscape and its ability to engender a sense of nationalism, pleasure and/or well-being in the visitor did not go unnoticed by theorists and enlightenment thinkers. These principles were used in the urban plan of London to influence the subjective response of the individual to the new urban landscape. The theorists had established the symbolic function of landscape and architecture, and here it was used in the service of monarch, state and nation, instead of that of an individual landowner. The educated population was already accustomed to reading the landscape, and it could have distinctly political associations. In his *Essays on the Picturesque* (1794) Uvedale Price represents these views as he aligns good government with naturalism in landscape:[6]

> A good landscape is that in which all the parts are free and unconstrained, but in which, though some are prominent and highly illuminated, and others in shade and retirement; some rough, and others more smooth and polished, yet they are all necessary to the beauty, energy, effect and harmony of the whole. I do not see how good government can be more exactly defined.

His sentiments were echoed by Humphry Repton, who was involved with the landscaping of London, especially of St James's Park and Russell Square:

> The neatness, simplicity, and elegance of English gardening, have acquired the approbation of the present century, as the happy medium betwixt the wildness of nature and the stiffness of art; in the same manner as the English constitution is the happy medium betwixt the liberty of savages, and the restraint of despotic government . . .[7]

The implications of these attitudes for the reading of urban landscapes come to the fore in the redevelopment of the royal parks and the Phoenix Park in Dublin. The direct association of landscape, politics and a sense of national identity was intensified by the metropolitan context of these parks. Here, the laying out of the landscape with an emphasis on axiality and vista, linking key monuments to national greatness, the nation's heroes and the impressive government offices and residences, created a new and important urban experience for both the upper and the middle classes. The positive remarks of contemporary commentators and guide books on the developments in the London parks may well have acted as an encouragement for the works undertaken in Dublin. *London Lions* (1826) gives a sense of this appreciation of urban landscapes: 'The plan and size of the [Regent's] Park is in every respect worthy of the nation.'[8] Alongside an improved metropolitan aesthetic, the public's access to royal land was also seen as a great bonus for city-dwellers. Percy's *History* remarked: 'It is fortunate for the inhabitants of London that the parks are royal demesnes', as they were, not least, the lungs of the metropolis.[9] Indeed, these feelings found official voice in the Committee on Public Walks in 1833:

> St James's Park, Green Park and Hyde Park . . . afford to the inhabitants of this Western portion of the Metropolis inestimable advantages as Public Walks. The two latter Parks are open to all classes. St James's Park has lately been planted and improved with great taste, and the interior is now opened, as well as Kensington gardens, to all persons well-behaved and properly dressed. Your Committee remarks with pleasure the advantage they afford to the Public.

The public gaze was to be directed to symbols of the nation that stood both inside and outside of the parks. The combined experience of 'common ownership' of these public open spaces and a coherent national identity gave both Londoners and visitors to the metropolis a sense of belonging.

These new urban landscapes were also intended to provide markers of this new national identity. According to a contemporary commentary (1816) these included: 'new palaces for the sovereign and the duke of Wellington – a national monument as memorial of our naval victories, another to the memory of generals, officers and soldiers, a new custom house, Post Office and several bridges'.[10]

All of the above underscored the role of the metropolis as a nexus of nationalistic sensibilities.[11] The importance of the urban landscape was not overlooked here, as the royal parks were the site for many of the plans for these new palaces and monuments. The Phoenix Park had some similar associations, as it was already the site of like buildings and the remnants of the old – pre-1798 – system of government, most notably the Vice Regal Lodge and the Chief Secretary's demesne. These symbols in the performance of the rituals of a patrician authority were now counterbalanced by the increasing political importance of the urban middle classes whose need for some kind of aesthetic expression of their identity had to be met. But the urban landscape of Dublin requires a more complex reading than does its London countersite because it is in a colonial context. Here, the heterotopic functions of the spaces of the Phoenix Park come to the fore as the re-ordered park both re-presents the royal parks and offers a tighter, more orderly, version of the same.

The national hero

The British military successes at Trafalgar and Waterloo prompted plans for monuments both to the victories and to the heroic leaders – Nelson and Wellington. Commemoration of these events was a nationwide phenomenon, but few of the projects to celebrate them planned for London were successfully completed.[12] In Dublin, however, monuments were erected to both Nelson and Wellington. William Wilkins's Nelson Column had been constructed in the centre of Dublin in 1808,[13] and in 1814 the Wellington Fund had been opened with the idea that there should be a monument also to the duke in the city. Wellington had long-standing connections with Ireland: not only was he was born there but, perhaps more significantly, he was made the country's chief secretary, a post he relinquished in 1808 when he was appointed commander of the peninsular. Moreover, it is important to remember the position of Ireland during the Napoleonic Wars, especially its comparative proximity to France and its hostility to the British colonial presence. These factors combined to promote the notion that Ireland might be a back door into Britain, and so a kind of weak spot in the armour of the empire. A monument to Wellington would, then, also serve as a reminder of British military might and of the forceful presence of the duke as commander of the army, in Ireland as well as throughout the rest of the empire.

The debates around the kind of monument that should be erected to the duke in Dublin shed light on how national identities can be expressed. The views of J. W. Croker, an MP and member of the committee that administered the Wellington Fund, on the subject of monuments are clearly set out in his letter to the secretary of the Dublin Wellington Fund dated 7 October 1814:

> I quite agree with the committee in its predilection for a pillar. I was one of the pillarists in the Nelson case and my only wish for our column to be one of more magnificent dimensions. Great height is the cheapest way and one of the most certain of obtaining sublimity. Ten thousand pounds will bring you the highest column in the world, and will produce an astonishing effect; fifty thousand pounds would serve to erect an arch, and when it was erected you would have it dated . . . Therefore, I exhort you to keep the column form. Whatever you do be at least sure to make it *stupendously* high; let it be of all the columns in the world the most lofty.
>
> Nelson's is 202, Trajan's about 150, Antonius' 132 or as some have it 180, Buonaparte's in the Place Vendôme is, I think, near 200. I wish therefore that you should not fall short of 250, and I should prefer to have it exactly from the first layer to the base of crown of the statue 300.[14]

The plans for the Wellington monument in Dublin were given fresh impetus by the victory at Waterloo, as seen, for instance, in the two designs for triumphal arches offered by James Gandon in 1815–16. The Phoenix Park was chosen as the appropriate site for the monument (whatever was to be its final form), as the secretary of state and his chief officers lived there; and, like Hyde Park in London, it was the scene of military exercises. However, the Dublin committee decided on a pillar to be designed by Robert Smirke, which was erected in the Phoenix Park. There are formal and ideological similarities between the placing of such a monument in the parks in London and Dublin. But the meaning of the Wellington Testimonial in the Phoenix Park is subtly different. It is a statement of national pride but one made within a colonial context – ironically, it is one of the more successful attempts to celebrate the duke, as the London monuments to his victory over the French were dogged by controversy, apathy and ridicule.[15]

The political backdrop to the Phoenix Park as a symbol of colonial rule

The works in the Phoenix Park can be set in the context of the turbulent English–Irish relations during the opening years of the nineteenth century.[16] The 1798 rebellion precipitated the abolition of the Irish Parliament, or College Green Assembly, and the transfer of government to London, although the Irish Exchequer was not amalgamated with the rest of Britain until 1816.[17] This meant that Ireland was now subsumed by British political and cultural identity. The nature of Ireland's colonial dependence changed as a metropolitan system of government was established. Although this was nominally run from Dublin it was clearly rooted in London. Moreover, the distinctly Protestant culture that emerged in the decades after the union became a driving force in urban politics.

The governmental structure in Ireland retained some facets of pre-union times. The viceroy, also known as the lord lieutenant, and his 'court' remained in place in Dublin, despite the transfer of power to London. The chief secretary maintained a powerful role – often augmented by good connections with the British cabinet.[18] The two posts did not always work well together. The chief secretary and his under secretary were more politically proactive and often used patronage of various kinds for their own political ends. Part of the development of a tighter governmental structure in Ireland in the post-union period was state involvement with improvements in education, public health and public works.[19] Here there was more decisive and extensive intervention than in mainland Britain, which helped ensure the implementation of a metropolitan system of rule. The Phoenix Park was, then, a site of both geographical and political importance in Dublin and can be seen as a focal point of the interaction between colonial rule and urban planning.

By 1828 the political and religious tensions in Ireland had escalated considerably. The Catholic question was becoming more of an issue as Daniel O'Connell, the Catholics' leader, had been elected to Parliament in 1828 in a by-election in County Clare. Roman Catholics were not allowed to sit in the House of Commons, but any attempt to bar O'Connell from doing so would be likely to strike up rebellion in Ireland. The alternative solution of calling a general election would only intensify the problem, as it was likely all of Ireland except Ulster would return Roman Catholic MPs. The duke of Wellington, by now prime minister, decided to admit Catholics to Parliament temporarily on condition that they taking an oath of loyalty. Further, the Catholic priesthood was to be licensed and paid for by government in an attempt to control their behaviour. Opinion had been moving some way towards Catholic emancipation as the House of Commons had voted in favour of it in 1821 and 1825, but the House of Lords had rejected it each time. The problem, in 1828, focused on Robert Peel, the leader of the House of Commons and home secretary, who was responsible for Ireland. He was known as 'Orange Peel', and therefore was hardly likely to be in favour of any toleration of the Catholics. But Wellington decided in the summer of 1828 that emancipation must be granted by the autumn, and he worked out proposals for this.

The terms offered by Wellington were that Catholic priests should operate under royal licence. Forty-shilling freeholders (i.e. most of the Catholic peasantry) should be disenfranchised and only the more substantial freeholders should be allowed to vote. Certain high offices – the lord chancellor, first lord of the Treasury, the chancellor of the Duchy of Lancaster and the lord lieutenant of Ireland – all controlled a high degree of patronage in the Anglican Church. These offices should remain in Protestant and, therefore, crown hands. Finally, the Catholic Association – O'Connell's political machine in Ireland – should be forbidden.

In 1829 the Act of Catholic Emancipation was passed, to which, despite much opposition, the duke of Wellington had given his support. Charles Arbuthnot had played an important role in ensuring the necessary support of the Whig opposition, especially Lord Duncannon and Earl de Grey. This act was quickly followed by the enfranchisement of the middle classes in the Reform Act (1832). The residency qualification of voters in this act made the Protestant bourgeoisie a significant force in Irish urban politics.[20] These social, religious and political changes highlighted the need for a tight metropolitan government in Ireland. It needed to be both effective and

[75]

have an appropriate symbolic presence in the cityscape to adequately represent British cultural identity. The Protestant middle class needed to find and appropriate aesthetic expression of its cultural identity, which was both located in and dislocated from mainland Britain. The redesign of the Phoenix Park had, then, to meet this need, as well as being a visual signifier of state authority and ideology. It was, at once, a mirror of London and its oppositional space.

The reform of the Irish Board of Works – a signifier of metropolitan systems of government

The escalating troubles in Ireland in the 1820s coincided with attempts to tighten control in the province – in particular the Irish Board of Works. Attention to the activities of the board coincided with the 1828 moratorium that had halted most of the major work being carried out in London by the Offices of Woods and Works. In the same year Lord Lowther was made first commissioner of the Office of Woods and Forests. Up until that point little attention had been paid to crown lands in Ireland. But Lowther made enquiries into the Phoenix Park, wishing to be informed on 'the extent, the income; the pasturage; number and names of lodges; whether any other ground is attached to the office of Lord Lieutenant; what extent of ground is attached to [the residences of] the Lord Lieutenant and his secretary'.[21] The enquiry was carried out by Lord Palmerston's agents in Leinster Street and sent back to Lowther via Mr Robinson, secretary to the Board of Works in Ireland, which was then responsible for the Phoenix Park. This enquiry may not have been totally innocent, as there were strong suspicions of mismanagement and financial irregularities on the part of the Irish Board of Works. And in 1829 the duke of Wellington launched an enquiry into the Irish Board of Works's activities that led to significant changes in the management of the Phoenix Park. Given the political situation, the symbolic function of the park and the nature of its residents, the attention paid to the Phoenix Park can be termed as being at least timely.

The death of George IV in 1830 facilitated the reorganization and financial restructuring of the management of all aspects of public works in Britain as well as Ireland. The English Offices of Woods and Works were merged in 1832.[22] In Ireland the Board of Public Works was established even earlier, in 1831, to replace the Board of Works, and the Phoenix Park was placed in its care. But the Government changed its mind quite quickly about who should have responsibility for the park, as in 1835 its supervision was shared. The enclosed grounds and buildings associated with the lord lieutenant and other

[76]

officers of state were put in the care of the Board of Public Works; all remaining areas of the park, where the greatest number of improvements were planned and to which the general public were admitted, were under the care of the Office of Woods.[23]

One of the main reasons for this shift in policy appears to have been funding. The improvements to the parks were to be paid for out of the Land Revenues' Account for Ireland, which was increasing at a fair rate at this time, and not out of a parliamentary grant. This pattern of funding and management followed that of the royal parks in London and obviated the problem of using public funds for such work. Moreover, the reform of the Irish Board of Works was part of the policy of economic development in Ireland. The board's remit was wide-ranging and included government-funded improvements to roads and railways, which would strengthen economic activity and growth.[24] The division of the care of the Phoenix Park was symbolic of the divided governmental structure of Ireland. On the one hand there was a system administered, albeit nominally, from Dublin Castle by offices and bodies established in pre-union days – in this case the chief secretary and under secretaries and the newly reformed Board of Public Works. On the other hand there were London-based authorities – specifically here the Office of Woods – whose concern it was to improve the quality of the urban fabric.

The 1832 and 1834 reports

It is against this background of social and political upheaval and the reorganization of the administration of crown lands in Ireland that a report on the state of the Phoenix Park with recommendations for improvements was commissioned from the architect Decimus Burton in August 1832. The commissioners found Burton to be the obvious choice and

> official instructions to that effect [i.e. the improvements] were issued to Mr Decimus Burton, who had previously been employed on a similar service in the Parks of the Metropolis, and who had designed and superintended the execution of the new lodges and other recent improvements there.[25]

Burton quickly followed up his initial report with a further survey, in September 1834, of the state of the Phoenix Park.[26] His remarks, written after a visit to Dublin in August 1834, give a clear idea of his overall vision for the park and have distinct resonance with his work in London. At this point it is important to remember the interconnectedness of the seemingly diverse government offices and officials, as this underscores the intentionality and complex relationships in and around the works in the Phoenix Park. For instance, the duke of Wellington was at once a celebrated war hero and the prime minister who prompted the reform of the Offices of Woods and Works in Britain and Ireland. His pragmatic view on the Act of Catholic Emancipation (1829) was contradicted by his strong objections to the 1832 Reform Act, yet he was concerned about rights of access of the urban middle class to the Phoenix Park. Charles Arbuthnot, another key player, was a close personal friend of Wellington who facilitated the 1829 Act.[27] Arbuthnot was also a prominent official in the Office of Woods who had done much to promote Decimus Burton as the architect in charge of the redevelopment of Hyde, St James's and Green Parks. And, finally, in this sequence, the architect Decimus Burton as the instrument or agent of the broader sociopolitical forces behind the redesign of the Phoenix Park.

The landscaping of the Phoenix Park

The work falls into three main categories: the drainage and general tidying and replanting of the park; the creation of pleasure grounds for the enjoyment of the public – especially women and children; and the re-landscaping of the area around the vice regal, chief and under secretaries' demesnes. Burton's scheme shows sympathy with the natural landscape of the area by creating views through to the countryside and the hills beyond, and the feeling of openness and space within the park. This was to be achieved by vistas stretching across the enclosed grounds of the official residences created through the use of sunken fences rather than high walls, the felling of tall trees and careful planting. In other, more remote, areas of the park Burton followed the lay of the land. For instance, the recommendations for the planting around Knockmaroon Glen in 1846 included thorns, furze and broom, 'to accord with the wild and natural scenery of that district of the park'.[28]

Although the plans to alter levels and improve drainage in the park received close attention, the main emphasis was on the public's enjoyment of the area and how people might use it. A letter to the Office of Woods towards the end of the work in March 1847 is indicative of this view:

> [T]he public would approve the enclosure of the plantation between the promenade ground and the zoo through which a direct footpath leads to the gardens from the city. If these groves were thus defended from incursions by horsemen it would become a favourite resort particularly in summer for promenades especially by women and children.[29]

[78]

This feeling for the good of the general public and of the importance of visibility influenced the landscaping around the vice regal, the chief and under secretaries' official demesnes within the park. Previously these grand buildings had been hidden from sight behind high fences that stopped views across the park. But the new designs recommended the felling of trees and the high fences were replaced with sunken fences (a kind of urban Ha Ha[30]) in order to open up vistas across the demesnes.[31] This allowed the official residences to be seen by the general public and recalls the techniques used in the design of country house landscapes, where impressive buildings became prominent signifiers of the power and wealth of the owner/occupant. This symbolic presence was further enhanced by the stage-set-style landscape that completed the panorama. Moreover, in common with country house landscapes, that of the Phoenix Park engendered a sense of belonging, or an illusion of inclusiveness and common ownership through the public's access to certain parts of the landscape and the visual accessibility of the whole scene. Indeed, that aspect of the design had been of paramount concern right from the inception of the project in the early 1830s. Attention focused principally on the fact that the opening up of the park for public enjoyment and the relandscaping of the areas around the official residences would impinge on the accommodation of the lord lieutenant. The lodge and barrack demesne in the north of the park, used by the lord lieutenant as a farm, denied the public access to parts of the park and potential revenue from the pasturage available there was desirable to fund the upkeep of the park. James Neale wrote to William Gosset stating:

> I am directed by the Board to signify to you with the view of obviating the complaints made in the House of Commons on the part of the public resorting to the parks for recreation as well as carrying into effect the improvements suggested by Mr Decimus Burton in his report dated 31 January last [1833]. The commons feel themselves required to resume possession of all the land comprised within the above mentioned enclosures [lodge and barracks] and to lay the same open again to the other parts of the park – but considering that the immediate execution of this measure may materially interfere with the comfort of his Excellency, the present Lord Lieutenant of Ireland whose domestic arrangements may have been formed upon an understanding that the farm was an authorized and permanent appendage to the Office the Commissioner trust that they shall be justified in consulting His Excellencies convenience by appointment of the measure during his administration of the Government of Ireland.[32]

But once the term of office is over the arrangement would no longer continue and therefore referring to Mr Burton's suggestions relating to this section of the park for your guidance, I am to communicate to you the Board's desire that whenever the Office of the Lord Lieutenant shall next become vacant you will remove walls and fences enclosing the farm preliminary to the execution of further improvements there recommended by Mr Decimus Burton.[33]

By the autumn things had moved on, as Duncannon, the First Commissioner of Woods, urged that instructions be issued for the Mountjoy Barrack demesne be opened to the public as quickly as possible as a new lord lieutenant might postpone it.[34] The reappropriation of land for the public's benefit is undoubtedly indicative of the use of landscape as tool to engender a feeling of inclusivity. But here it is also representative of the way in which political control in Ireland was both tightened and overseen more closely by government in London. Once again the aesthetic considerations of the landscape and issues of accessibility come to the fore in the repair of the boundary wall of the park, which was to act

> as a means of preventing trespass and at the same time of increasing the beauty of the park, an irregular belt of plantation should by degrees, be formed, having a deep ditch next [to] the wall, and another next [to] the park. These ditches would, at the same time, be extremely serviceable in draining the land, which is in the most parts of a damp and spongy nature.[35]

The architecture of the park also received aesthetic attention, not unlike the remodelling of farm buildings and workers' housing on country house estates.

> The lodges and gates throughout the park are of a mean character, and for the most part, the former are far larger than is necessary, either for the purpose they are intended for, or for appearance. They should be gradually rebuilt in an appropriate style of architecture, and no walled gardens, cowhouses or outbuildings allowed to be attached to them.[36]

One of the hallmarks of Burton's redesign of the royal parks in London had been their new entrances. These classically inspired compact lodges helped shape the character of the parks. This was also the case in Dublin, and the Chapelizod Gate and Lodge amply demonstrate what Burton had in mind.[37] The new lodge had no outbuildings; instead a sunken court provided storage and a small garden laid to turf replaced the plot that had been used for cultivation. Here, as in the Castleknock and Knockmaroon Gates and Lodges, the creation of an ordered public cultural space with which to replace a more disordered private useful space was of paramount importance. Chapelizod Lodge was the first to be re-sited in alignment with the Hibernian Military School.[38] Although the new lodge was smaller than its predecessor, it created a more impressive and secure entrance as a turnstile gate, locked each night by the Chapelizod gatekeeper. The alignment of Chapelizod Gate and the military school is important here, as axiality is a recurrent feature of the plan for the park. Moreover, the amount of remodelling of the landscape required to enable the new plan is once again reminiscent of the huge undertakings in the laying out of country house landscapes.

The idea of aligning the new entrance to the Hibernian Military School was ambitious and typifies the amount of work undertaken in each stage of the redevelopment of the Phoenix Park. It involved moving to the side the farm situated at the front of the school and concealing it by planting. A sloping lawn was also created to take account of the steep terrain at the front of the school, so affording an axial view of the building from the new entrance gate. This line continued through an ornamental garden laid out at the rear of the school and a small church. The design of the lodge itself was typically compact and symmetrical, with a temple portico front – not dissimilar to the Cumberland Lodge (1825) designed by Burton for Hyde Park in London.

The Straight Avenue

There was general concern about the roads and the provision for the public of convenient access through the park. Several new roads were proposed, along with a widening of existing roads, which required taking small tranches of land from the grounds of the official residences. The most impressive proposal for the road system was the new Straight Avenue, which, despite its importance to the overall plan, was formed only gradually, as work in the park progressed. It was necessary to alter the line of the existing road through the park and, where necessary, to sow over it with grass and to carry out substantial tree-felling and replanting to create the desired effect The avenue was the essential backbone of the park, giving to the through-flow of traffic a directional logic. Indeed, other avenues and roads in the park, which were also improved, met with the Straight Avenue at its virtual centre point. Here, Burton resited the Phoenix Pillar, the very symbol of both the park itself and of Dublin the capital city of Ireland and the second city of empire.[39] The pillar was surrounded by four iron standard lamps with burners, to align with the new line of the road – a kind of metaphorical re-enactment of the process of annexation and re-ordering experienced by the colonized at the hands of the colonizer. By 1846 the Straight Avenue was completed between the Phoenix Pillar and the Dublin Gate,[40] where the unfinished Wellington Testamonial was situated, so creating an ambiguous axis between a monument to Dublin, albeit resited, and a potent, but incomplete, symbol of colonial presence. Although he lamented that the monument was unfinished, Burton suggested that the whole area be replanted and the Dublin Gate redesigned so that 'the *tout ensemble* would have a spacious and noble effect'.[41] Even so, the remaining portion of the road leading to the Castleknock Gate still awaited completion a year later.[42]

Burton's vision was in accord with the Office of Woods' aim to 'render the park more attractive and better suited to those objects (lodges, gates, drives &tc) than it was represented to be'. This, it was stated, followed the wishes of Charles II, who had purchased the Phoenix Park 'expressly with the view of consulting the taste, and promoting the health and enjoyment of the people'.[43] But this went beyond a simple desire to beautify the only park in Dublin. Perhaps, as might be expected, there was a strong political motivation behind the instigation of such works. The recent works in the royal parks in London were intended to underline governmental authority and be of benefit to the public. Likewise, the Government felt that this should be extended to 'the inhabitants of Dublin [who] are justified in their expectation they entertain that the favour and liberality of the Government will not be withheld of the only park attached to their capital'.[44] This 'liberality' is evident in the careful use of improved landscape and increased public access. Moreover, the relationship between the London parks and the Phoenix Park went beyond the uniformity of their landscaping and architectural improvements, and their architect. The outfits worn by the gatekeepers, which it was decided early on in the works should be the same as those worn in St James's Park and Regent's Park, demonstrate the importance of the image of the parks and the strong connection between the works in the two cities. In this way the re-use of the design principles of the London parks can be seen as one way in which authority was exported to a colonial capital. The Phoenix Park helped forge an aesthetic identity for the urban Protestant bourgeoisie whose political empowerment had been augmented both by the Act of Catholic Emancipation and the Reform Act (1832).

All of the works discussed thus far were funded by the State, the only revenue yielded by the park being from the pasturage and tollgates.[45] Yet, like the royal parks in London, there was room for speculative private development. In 1837, in an uncanny imitation of Regent's Park in London, Burton recommended that an area between the Castleknock and Colonel White's Gates (some 12 acres) should be appropriated for building villas;[46] importantly these should be constructed 'without interference with the views across the park'.[47] More-over, as in Regent's Park, the commissioners would be responsible for the construction of a road leading to the plots. No villas were built in the park, although a Dublin-based builder, Jacob Owen, did tender for some of the plots. Perhaps the dislocation from central Dublin, a geo-graphical disadvantage no amount of landscape re-design could change, blighted these plans, as it did the impact of the park on the urban fabric of the city itself.

Conclusion

The remodelling of the Phoenix Park drew to a close in 1849. The points of contact between the Phoenix Park and the royal parks in London are manifold. The emphasis in this study has been on the expression of colonial authority now exercised through a metropoli-tan system of government and how this, in turn, found expression in the urban landscape. The decisions made in the remodelling of the Phoenix Park offer a mirror image of those effected in London, pro-viding us with a reading of the Phoenix Park as a countersite where the sociopolitical co-ordinates of the re-imaging of London in the opening years of the nineteenth century are enacted as an inverted vision. Here the democratizing principles of urban landscape develop-ment transform into the colonizing authority of a new social elite. The newly remodelled park made the official demesnes of the Protestant officers of the British government more visible. And these residences were placed in an improved landscape setting designed for the conve-nience and pleasure of the public – especially the Protestant bour-geoisie. The park and its intended public are important statements when seen against the backdrop of the religious and political situation in Ireland. The landscape design principles used to achieve the desired results correspond to those Burton employed in the royal parks. More-over, the plans for the inclusion of speculative private development as seen in the villas and the inclusion of premises for learned societies – for example in the zoological gardens, which were also laid out by Burton in both London and Dublin – tie the Phoenix Park more closely to London, in particular the distinctive social environment created in Regent's Park.[48] The commissioners were successful in their intention to stimulate use of the park, causing Burton to remark that 'since the improvements in the appearance and police in the park have been effected the public generally are accustomed to frequent it in far greater numbers than formerly – and that the difference in this respect is more particularly observable in regard to the upper classes'.[49] In this way the park becomes a colonizing heterotopia, a meticulous space where all that was planned, but not always realized, for the London parks is mirrored in a discrete location away from the main centre of Dublin.[50] Both the order imposed on the space through the re-landscaping, and the conditions of entry and social conduct within the park, made possible through improved perimeters and boundaries, are parts of the colonizing process and of a heterotopia. But the Phoenix Park remains a distinct urban landscape with its own identity. Perhaps here more than anywhere else Burton's work is the physical expression of the political metaphors of landscape design used by the critics of Capability Brown and Humphry Repton. The attempts by the British government to impose its political will on Ireland could not be better represented than by Burton's 'smoothing and levelling' of the rugged Irish terrain.

Notes

1 The royal parks in London included Regent's Park as well as Hyde, St James's and Green Parks. All these parks were relandscaped and generally improved in the opening decades of the nineteenth century.

2 For a discussion of the social, cultural and political significance of the royal parks in London in the early nineteenth century, see D. Arnold, *Re-presenting the Metropolis: Architecture, Urban Experience and Social Life in London 1800–1840*, Aldershot, Ashgate, 2000.

3 Throughout this chapter I use 'bourgeois' and 'middle class' interchangeably; see R. Williams, *Keywords: A Vocabulary of Culture and Society*, London, Fontana, 1976.

4 See M. Foucault, 'Des espaces autres', trans. Jay Miskowiec as 'Of other spaces', *Diacritics*, spring 1986, pp. 22–7.

5 For a fuller discussion of the ways in which the middle and upper classes were taught to view the landscape see M. Andrews, 'A picturesque template: the tourists and their guidebooks', in D. Arnold (ed.) *The Picturesque in Late Georgian England*, London, Georgian Group, 1995.

6 Price published follow-on volumes to his 1792 *Essay on the Picturesque* under the title *Essays on the Picturesque*, London, 1794. This statement is from vol. 1, p. 39.

7 From a letter from Repton to Uvedale Price Esq., London 1794, in J. C. Loudon, *The Landscape Gardening and Landscape Architecture of the Late Humphry Repton Esq., Being His Entire Works on These Subjects*, London, 1840, p. 106.

8 *London Lions for Country Cousins and Friends about Town, New Buildings, Improvements and Amusements in the British Metropolis Illustrated with Wood Engravings by Horace Wellbeloved*, London, 1826, pp. 20 and 22.

9 S. Percy and R. Percy, *The Percy History and Interesting Memorial on the Rise, Progress and Present State of All the Capitals of Europe*, 3 vols, London 1823, vol. 3, p. 355.

10 Richard Crutwell, *Remarks on the Buildings and Improvements in London and Elsewhere*, London, 1816, p. iii.

11 Many of these plans – some of them quite improbable – are outlined in F. Barker and R. Hyde, *London as It Might Have Been*, John Murray, London, 1982.

12 For a discussion of the national celebration of Nelson and Wellington, see A. Yarrington, *The Commemoration of the Hero 1800–1864: Monuments to the British Victors of the Napoleonic Wars*, New York and London, Garland, 1988.

13 R. W. Liscombe, *William Wilkins*, Cambridge, Cambridge University Press, 1980, pp. 57–8.

14 B. Pool (ed) *The Croker Papers 1808–1857*, London, Batsford, 1967, pp. 21–2.
15 For a discussion of the different ways in which the duke of Wellington was commemorated in London, see Dana Arnold, *The Duke of Wellington and London*, Wellington Lecture Series 13, Southampton, University of Southampton, 2002.
16 For a detailed discussion of Anglo-Irish politics at this time, see W. E. Vaughan (ed.) *A New History of Ireland*, vol 5: *Ireland Under the Union, I: 1801–1870*, Oxford, Clarendon Press, 1989.
17 For a fuller discussion, see R. F. Foster, *Modern Ireland 1600–1972*, Harmondsworth, Penguin, 1988, p. 282 ff.
18 Foster, *Modern Ireland*, p. 289.
19 Foster, *Modern Ireland*, p. 290.
20 Recent debates have queried the relationship between the Reform Act (1832) and the rise of middle-class power (see, among others, Dror Wahrman, *Imagining the Middle Class: The Political Representation of Class in Britain, c.1780–1840*, Cambridge, Cambridge University Press, 1995), claiming that this Act facilitated the 'invention' of the ever-rising middle class rather then having been precipitated by this social group. It is not my intention here to debate the merits of these revisions of historical constructions of class identities and their broader ramifications. But, in this instance, the case for the combined influence of the Act of Catholic and Emancipation and the Reform Act on the sociopolitical context of the Phoenix Park is compelling, particularly within a colonial framework.
21 In 1994 a substantial amount of documentary material became available in the Office of Public Works' Collection, the National Archives of Ireland. The collection of letters, plans and designs for the works carried out in the park in 1832–49 sheds new light on the nature of these improvements, and on the role played by Decimus Burton and his relationship with other parties also employed in the improvements to the park. The material comprises six boxes of letters and six folders of drawings. The letters are as yet uncatalogued. A temporary reference of OPW5/Decimus Burton/Phoenix Park has been given to them (hereafter OPW). A statement of my preliminary findings appeared as D. Arnold, 'Decimus Burton's work in the Phoenix Park, 1832–49', *Bulletin of the Irish Georgian Society*, vol. 37, 1995, pp. 57–75. OPW Letter from Mr Philipps, Office of Woods, to Mr James Neale, 19 September 1828.
22 On this point see M. H. Port, 'Retrenchment and reform: the Office of Woods and Works', in J. Mordaunt Crook and M. H. Port, *The History of the King's Works*, vol. 6: *1782–1851* (general editor H. M. Colvin), London, HMSO, 1973, pp. 179–207.
23 *Report of the Commissioneres of Woods, &c., to the Lords of the Treasury*, 1835. This report also suggested improvements to the Phoenix Park and requested authority to spend £15,000 to execute them (abbreviated hereafter as 1835 *Report*).
24 For instance, in 1835 a Commission on Railways was set up for Ireland.
25 1835 *Report*.
26 This report by Burton, dated 27 September 1834, was printed as an appendix to the *Twenty Second Report of the Commissioners of Her Majesty's Woods, Forests and Land Revenues*, 1845. Abbreviated hereafter as Burton's 1834 report.
27 The friendship between the duke of Wellington and Charles Arbuthnot and his wife Harriet is well documented. They were known to have been his confidantes from whom he sought advice. See, among others, E. Smith, *Wellington and the Arbuthnots*, Stroud, Sutton, 1994; and Harriet Arbuthnot, *The Journal of Mrs Arbuthnot, 1820–1832*, ed. Francis Bamford and the Duke of Wellington, London, Macmillan & Co., 1950, 2 vols.
28 OPW 6 January 1846, Burton to the commissioners of woods.
29 OPW March 11 1847, Burton to the commissioners of woods.
30 'A Ha Ha' is a term to describe a sunken ditch used to separate the landscaped area of a country house estate from the working farmland without creating a visual barrier.
31 For instance OPW 5 June 1838, Burton to the commissioners of woods, outlining his plans for the felling of trees and new planting around the chief secretary's

demesne. This was agreed to as the first commissioner felt the vistas were for 'the general good of the public'.

32 OPW 29 April 1833, James Neale, Office of Woods to William Gosset.
33 OPW 29 April 1833, James Neale, Office of Woods to William Gosset.
34 OPW 7 September 1833, Lord Duncannon, Office of Woods, to Mr Adams.
35 Burton's 1834 report.
36 Burton's 1834 report.
37 Burton also produced designs for the Cabragh Gate and Colonel White's Gate with his report of 27 February 1839. Drawings for these submitted with Burton's report are held in the National Library of Ireland (NLI 2123, 2124, 2126 and 2127).
38 A drawing by Burton dated January 1836 showing this is held in the National Archives of Ireland, OPW 5 temporary folder HC/2/65.
39 He received permission to resite the pillar on 11 March 1843 in a letter from Alexander Milne (OPW). Mr Hayden provided the standard lamps and burners. OPW 31 October 1843, Burton to the commissioners of woods. Mr John Butler was responsible for taking down the Pillar and re-erecting: OPW 20 December 1843 Burton to the commissioners of woods.
40 OPW 15 March 1847, Burton to the commissioners of woods.
41 Burton's 1834 report.
42 OPW 15 March 1847, Burton to the commissioners of woods.
43 1835 *Report*.
44 1835 *Report*.
45 Little mention is made of the tollgates but there were problems with avoidance of payment; Burton intended to speak to Jacob Owen on the matter. OPW 12 February 1838, Burton to the commissioners of woods.
46 OPW 9 June 1840, Burton to the commissioners of woods. Burton refers to his original suggestion for villas in his report of 1837. A drawing by Burton, dated 10 September 1840, showing the proposed villa plots, is held in the National Archives of Ireland: OPW 5 temporary folder HC/2/84.
47 OPW 30 June 1840, Burton to the commissioners of woods.
48 The Dublin Zoological Society had first approached Burton in August 1830 about a suitable layout for their gardens. Burton submitted his plan and report on 27 October 1832. A transcript of his report exists in Trinity College Library: Zoological Society Minute Book May 1830–July 1840 10608/2/1 TCD. I am most grateful to Dr F. O'Dwyer for this reference and to Dr S. O'Reilly for transcribing the document for me. Burton designed the Zoological Society Gardens in Regent's Park (1826–41). The original plan is held in the Public Record Office: MPE 906. Although these provide further examples of the dialectical relationship between London and Dublin they stand outside of the concerns of this chapter which are confined to the State's intervention in the landscapes of the urban parks in both cities.
49 OPW 15 June 1842, Burton to the commissioners of woods.
50 Foucault, 'Des espaces autres', p. 27.

CHAPTER FIVE

Two nations, twice: national identity in *The Wild Irish Girl* and *Sybil*

Andrew Ballantyne

This chapter offers a comparison of two novels that share a surprising number of features, and which both have strong links with aesthetic theory. The first is *The Wild Irish Girl: A National Tale*, by Lady Morgan (1776–1859), which was first published in 1806 and is the most self-consciously picturesque novel ever written. The second is *Sybil, or the Two Nations* by Benjamin Disraeli (1804–81), from 1845, which has a Gothic revivalist slant. One of the features common to both novels is a highly political intent, an aspect one can hardly fail to miss, even if absorbed in the plot. Indeed their plots are similar, both having, in important respects, the same contours, though the circumstantial detail in each is distinctive. Each novel has a heroine who is an embodiment of the national identity, and in either case she is endowed with innately aristocratic dignity, even though she is without money. She is associated with ruined buildings, and turns out to belong to the ancient autochthonous nobility, which has been dispossessed. In both novels the hero belongs to the class which has done the dispossessing. He is enthralled by the heroine, but has much to learn before he is worthy of her. In the end they marry and the two cultures are united. In each case the hero's learning is the politically significant part of the tale. Both novels depict him initially as accepting the commonly held views of the day, and by confronting a series of experiences he is educated out of them. The reader is, of course, a vicarious witness to these experiences, and the persuasion is likely to work on the reader as it does on the hero, so that there was an implicit role in practical politics for each novel, persuading the reader to see the merits of a political cause, as the fictional political narrative unfolds on the page.

In *The Wild Irish Girl* the two protagonists' identities belong to two nations: the Irish and the British, or more specifically the Irish Catholics and the Anglo-Irish Ascendancy. The novel was written soon after the Act of Union had been ratified, at which time the land was owned by the Anglo-Irish aristocracy. The Catholics in Ireland, as in mainland Britain – and in common with all non-Anglicans (including Protestant nonconformists) as well as all non-Christians – had no vote and were not allowed to buy land, or to sell inherited land to non-Anglicans. The reason for this state of affairs was that the head of the Anglican Church was (and still is) the monarch, and in those days a refusal to accept the state religion was seen as a symptom of potential disloyalty to the State.

The plot of *The Wild Irish Girl* is worked around the English hero; he arrives with his unconsidered and prejudicial national stereotypes in place, and is won over by the heroine – Glorvina – whose social exclusion is, at the narrative's end, resolved at the personal level by marriage into the British aristocracy. Her fate is presented as emblematically hopeful for the future of relations between the two nations. The novel's political importance stems from its tremendous popularity and its invention of a positive national stereotype for the Irish, as a natural place-bound aristocracy, which Lady Morgan – an Irish girl who married an English nobleman – then adopted in her own persona, and enacted it in drawing rooms in Dublin and London. She *became* the wild Irish girl, and performed the role by acting vivaciously and dressing in her own eccentric way. 'I thought her pretty at first', said one of her female acquaintances, 'and now I think her frightful . . . her eyes would be very pretty if they did not squint *à faire dresser les cheveux*. Her figure is not the better of being obtrusively crooked, and her head is ornamented with a frightfully ill-cut crop.'[1] She was certainly charming and vivacious, but did not conform to the template of beauty and so was seen as 'picturesque' – the description of her here corresponding closely with the picturesque charm of the parson's daughter described by Sir Uvedale Price in his *Essays on the Picturesque*.[2]

While the role of wild Irish girl could be burdensome when she was called on to perform it, she managed by way of it to escape from many of the confinements which a woman of her rank would have expected, and although she moved in high society, her position therein was not that of a model of polite accomplishment: 'People flock to her house as they would to a wild beast show', said one who was not invited.[3] She had an income from writing, which she continued to control even after her marriage, and she was the first woman writer in Britain to be given a state pension, which is equally remarkable whether it was given for her writing or, as was suspected, in recognition of her political work – 'a just compensation for the sacrifices she had made to liberal principles, as well as for the uninterrupted stream of slander which John Wilson Croker and his Tory colleagues had long brought to play upon her reputation'.[4] Being a woman, she could not hold political office, but she moved in the political circle associated with the household of Lord Abercorn, where she came into contact with a great many people, including Lord Aberdeen, who as a young man lived as part of that household and was to become one of Queen Victoria's prime ministers.

Disraeli, of course, became another. By the time that *Sybil* was published, the Reform Bill had widened the franchise a little, and the Act of Toleration had put Roman Catholicism on a better footing. Both of the nations which are in conflict in *Sybil* are British – we might now prefer to call them two *cultures* – the rich and the poor. Disraeli, however, configured the problem with the mindset of his day. If we go along with the common sense of his day in seeing identity as largely a matter of national identity, of heredity and place, then it becomes a boldly imaginative move to notice that there are two entirely distinct group identities being formed side by side:

> 'Well, society may be in its infancy,' said Egremont slightly smiling; 'but, say what you like, our queen reigns over the greatest nation that ever existed.'
>
> 'Which nation?' asked the younger stranger, 'for she reigns over two.'
>
> The stranger paused; Egremont was silent but looked inquiringly.
>
> 'Yes,' resumed the younger stranger after a moment's interval. 'Two nations; between whom there is no intercourse and no sympathy; who are as ignorant of each other's habits, thoughts, and feelings, as if they were dwellers in different zones, or inhabitants of different planets; who are formed by a different breeding, are fed by a different food, are ordered by different manners, and are not governed by the same laws.'
>
> 'You speak of –' said Egremont, hesitatingly.
>
> 'THE RICH AND THE POOR.'[5]

In a different language, this could be made to sound postmodern: what we have here is the idea of a plurality of identities being performed in the same place, producing distinct social spatialities. Now that we know some Marx, we might think that the difference between the rich and the poor was a class divide, but Disraeli was no proto-Marxist, and he complexified that issue by making Sybil a dispossessed aristocrat, whose hereditary lands had been confiscated at the Reformation, so Sybil, though emblematically allied with the poor, is presented as being actually more truly aristocratic than the hero. Moreover, at the end of the novel, when his elder brother is killed in a riot, the hero succeeds to his title, so that the marriage works to unite the old and new aristocracies, rather than the bourgoisie and the proletariat, and Sybil ends up as a countess. From a Marxian standpoint, the novel is politically confused. According to the unfolding story of *Sybil*, the true aristocracy understands the poor, and looks after them; but the true aristocracy has been displaced since the Reformation, and the modern industrialists of Disraeli's day had no real understanding of the poor, exploiting them mercilessly. The novel makes it clear that there is a need for reform, and the reform is proposed via the traditional alliance of old genes and new money. The marriage is symbolic of the ancient aristocracy which represents the interests of the poor being allied with commercial interests in order to bond as 'one-nation' tories. The interests of the labouring poor, who were still at this stage excluded from the electorate, are presented as being in line with those of the ancient dispossessed aristocrats, and therefore adequately represented by them.

Going back the *The Wild Irish Girl*, now, the opening pages announce its themes. After a prefatory letter from the hero's father, making it clear that the son has been sent into exile in Ireland, the narrative is put into the words of the hero, Horatio, as he approaches Dublin by boat. At this point his head is full of English stereotypes, so he sees the muscular boatmen as descendants of ancient giants. He is, however, a painter, and his response to the scenery is immediately appreciative, being mediated through positive associations of ideas, so that he is made to say of his first view of Ireland:

> [N]ever was I more pleasantly astonished, than when the morning's dawn gave to my view one of the most splendid spectacles in the scene of picturesque creation I had ever beheld, or indeed even conceived – the bay of Dublin.
>
> A foreigner on board the packet, compared the view to that which the Bay of Naples presents; I cannot judge of the justness of the comparison, though I am told one very general and commonplace; but if the scenic beauties of the Irish bay are exceeded by those of the Neapolitan, my fancy falls short in a just conception of its charms. The springing up of a contrary wind kept us for a considerable time beating about the coast: the weather suddenly changed, the rain poured in torrents, a storm arose, and the beautiful prospect, which had fascinated our gaze, vanished in mists of impenetrable obscurity.[6]

The picturesque is explicitly invoked at this early stage, and the image of the true beauty of the place being temporarily obscured by volatile local conditions is thematically important, as well as giving us an aesthetic allusion to the realm of the sublime, and in showing a susceptibility to this sort of thing giving (with hindsight) a hint of the fact that Lady Morgan would later write a biography of Salvator Rosa.[7] Thematically it is an image which shows Ireland as more or less the promised land, but with its promise occluded by troubles. Horatio, however, arrives in Ireland in a negative frame of mind, banished there by his father as a punishment, believing the Irish to be unsophisticated, and slow to submit to the salutary and ennobling influence of the arts.[8] He sets out for the west coast and finds, and by degrees comes to appreciate, the genuine, uncontaminated, Irish culture which is still alive there.

At first, however, the descriptions contrast the magnificence of the scenery with the wretchedness of the lives of the peasantry, treated like slaves by the English landowners or their agents. 'It is certain', Horatio says, 'that the diminutive body of our worthy steward is the abode of the transmigrated soul of some *West Indian* planter.'[9] There are harrowing descriptions of everyday life, with copious footnotes to make the point that the descriptions are not fictional – although one note does cite 'Ossian' as an authority, but only on a point of minor detail.[10] (Elsewhere in the novel, incidentally, a priest explains that although the English seem to be divided in opinion as to whether Ossian's works were written by MacPherson or by an ancient Scottish bard, nevertheless Ossian was actually Irish – 'from proofs of historic fact, and above all, from the internal evidences of the poems themselves'.[11]) The scenery, however, is always described appreciatively and its magnificence is evoked by calling to mind the work of landscape painters who were well known to Lady Morgan's friends and readers.

> To him who derives gratification from the embellished labours of art rather than the simple but sublime works of nature, *Irish* scenery will afford little interest; but the bold features of its varying landscape, the stupendous altitude of its 'cloud-capt' mountains, the impervious gloom of its deep-bosomed glens, the savage desolation of its uncultivated heaths and boundless bogs, with those rich veins of a picturesque champagne, thrown at intervals into gay expansion by the hand of nature, awaken, in the mind of the poetic or pictorial traveller, all the pleasures of tasteful enjoyment, all the sublime emotions of a rapt imagination. And if the glowing fancy of Clause Lorraine would have dwelt enraptured on the paradisaical charms of English landscape, the superior genius of Salvator Rosa would have reposed its eagle wing amidst scenes of mysterious sublimity with which the wildly magnificent landscape of Ireland abounds.[12]

And then a little later:

> All was silent and solitary – a tranquillity tinged with terror, a sort of 'delightful horror', breathed on every side. I was alone, and felt like the presiding genius of desolation![13]

[91]

Lady Morgan had clearly been reading Burke on the beautiful and the sublime, and knew her picturesque theory, too.[14] She had probably read Richard Payne Knight's *Analytical Inquiry on the Principles of Taste* (it was his best-selling book, and she would describe him, when they met, as 'the famous Mr. Knight'); and she had certainly read much else besides.[15] Although some passages might bring to mind the work of Ann Radcliffe, *The Wild Irish Girl* is not a Gothic novel, romantic though it is. It does not depend on the supernatural, but is a serious work of political education, which enlists the charms of narrative in order to spread its message. (The book has been charged with giving shape to the arguments which have been played out in Northern Ireland.[16])

The Wild Irish Girl also has a neo-classicizing vein: Dublin is likened to an Ionic temple in the novel's opening pages;[17] the appeal of 'Ossian' was strong because he made a local substitute for Homer; and there are claims for the antiquity, dignity and grammatical rigour of the 'Celtic dialect used by the native Irish'.[18] There seems to be something Boeotian in the air.[19] More surprisingly, the comparisons are not confined to the *ancient* Greeks. Travel in Greece was still far from common, and Lady Morgan did not go there herself. She did, however, write a novel (the apparently eternal oppression of women was one of its themes) called *Woman, or Ida of Athens*, which had specifically neo-classical ambitions. She is supposed to have adopted that subject because her friend Sir William Gell suggested it to her, and he had travelled extensively in Greece.[20] The Irish, like the Greeks, 'are only debased because they are no longer free'.[21] The usual reaction of travellers was to deplore the state of the modern Greeks, and to find them altogether unworthy of their ancient past.[22] A more sympathetic understanding acknowledged the decline but saw it as being due to Turkish oppression; and, of course, the sorry state of the Irish was comparably due to British oppression. In Dublin we find Greek revival buildings being designed for Catholic institutions, on account of this fellow-feeling for the modern Greeks.[23] This fellow-feeling was helped along, if it was not actually started by, *The Wild Irish Girl*, in which the Irish are likened to the modern Greeks, in their fondness for fables, in confirming every assertion with an oath and in their dancing at festivals.[24] It is exactly a Byronic view of Greece, transplanted to Ireland, and Irish politics.

The architectural complement to this state of society, is the ruin – again in Ireland as in Greece. The wild Irish girl, the Lady Glorvina, is the daughter of the prince of Inismore, and they live in a spectactularly picturesque ruined castle. Moreover this castle is far from being the only ruin. One character speaks with rapture of the many fine views this country affords to the genius of the painter, he dwells with melancholy pleasure on the innumerable ruined palaces and abbeys which lie scattered amidst the richest scenes of this romantic province: he generally thus concludes with a melancholy apostrophe: –

'But the splendid dwelling of princely grandeur, the awful asylum of monastic piety, are just mouldering into oblivion with the memory of those they once sheltered. The sons of little men triumph over those whose arm was strong in war, and whose voice breathed no impotent command; and the descendant of the mighty chieftain has nothing left to distinguish him from the son of the peasant, but the decaying ruins of his ancestors' castle; while the blasts of a few storms, and the pressure of a few years, shall even of them leave scarce a wreck to tell the traveller the mournful tale of fallen greatness.'[25]

The theme of an oppressed and diminished civilization is linked with the ruins as material objects that carry a symbolic charge by way of the association of ideas, which is explicitly linked with picturesque themes, not only in Lady Morgan's manner of describing landscapes but by having the hero adopt a disguise. He does not give his real name, which would instantly have declared him to be an oppressor and an enemy, but explains that he is travelling as an artist – and one means of his acquaintance with Gorvina developing is by him teaching her to sketch. The views turn into landscapes, and when ruins are there the scenes also have a moral character – and this is made explicit in the narration. To take one characteristic sentence:

I cast my eyes around, all still seemed the vision of awakened imagination – surrounded by a scenery, grand even to the boldest majesty of nature, and wild even to desolation – the day's dying splendours awfully involving in the gloomy haze of deepening twilight – the grey mists of stealing night gathered on the still faintly illiminated [sic] surface of the ocean, which awfully spreading to infinitude, seemed to the limited gaze of human vision to incorporate with the heaven, whose last glow it reflected – the rocks, which on every side rose to Alpine elevation, exhibiting, amidst the soft obscurity, forms savagely bold, or grotesquely wild, and those finely interesting ruins, which spread grandly desolate in the rear, and added a moral interest to the emotions excited by this view of nature in her most awful, most touching aspect.[26]

This is the west of Ireland seen by way of the paintings of Salvator Rosa, and the hero's response to the land is a steeped in a romantic aesthetic sensibility. We have the particular lighting conditions of twilight which make the scene's pigmentation more harmonious than would the glare of full sunlight, and also references to the spectator's point of view. The scenery is seen to have a visual appeal, but also to

[93]

awaken moral sentiments, which, if it were art, would put it in a high class of art.

Disraeli wove together some of the same elements in his description of the momentous occasion when his hero first sees Sybil. It is set at the same moment of the day, when the forms of the landscape are softened and melt into one another in a definitively picturesque manner, here coupled with the effect of a follow-spot from stage lighting:

> At this moment a sudden flush of rosy light, suffusing the grey ruins, indicated that the sun had just fallen; and through a vacant arch that overlooked them, alone in the resplendent sky, glittered the twilight star. The hour, the scene, the solemn stillness and the softening beauty, repressed controversy, induced even silence. The last words of the stranger lingered in the ear of Egremont; his musing spirit was teeming with many thoughts, many emotions; when from the Lady Chapel there rose the evening hymn to the Virgin. A single voice; but tones of almost supernatural sweetness; tender and solemn, yet flexible and thrilling.[27]

The scene has been carefully prepared – there is a long build-up to this moment, with an evocative description of Fountains Abbey in north Yorkshire (presented as the fictional Marney Abbey). This is followed by Disraeli's idiosyncratic explanation of the political background to the current state of affairs, in which the monks are presented as benevolent institutional landlords, who were dispossessed by the new aristocracy against the interests of the common people. This section concludes with the announcement of the existence of two nations, quoted above, and then cuts to the gleam of light, the ethereal voice and the appearance of Sybil, 'the fair phantom of some saint haunting the sacred ruins of her desecrated fane'.[28] Sybil actually lives in a modest dwelling in the nearby industrial town, but is strongly associated with the ruins, which are presented as her spiritual home. Sybil, like Glorvina, is poor but dignified and aristocratic, from an ancient and unvalued nobility. She is apparently politically close to, but remains culturally apart from, the labouring poor of the town, who have raucous and gaudy entertainments which keep their spirits up in the face of cruel oppression from the industrialists (allied to the new post-reformation aristocracy). The workers' entertainments are clearly described as what we would want to call *kitsch*, though the word was not available to Disraeli. In 1939 Clement Greenberg set out the idea that *kitsch* developed in the mid-nineteenth century as the counterpart to the emergence of the avant-garde, as a consequence of industrialization:

The peasants who settled in the cities as proletariat and petty bourgoisie learned to read and write for the sake of efficiency, but they did
not win the leisure and comfort necessary for the enjoyment of the city's
traditional culture. Losing, nevertheless, their taste for the folk culture
whose background was the countryside, and discovering a new capacity
for boredom at the same time, the new urban masses set up a pressure
on society to provide them with a kind of culture fit for their own consumption. To fill the demand of the new market, a new commodity was
devised: ersatz culture, kitsch, destined for those who, insensible to the
values of genuine culture, are hungry nevertheless for the diversion that
only culture of some sort can provide.[29]

Disraeli described some effects of this process at an early stage in its
development, long before it had been theorized, and shortly before the
great festival of *kitsch* that the Great Exhibition of 1851 turned out to
be, and which led directly to the foundation of the Victoria and Albert
Museum, as an institution for the education of the taste of industrial
designers. In *Sybil* the workers with spending-money frequent the
Temple of the Muses, a hall behind a public house (Cat and Fiddle)
which was used for popular entertainments, such as

a lady in a fancy dress who sang a favourite ballad; or a gentleman elabo-
rately habited in a farmer's costume of the old comedy, a bob-wig, silver
buttons and buckles, and blue stockings, and who favoured the company
with that melancholy effusion called a comic song. Some nights there
was music on the stage; a young lady in a white robe with a golden harp,
and attended by a gentleman in black mustachios. This was when the
principal harpiste of the King of Saxony and his first fiddler happened to
be passing through Mowbray, merely by accident, or on a tour of pleasure and instruction, to witness the famous scenes of British industry.
Otherwise the audience of the Cat and Fiddle, we mean the Temple of
the Muses, were fain to be content with four Bohemian brothers, or an
equal number of Swiss sisters. The most popular amusements however
were the 'Thespian recitations:' by amateurs, or novices who wished to
become professional.[30]

These entertainments, which satisfied their audience, took place in a
hall which was entered by way of a portal 'of considerable dimensions
and of architectural pretension', painted bright green, with gilt panels.
The 'temple' itself was not finely judged, being 'very long and sufficiently lofty, though rather narrow for such proportions'.[31] The decoration continued the theme of pretentious aspiration, with panels
depicting scenes from Shakespeare, Byron and Walter Scott, painted by
a brush 'of considerable power' – but perhaps implicitly without refinement. This is commercial entertainment, and everything about it is
just good enough to keep people happy, but no better than that, so

there is no unprofitable expenditure. The food and drink on sale here are presented as equally commercial. Nourishment is not the point. If the characters are not hungry, then 'a sharp waiter' invites them to buy a drink to give them an appetite; if they seem uninclined to drink, he suggests that they have something to eat to work up a thirst.[32] The architecture, entertainment and food are all generated by the same values, which are a world away from those of the rich, who can afford to surround themselves with high-quality products, and a world away also from those of Sybil wandering in the ancient ruins, whose high-mindedness needs no support from fine artefacts, but who communes with the high architecture of the Middle Ages. Her system of values is that of the traditional countryside, where money may be scarce but what there is of it is sensibly directed into sustenance.

Disraeli's view of the Middle Ages was close to that set out by Augustus Pugin (1812–52) in *Contrasts*,[33] and had particular import because when *Sybil* was published (1845) the new Palace of Westminster, designed by Pugin and Sir Charles Barry (1795–1860), was actually under construction. When the new building is seen through the refractions of Disraeli's narrative, then the whole edifice becomes a work of propaganda for Disraeli's one-nation toryism, as the ancient past is restored to face the future with unparalleled magnificence. The building allied the production methods of modern industry with the aesthetic aspirations of the ancient past in exactly the same way as the marriage at the end of Disraeli's novel.

What we see in both these novels are attempts to reformulate the idea of national identity in order to bring about political change, and in each a beautiful woman is designated as a symbol of the ancient but oppressed national spirit – a symbol of the true, essential and distinct national character (an idea which is now of course problematical). In each case the condition of this 'true' national character is associated with buildings in a ruinous state, and in each the situation is remedied by marriage to a high-ranking representative of the current ruling class. In each, curiously, the story is narrated from the viewpoint of the hero, for whom rank is a problem in his winning the affections of the afflicted national symbol.

More important than the similarities in the means, however, are the similarities in the ends. Lady Morgan and Benjamin Disraeli perhaps thought that they were revealing the true character of the nation in their works. We might now prefer to say that each was deploying whatever means were available to construct a distinctive national identity, which was attractive to their readers and was ostensibly deeply rooted in the place. The fact that the invention of an indigenous national identity, one other than that of the current ruling class, could be seen to lead directly to a call to revolt – in order to throw off the non-legitimate, non-national, incomers – but in each case the narrative proposes the advantages of union in cultural hybridity, rather than any form of nationalistic purity or 'ethnic cleansing'.

Novels do not, however, finally control events, and happy endings are strictly confined to fiction. The new stereotypes in *The Wild Irish Girl*, which clarified identifying markers for natives and interlopers, have done as much to demarcate divisions in Ireland as they have helped to resolve problems there, while it seems to be Disraeli's purveyors of *kitsch*, rather than any sort of aristocracy, who have inherited the earth, and two cultures seem to be remarkably few now that we think in terms of multiculturalism. Each novel, however, made a political argument more persuasive by enlisting architecture and aesthetic theory in the service of constructing a national identity with which its readership was, in turn, invited to identify.

Notes

1 Charlotte Clavering to Susan Ferrier, quoted in Lionel Stevenson, *The Wild Irish Girl: The Life of Sydney Owenson, Lady Morgan (1776–1859)*, London, Chapman & Hall, 1936, p. 137.

2 The parson's daughter appeared in Price's *Dialogue on the Distinct Characters of the Picturesque and the Beautiful*, 1805, which was reprinted in Sir Uvedale Price, *Essays on the Picturesque*, 3 vols, London, Mawman, 1810, vol. 3, pp. 291–2. She was taken up by Knight, whose satirical remarks about her led to Price breaking off his friendship with Knight – the episode is set out in Andrew Ballantyne, *Architecture, Landscape and Liberty: Richard Payne Knight and the Picturesque*, Cambridge, Cambridge University Press, 1997, pp. 153–6.

3 Marianne Spencer-Stanhope, quoted by Stevenson, *The Life of Sydney Owenson, Lady Morgan*, p. 204.

4 £300 a year, awarded by Earl Grey's ministry under William IV in 1830; see William John Fitzpatrick, *Lady Morgan; Her Career, Literary and Personal, with a Glimpse of Her Friends and a Word to Her Calumniators*, London, 1860, p. 260. See also Sidney Lee (ed.) *Dictionary of National Biography*, 63 vols and supplements, London, 1894, vol. 39, p. 28.

5 Benjamin Disraeli, *Sybil; or, the Two Nations*, Harmondsworth, Penguin, (1845) 1980, p. 96.

6 *The Wild Irish Girl*, p. 2. (With the exception of note 16, below, page numbers given for *The Wild Irish Girl* are to the 1986 edition, published by Routledge (Pandora), with an Introduction by Brigid Brophy. The Introduction is also collected in Brigid Brophy, *Baroque-'n'-Roll and Other Essays*, London, Hamish Hamilton, 1987, pp. 51–5. There is another recent reprint of the novel, with an Introduction and notes by its editor Kathryn Kirkpatrick: Sydney Owenson, Lady Morgan, *The Wild Irish Girl: A National Tale*, Oxford, Oxford University Press, 1999.)

7 Lady Morgan, *The Life and Times of Salvator Rosa*, 2 vols, London and Paris, 1824.

8 *The Wild Irish Girl*, p. 1.

9 *The Wild Irish Girl*, p. 23.

10 *The Wild Irish Girl*, p. 16. 'Ossian' is now known to be a fictional character, fraudulently presented as an ancient Gaelic poet by his creator James MacPherson (1736–96).

11 *The Wild Irish Girl*, p. 98.

12 *The Wild Irish Girl*, pp. 6–7.
13 *The Wild Irish Girl*, p. 7.
14 Edmund Burke, *A Philosophical Enquiry into the Origin of Our Ideas of the Sublime and Beautiful*, London, 1757.
15 Richard Payne Knight, *An Analytical Inquiry into the Principles of Taste*, 1805.
16 Kirkpatrick, Introduction, *The Wild Irish Girl*, p. xiv.
17 *The Wild Irish Girl*, p. 3.
18 *The Wild Irish Girl*, p. 78.
19 *The Wild Irish Girl*, p. 128.
20 Sydney Owenson, Lady Morgan, *Woman; or Ida of Athens*, 4 vols, 1809; Lionel Stevenson, *The Wild Irish Girl*, London: Chapman & Hall, 1936, p. 108.
21 *Woman*, vol. 1, pp. 2–3.
22 See for example David Constantine, *Early Greek Travellers and the Hellenic Ideal*, Cambridge, Cambridge University Press, 1984; and Fani-Maria Tsigakou, *The Rediscovery of Greece: Travellers and Painters in the Romantic Era*, London, Thames & Hudson, 1981.
23 Joseph Mashek, 'Politics of style: Dublin pro-cathedral in the Greek revival', in *Building-Art: Modern Architecture Under Cultural Construction*, Cambridge, Cambridge University Press, 1993, pp. 29–46.
24 *The Wild Irish Girl*, pp. 98n, 113, 143, 144.
25 *The Wild Irish Girl*, p. 54.
26 *The Wild Irish Girl*, p. 42.
27 *Sybil*, p. 96.
28 *Sybil*, p. 97.
29 Clement Greenberg, 'Avant-garde and kitsch' (1939), in Clement Greenberg, *Art and Culture: Critical Essays*, Boston, MA, Beacon Press, 1961, p. 10.
30 *Sybil*, p. 125.
31 *Sybil*, p. 125.
32 *Sybil*, p. 126.
33 A. W. N. Pugin, *Contrasts; or, A Parallel Between the Noble Edifices of the Middle Ages and Corresponding Buildings of the Present Day*, London, 1836.

CHAPTER SIX

Monumental nationalism: Layard's Assyrian discoveries and the formations of British national identity

Frederick N. Bohrer

> Because there is no Originator, the nation's biography cannot be written evangelically, 'down time', through a long procreative chain of begettings. The only alternative is to fashion it 'up time' – towards Peking Man, Java Man, King Arthur, wherever the lamp of archaeology casts its fitful gleam. (Benedict Anderson, *Imagined Communities*)[1]

'What is the force that moves nations?'[2] This question was still new when Tolstoy posed it in 1869, in the second epilogue to *War and Peace*. Like nation states themselves, the motives behind national identity presented a new challenge to conventional wisdom. Tolstoy's essay may be contrasted with Ernest Renan's slightly later one, entitled 'What is a nation?'[3] It is noteworthy that both are framed around a question, a reflection of the pressing indeterminacy, the still-evident questionableness, attaching to the concept of nationhood in the later nineteenth century. But the two provide very different sorts of answers. Renan's prescriptive, even quasi-spiritualized, account of the nation as a commonality of past heritage and present will is well known today. It serves as a common reference point in much contemporary writing on nationalism. Tolstoy's approach, however, is less cited. It is, by contrast, critical and highly sceptical of theories of great men and national will on which much theorizing of the nation then depended. Indeed, Tolstoy's view verges on a critique of historical causation as such.

> Why does a war or a revolution come to pass? We do not know. We only know that to bring either result to pass, men form themselves into a certain combination in which all take part; and we say that this is so because it is unthinkable otherwise; because it is a law.[4]

Surveying the momentous, confused and bloody stage of national assertions from the French Revolution through to 1848, Tolstoy saw, much unlike Renan, that there is no pure 'force' that moves nations, but that rather our later accounts of such events are construed as a 'law', one designed not merely to distinguish the essential cause within the event, but actually to create it, within a situation far more ambivalent and complex. A situation in which 'men form themselves into a certain combination' figures the very chain of causation in which this law is embodied and through which the later account is constructed. As I show, it also describes, quite literally, a visual idiom of national monumentalizing representation.

Tolstoy's essay could be said to anticipate a number of themes of the contemporary critique of nationalism associated with Anderson, as well as with figures such as Ernest Gellner, Homi Bhabha and Edward Said. While Tolstoy himself is hardly an innocent figure on the question of nationhood, his essay is important here for it serves to root the concerns of these contemporary critics within the milieu of the later nineteenth century. Far from monolithic, the cultures of nineteenth-century Europe, in Britain as elsewhere, were riven with fissures related to class, gender and many other forms of cultural difference. The 'nation' is a signifier floating through these constituencies, a loose consensus that is contingent and changeable, and all the more powerful for that. In forms both the same and different, it is everywhere and nowhere: a continuity of discontinuities.

In this chapter, I examine the multiple workings of a concept of nation which underlay at key points the overwhelmingly positive response to the ancient Assyrian discoveries made by Austen Henry Layard in the 1840s, and enshrined in the British Museum in the years around 1850. Strangely enough, to consider the public sponsorship and reception of a major archaeological project slides almost seamlessly into a study of the varieties and motivations of nationhood behind the very project, and which demanded in various ways its assimilation into the museum whose very name evoked the unified body of Britain: the British Museum. Why, indeed, would the British Museum be a museum of antiquities at all (and few of them British)? Many things are at play here, but not least is the anxious, uneasy dialectic of modernity and tradition, each both supporting and undermining the other, built into the very structure of the modern nation. With characteristic irony, Anderson probes the condition. 'But why', he asks, 'do nations celebrate their hoariness, not their astonishing youth?'[5] The modern nation's near-obsession with the distant past fulfils a number of different needs. Examining the process of fixing nationhood through temporal projections like those triggered by Assyria magnifies and makes even more evident the discontinuities upon which a nation itself can be constructed.

Layard's discoveries were made in Mesopotamia at the behest of Stratford Canning. Canning was then British ambassador to the Ottoman empire, an eminent figure in the British Foreign Service who was then at the height of his power. Layard, by contrast, was an unpaid and irregular assistant, employed by Canning for a number of covert operations. These included various sorts of intelligence gathering in Balkan countries; but certainly the most momentous were his archaeological activities, digging first into the great mound of Nimrud, opposite Mosul on the Tigris, in northern Mesopotamia. This archaeology was just as fraught with contemporary political significance, with national interest, as was Layard's other employ under Canning. It was, first of all, illegal. Thus Layard's tools were fashioned in secret and his party travelled under a cover story. Only after his spectacular success did Canning arrange, retroactively, to obtain permissions from the Ottoman governors for the finds.

None of this, to be sure, is unique to Layard's particular case. To the contrary, what is striking is how much it exemplifies the norm, in which European nations dug into Mesopotamia and took away their finds, more or less with impunity, as justified on grounds of national interest. Indeed, Layard's finds were not the first of their kind, but were rather a response to the extraordinary, and truly unprecedented, finds of Assyrian antiquities made by the Frenchman Paul-Emile Botta at nearby Khorsabad. Botta's finds were quickly transported to the Louvre. There they became the core of the first real museum display of ancient Near Eastern artifacts ever presented to European eyes: the Louvre's 'Musée Assyrien', first opened in 1847. Canning's sponsorship of Layard was a direct response not merely to the discovery itself but to its French enshrinement. His first official correspondence to Sir Robert Peel, describing Layard's discoveries, presents them as a means by which to outdo their rival country. As Canning wrote: 'M. Botta's success at Nineveh has induced me to adventure in the same lottery, and my ticket has turned up a prize . . . there is much reason to hope that Montague House [the British Museum] will beat the Louvre hollow'.[6]

This passage is revealing on two counts. First, it refers to the discovery solely as a way by which to compete with the French. Mesopotamia itself, to some the renowned cradle of civilization, serves here only as a sort of blank tablet on which Britain can do whatever France did, but do it even better. Indeed, Canning was rather vague on the values, either aesthetic or antiquarian, of Layard's discoveries themselves. Second, both the assumptions and the breezy tone of Canning's letter reveal just how this national competition is to be waged. Canning's off-handed and jocular tone resembles, to me at least,

[101]

nothing so much as a kind of tourist postcard, a rather proud, self-satisfied, dispatch. The touristic analogy, indeed, taps into a fundamental feature of cross-cultural sightseeing: the demand for objectification and mastery of the place viewed. In the West, on an individual level, photography came to serve this need. As Susan Sontag has noted, in modern times '[t]ravel becomes a strategy for accumulating photographs'.[7] Similarly, in a particular correlate of the age of imperialism, diplomacy becomes a national strategy for accumulating artifacts. Sontag points to the scene in Godard's *Les Carabiniers* in which travellers return home after a long journey and open their suitcases, which contain nothing but photographs. Artifacts may serve a nation in a way analogous to photographs for an individual, offering a sort of possession of a larger cultural whole fixed by the power and agency imparted by the traveller. At the same time, it is just as important to consider the role of the suitcase, the carrier and context maker. As Canning clearly indicated, that is surely the British Museum itself, the 'noble cabinet' in which the treasures were (and still are) assembled. Accordingly, I move now to another national viewpoint on the Assyrian discoveries, in which container and contained are seen one through the other.

Layard's discoveries were followed in almost breathless detail in the *Illustrated London News* (*ILN*), the uniquely successful new journal of visual presences (as proclaimed even in its name), just then, at mid-nineteenth century, entering its first golden age. The overwhelming success of the *ILN* is just starting to be adequately described.[8] It is an important supplement, and complication, to theories of mass communication based on the rise of photography. The *ILN*'s engravings were, in fact, sometimes even referred to as photographs by its readers, but the palpable differences between media, so obvious today, are important to understanding the magazine's function.

Between the arrival of the very first shipment of Layard's discoveries, in 1847, and the British Museum's ultimate enshrining of them in a purpose-built series of galleries, in 1853, the *ILN* devoted more than a dozen illustrated features to this collection (far more than to any other aspect of the museum at the time). As the *ILN*'s own language clearly acknowledged, the coverage did not merely gloss or describe metropolitan events for those with independent knowledge of them (as was clearly intended in higher-echelon publications), but rather was fundamentally constitutive of them, literally creating knowledge of events in circles where it would otherwise have been absent. The magazine's first major notice of the Assyrian discoveries states: 'when we consider that this description may have to meet the eyes of many who may never have the opportunity of seeing the originals, we are satisfied that no other apology will be requisite for so far extending this paper'.[9]

This acknowledges many of the paradoxes of reality and media coverage that today bedevil things like advertising and political campaigns. A foreigner long ago told me that he imagined in America nothing happened if it was not publicized. It was striking then, but now seems strangely commonplace from politics to advertising. This kind of representational brokering now so familiar was unleashed in perhaps its first full-scale form in England in the pages of the *ILN*. It was a format soon emulated, to similarly great success, throughout Europe and the rest of the world. The *ILN* itself has survived to the present day. Looking at it in its early years, though, we find an additional function, today seemingly submerged (or perhaps too familiar to sense): the constitution of place and nation. Anderson, in particular, has stressed the crucial role of literacy, and specifically of periodical publishing, in the rise of nationalism. While we today might look at the content of a nineteenth-century daily newspaper or weekly journal as a mere miscellany, a jumble of events, its significance in the mid-nineteenth century lay in its very ability to gather together such spatially and socially disparate events in a single synchronic frame. The chronotope of nation emerges in a secularized framework valuable precisely for its ability to convince the individual reader of the simultaneity of events both spatially and socially disparate. Thus arises a conception of national interest, overlapping and extending personal individual interests and identities.

Coverage of the Assyrian discoveries in the *ILN* exemplifies the spatio-temporal span of the new consciousness it represented, as well as the force of the specifically *national* identity which drove it. The *ILN*'s many articles on the artefacts covered and reproduced, in the main, objects as they were brought into the British Museum. Indeed, the artefacts were far more accessible to lower- and middle-class viewers in the pages of the magazine than in the museum itself. This is true, first, because the museum was at the time distinctly unwelcoming to the general public, being open only at times when most people had to work, and even then strictly limiting tours to chaperoned groups. Second, and equally important, the *ILN* actually did transform the artefacts from their state of display within the museum itself. A case in point occurs with the coverage of the great winged Assyrian animals, the virtual hallmark of the discoveries. When these colossal bulls and lions were first put on display in the British Museum, the museum's trustees directed that the objects were 'to be there protected by a sufficient fence'. The works were immediately represented in the *ILN*, but they were depicted without any such

[103]

encumbrance – indeed, with middle-class viewers standing directly in front of them, their gazes unmediated.[10]

As this incident just begins to suggest, one can see in the *ILN*'s coverage a degree of transformation of the reality of the museum's installation, and indeed a contestation of the socially restrictive policies of the museum's directorship. This climate of fracture and opposition is symptomatic of the inherent tensions in Britain of the period, as figured in the swirl of interests around the museum itself: of learned v. popular audiences. Yet looking elsewhere at the *ILN*'s coverage of the Assyrian discoveries, one finds evidence of what constrains this difference from breaking out into a full-scale war: a sense of national purpose and pride, further defined by contrast with an Eastern 'other'.

The magazine covered both the artefacts in the museum and the triumphant process of transport. Most salient here is an article of July 1850 on the shipping of the Great Bull. The article was accompanied by an engraving (Figure 10) showing HMS *Apprentice* moored at a spot in Mesopotamia already staked out for Britain: Morghill, on the Euphrates, just north of Basra. Morghill had been the residence of

10 'Shipping the Great Bull from Nimroud, at Morghill, on the Euphrates', *Illustrated London News*, 27 July 1850, p. 72

Colonel Taylor – who had originally sent Layard to Canning – before being leased to the British East India Company to service ship traffic.

The engraving dramatizes the weight of the object by showing the *Apprentice* listing somewhat, as the Great Bull is gradually hoisted over the gunwales. The workers and distant spectators are not depicted in any detail, though there is a suggestion that turbans are worn by some of the workers. The only people identified with a measure of clarity are a *repoussoir* group of four or five Arabs at the lower left. They are spectators of the general scene, a nearby canoe suggesting their mode of transport. The Arabs appear mute, engaged solely in regarding the loading of the Bull.

The topos of lyrical longing in the face of loss is common in aspects of Orientalism, from the many illustrations of Psalm 109 to paintings like Wright of Derby's *Indian Widow*. Such a projection works here not so much to highlight the Arabian as to efface the presence of the British in the entire affair. This incident seems to take place as result of abstract necessity rather than individual volition. Such a scheme offers testimony to the text's claim for a sort of omnipotence of Captain Jones of the Nitocris – '[his] influence with the natives is all powerful'. Power so subsumes the scene that the British are made explicit only through their property, such as Colonel Taylor's mansion or the ships. Following this metonymous strategy brings out subtler relations of dominance in the image, as in the scale by which the building dwarfs the spectators and, more directly, in the contrast between the vast British sailing ship and the native canoe.

But what is even more striking, especially in contrast to the rest of the *ILN*'s coverage of the Assyrian discoveries (which was largely factual and descriptive), is the voluminous national praise which takes up most of the accompanying text in this article. A small sample will be more than enough.

> It is gratifying . . . to consider, that, while her [England's] ports and magazines are full of the products of the most distant lands – while each of her busy citizens is constantly engaged in contributing to the aggrandisement and stability of the country, she does not neglect those arts and sciences which, though not distinguished by the appellation of *useful*, tend to cultivate and polish the understanding, and to humanize and socialize our fellow creatures, and without which the greater blessings of civilization would be lost to us. It was the knowledge and practice of this principle which so distinguished the ancient Greeks; and while many equally or more powerful nations have passed into oblivion, has caused their name to be handed down as a precious heirloom to perpetual generations. May our land, therefore, long continue to cultivate

with equal assiduity the useful as well as the polite arts, and to earn thereby, not the hatred and envy, but the esteem and admiration of foreign countries, and to ensure the praises of a grateful posterity.[11]

This act of appropriation is made in the name of civilization. The principle of aggrandizement as a marker of national achievement was widely shared in the age of imperialism, and thus might well have been expected to inspire 'the esteem and admiration of foreign countries'. Here, moreover, is one thing on which the *ILN* and the ruling classes represented by Canning could agree. Implicit here though, and no doubt widely shared as well, is that Mesopotamian Arabs do not have a country, that nationhood itself belongs to the progressive West.

This argument, that Britain's attentiveness to the Assyrian discoveries distinguishes it as the proud successor to the ancient Greeks, takes the subject into another field for national assertion (and misrepresentation). First, of course, it projects a conception of classical Athens, a city–state, on to a putative ancient Greek *nation*. Such national solidarity would be more appropriate for, say, the ancient Romans or, for that matter, the Assyrians. But the attempt to tie the Assyrian artifacts with the notions of cultivation and humanity, deemed as essential to civilization as any utilitarian concerns, had particular ramifications for Assyria's reception. It brings Assyria into the realm of the aesthetic, itself mobilized in many ways on behalf of the nation at the time. One such project is the focus of my concluding remarks.

The Albert Memorial (Figure 11), whose overall design was submitted to Queen Victoria by George Gilbert Scott in 1863, has been called an 'exquisite summary of the aspirations of English art'.[12] This monument to the beloved prince consort, whose patronage had been crucial for the arts in England, brought together a comprehensive spatial and historical array of figures both typical and individual. On behalf of art, and to honour the great national patron, the monument presented what Bhabha (via Bakhtin) calls a 'national time–space', a spatialized history fixed through Albert and the artistic realm he embodies.

Mesopotamia's fit within the commodious structure exemplifies the consequences of the *ILN*'s association of Assyria with the 'polite' arts. It places it, moreover, in a larger framework in which national and historical forces themselves are put on display. Albert was enshrined within a realm of glory both spatial and temporal. The former was manifest in the groups at the corners of the monument's main platform, representing the four continents of Asia, Africa, Europe

11 The Albert Memorial, Hyde Park, London, 1860s

and America. Albert, whose figure rose at the centre of these four, mediates between them, in the process positioning Britain as emerging from the full world-span which it considered its proper stage. But this identity was defined also, and more specifically, in the interlocking historical display which is no less integral to the monument. The expanse of the Albert Memorial's remarkable podium contained 169 portrait figures of those deemed to have excelled throughout history in poetry, music, painting, sculpture and architecture. Poetry and music were combined on one of the fronts of the square podium, while the other three arts had a side each. Architecture was depicted on the north front and sculpture on the west. At the north-west vertex, the start of the temporal span for both arts, stood an Egyptian and an Assyrian, traces of the origin and unity of the two arts at the virtual

[107]

origin of civilization. Assyria was thus involved in buttressing a concept of origin, the fount of a tradition which Victorian England saw as its legitimate inheritance. It is a lineage including Phidias, Michelangelo and Canova, among the sculptors, and Ictinus, Brunelleschi and Palladio among the architects. Alone of the entire crowd the Egyptian and the Assyrian are depersonalized, presented generically as ethnographic types comparable to the allegorical figures of the continents.

Assyria was too important to be confined to the farthest edge of the monument's spatio-temporal scope. But what is notable is *how* it was brought to further attention. Assyria was channelled specifically into the realm of architecture. Farther down the north front, among Menesicles, Theodorus and Hiram, appeared Sennacherib. As the official guide to the monument explains: 'He was a great builder, and greatly adorned the city of Nineveh. His palace, which was discovered by Mr. Layard, was of great extent and magnificence. Many sculptures from this palace are now in the British Museum.'[13]

Sennacherib's palace had been the great discovery of Layard's second expedition. Though the individual works were described as 'sculptures', it was architecture in which the great achievement is deemed to lie, perhaps not least because the contemporary paradigm of valorization required an agent, an artist or maker, to celebrate. And while the individual sculptors and painters were unknown, as in much of the rest of pre-classical art, a case could be made in architecture for the patron as *auteur*. And yet, at the same time, even more striking is the almost immediate insertion of the name of Layard. As much as this figure stands for something about antiquity, both Layard and the British Museum are lionized through it.

However much these are figures of an extra-national far-spread antiquity, then, they also amount to a nationally motivated assembly of contemporary significance, a particularly high Victorian Parnassus. The Albert Memorial, that is, is a national monument, but not precisely a purely *nationalist* monument. Rather, it fixes a specific national project of definition by means of the larger vocabulary of time and space available for national appropriation in the great age of European expansion. It is an ideal, clean and frictionless, version of the ideological work of archaeology.

In constructing the national chronotope, Bhabha states that 'the difference of space returns as the sameness of time'.[14] That is, within the interplay of spatial and temporal reference in fixing the monument itself, the variety, contingency and sheer incommensurability of hugely divergent cultural practices is homogenized and flattened for contemporary legibility.

[108]

In this very act – this construction of sameness – we see the observation of Tolstoy, with which I began, realized quite literally. The temporal chains of artistic worthies on the podium of the Albert Memorial precisely illustrate Tolstoy's observation: 'Men form themselves into a certain combination' in a way that is seen, and here displayed, as 'the law'. And observing this combination of men, it is clearly a law regulated by and for contemporary British purposes. Each of these chains leads to contemporary British artists. Most remarkably, the chain of architects, representing the medium in which Assyria plays its largest role, leads ultimately to a group of contemporary British architects, not the least of them George Gilbert Scott himself, depicted at the end of the podium's line of architects.

More generally, considering Canning's sponsorship of Layard, the *ILN*'s coverage and the sculptural programme of the Albert Memorial, however much Assyria may have offered a surprise to contemporary expectations, whatever different challenges it may have posed to different groups, it was not only brought home but was incorporated within a narrative of Britain. Whatever it said about antiquity, it was also made to speak to, and for, the culture that had newly appropriated it.

Notes

1 Benedict Anderson, *Imagined Communities: Reflections on the Origin and Spread of Nationalism*, revised edn, London and New York, Verso, 1991, p. 205.
2 Leo Tolstoy, *War and Peace*, trans. C. Garnett, New York, Modern Library, 1983, p. 1104.
3 In Homi K. Bhabha (ed.) *Nation and Narration*, London and New York, Routledge, 1990, 8–22.
4 Tolstoy, *War and Peace*, p. 1122.
5 Benedict Anderson, 'Narrating the nation', quoted in Bhabha, *Nation and Narration*, p. 293.
6 Cited in Stanley Lane-Poole, *The Life of the Right Honourable Stratford Canning*, 2 vols, London and New York, Longmans Green, 1888, vol. 2, p. 149: Canning to Sir Robert Peel, 18 April 1846.
7 Susan Sontag, *On Photography*, New York, Farrar, Straus & Giroux, 1977, p. 9.
8 See Peter W. Sinnema, *Dynamics of the Pictured Page: Representing the Nation in the Illustrated London News*, Aldershot and Brookfield, VT, Ashgate, 1998.
9 *Illustrated London News*, 26 June 1847, p. 412.
10 British Museum Archive, Committee, 8 October 1850, p. 8067. For the ILN's image, and more discussion of its implications, see Frederick N. Bohrer, 'The times and spaces of history: representation, Assyria, and the British Museum', in D. Sherman and I. Rogoff (eds) *Museum Culture: Histories, Discourses, Spectacles*, Minneapolis, MN, University of Minnesota Press, 1994, especially pp. 206–9.
11 *Illustrated London News*, 27 July 1850, p. 71.
12 Stephen Bayley, *The Albert Memorial: The Monument in its Social and Architectural Context*, London, Scolar Press, 1981, p. 14; on the monument, see Chris Brooks (ed.) *The Albert Memorial, the Prince Consort National Memorial: Its*

History, Contexts, and Conservation, New Haven, CT, and London, Yale University Press, 2000.

13 *Handbook to the Prince Consort National Memorial*, London, John Murray, 1872, p. 71.

14 Bhabha, *Nation and Narration*, p. 300.

CHAPTER SEVEN

Union and display in nineteenth-century Ireland

Fintan Cullen

Recognition of the relationship between Ireland's colonial status in the nineteenth century and the display of art and material culture is slowly gaining ground in scholarly research.[1] In a recent publication on the early history of what is now the National Museum of Ireland in Dublin, its present director has usefully reminded us that, at the end of the nineteenth century, 'pride of place' at the centre of the entrance rotunda to the Kildare Street building was 'given to a pair of six pounder field guns captured by the British from the Sikhs in India in 1845'.[2] In this chapter I examine nineteenth-century reactions to the display of visual imagery in Ireland during the first century of union, the focus being on two exhibitions of English paintings that attracted considerable public attention in Dublin and Belfast. The first example looks at a peculiarly nineteenth-century phenomenon, the display in 1801 of a huge panorama celebrating British military success (Figure 12); while the second jumps forward to the middle of the century and, with the aid of Queen Victoria (Figure 13), discusses a more domestic visualization of empire.

College Green

For a short period in the late eighteenth century, Dublin's College Green, an open space defined by the old Parliament House, the façade of Trinity College and Grinling Gibbons's now-destroyed bronze equestrian statue of William III, became a much-represented locus for oppositional politics. The space was possibly best captured by Francis Wheatley in his well-known canvas, now in the National Gallery of Ireland, celebrating a Volunteer gathering in 1779, but College Green continued to feature as a backdrop in a number of satirical prints well into the 1790s.[3] Ironically, as soon as the Irish Parliament was removed, College Green was no longer to feature as an active

12   John Vendramini after Robert Ker Porter, *The Storming of Seringapatam* (1802) (centre engraving), stipple engraving, 59.8 × 270 cm

subject in Irish visual productions but played the more passive role of a venue for the display of art. In switching from subject to venue, College Green lost its association with oppositional politics to become, if only for a short time, the site for the display of a celebration of union.

For a few years between the dismemberment of the Irish Parliament in 1800 and the subsequent transformation of Parliament House into the headquarters of the Bank of Ireland, the fine building of Edward Lovett Pearce and James Gandon was the venue for a number of public exhibitions of works by Irish artists. In July 1801, an elusively anonymous Dublin art connoisseur, possibly a member of the Tighe family of County Wicklow, described a visit to one of these exhibitions organized by the Society of Artists in Ireland. He was clearly knowledgeable about art and personally knew many of the artists exhibiting. Commenting on Hugh Douglas Hamilton's splendid full-length oil portrait of Richard Mansergh St George (National Gallery of Ireland,

13 Thomas Jones Barker, *The Secret of England's Greatness* (c.1863), oil on canvas, 16.76 × 21.38 cm

Dublin), murdered in early 1798, the diarist writes in spiritedly loyalist terms:

> The Colonel is in his light horse uniform, his helmet on the ground; he is drawn leaning against his wife's tomb – the expression of the countenance is admirably delineated, it is that of a man versed in misfortune, whose accounts with this world are closed and who cares not how soon he should be removed to another. This, with the solemn scenery in which he is placed and the recollection of the late shocking termination of his existence by the hands of assassins, combine to fill one while gazing on it, with the most melancholy sensations.[4]

The author of this anonymous diary returned to College Green a few weeks later to spend 'a couple of hours' in viewing yet another display of paintings. On that occasion he enjoyed 'a Panorama', which, he wrote, 'at present engages the attention of everyone here'.[5] Exhibited in College Green in a building 'erected for the Purpose near the College',[6] the subject of the panorama was the storming by the British army of the fortress at Seringapatam two years earlier and the defeat of Tipú Sultán, ruler of Mysore. The capturing of Tipú's city was an important moment in the consolidation of British power in India while his death during the course of the siege allowed for greater British expansion in the southern half of the subcontinent.[7] Back home, the defeat and ensuing death of Tipú were major forces in the galvanizing of public opinion regarding the value of imperial expansion. As P. J. Marshall and others have shown, a more 'authoritarian nationalism' began to emerge in 1790s' Britain with the ending of the long-running Mysore Wars that suggested a growing 'pride in British rule in India as well as a pride in British military successes'.[8] That sense of developing pride was felt also in Ireland.

Painted by the English artist Robert Ker Porter (1777–1842), the panorama shown in Dublin's College Green measured 120 feet in length and covered 2,550 square feet of canvas. It is thought to be have been destroyed not long after its exhibition and is now known only by means of three engravings, made from the original, by John Vendramini.[9] In the first engraving, Sepoys backed by British artillery attack a party of Tipú's grenadiers. Tipú himself stands on the ramparts, 'directly above the gateway, in which he afterwards fell', as the *Narrative Sketches of the Conquest of the Mysore* which accompanied the exhibition informs us.[10] In the second or central engraving (Figure 12), General Baird, pointing his sabre towards the fortress and 'surrounded by his staff ... animat[es] the troops to follow Serjeant Graham ... who, having planted the British colours on the rampart, is shot by an Indian at the moment he is giving the huzza of victory'. In the third and final engraving, we see the mortar battery and a 'brave Colonel Donlop, borne off the breach, wounded, by two grenadiers'.[11] 'You are placed', the Dublin diarist tells us,

> as it were in the middle of the battle before the ramparts and without the danger ... precisely as in reality ... The artist will observe in it the finest specimen of shading, perspective, foreshortening, etc. It contains beside the innumerable small ones, several hundreds of figures of which those in the foreground are large as life, and those of all the officers, and the most distinguished subalterns, much esteemed portraits. The rich and fanciful dresses of the East, the curious and magnificent architecture of their Mosques and Zenanas, and other novelties in European eyes contribute to render this noble picture more interesting.[12]

Prior to its exhibition in Dublin, Porter's panorama had been viewed to popular acclaim for a full year at London's Lyceum. Remembering its exhibition some thirty years later, a friend of the artist delighted in the panorama's visual excitement:

> The learned were amazed, and the unlearned were enraptured ... You longed to be leaping from crag to crag with Sir David Baird, who is hallooing his men on to victory! Then, again, you seemed to be listening to the groans of the wounded and the dying – and more than one female was carried out swooning. The oriental dress, the jewelled turban, the curved scymitar – these were among the prime objects of favouritism with [the artist's] pencil.[13]

Its popularity assured at the heart of empire, in 1801 the panorama began a tour of the cities of the United Kingdom that lasted some three to four years. For the first half of 1801 Porter's canvases were on display in a purpose-built structure on the Mound in Edinburgh before moving on to Dublin for the rest of the year. Early 1802 saw it in Cork in another specially built 'Panoramic Building' on the 'North-side of St Patrick's Bridge' while it was on display in Belfast's South Parade from April to June.[14] On show in Ireland for at least twelve months and exhibited throughout the United Kingdom over a period of years, *The Storming of Seringapatam* panorama was soon followed by another of Porter's 'all embracing views', this time the even larger *Siege of Acre* which measured almost 3,000 square feet of canvas.[15]

The anonymous Dublin diarist stated that the exhibition of the *Seringapatam* panorama engaged 'the attention of everyone' in Dublin, and indeed an entry of ten days later says that the panorama 'is still the rage'. Porter himself accompanied the exhibition to Dublin, and our diarist relates how he engaged him in conversation. Deposits of 6 guineas a set were already been taken for the three engravings, which, when joined together, reached almost nine feet. The diarist also tells us that sales of an accompanying booklet on the battle were good in Dublin. Copies of this brochure supplied orientation sketches and a lengthy description of the battle.[16] What are we to make of such evident liking in Dublin for imperial celebration? It is, of course, important to note that the exhibition of *The Storming of Seringapatam* began only six months after the Act of Union had come into effect and was in fact but one of a number of displays or theatrical representations of 'Tipú as bogeyman' in Dublin around this time.[17] Indeed, only a decade earlier, during the third Mysore War, *Walker's Hibernian Magazine* had carried a portrait of Tipú accompanied by a lengthy account of his military might.[18] More popular interest in Tipú was also in evidence: specially penned songs with an Irish flavour, such as 'Patrick O'Conner's Description of the India

Campaign with his friend Tippoo', were sung in London and possibly in Dublin in 1792:

> From sweet Tipperary, to pick up some honour,
> I am here to be sure, little Patrick O'Conner
> With Dennis O'Neal, Trupy Blane and O'Carty,
> By my soul we have routed the black-a-moor party.[19]

Ireland at the end of the eighteenth century, it can be said, was fully aware of other imperial troublespots, while it can also be argued that the popularity of Porter's panorama shows how Dublin, only three years after rebellion had stalked the streets of the city, was seen as a highly acceptable venue on the imperial commercial roundabout. Also, it indicates how, as the nineteenth century develops, the discussion of the visual arts in Ireland is as much a case of analysing British art, or an art of union, as it is one of unearthing a seemingly forgotten national visual tradition.

A 'sovereign gaze'

The union of 1801 conveniently updated the political relationship between Ireland and Britain for a new century. An art of union was equally updated by the display of Robert Ker Porter's panorama throughout Ireland in 1801 and 1802 due to the modernity of the panorama as an exhibition concept. The three-quarter-circle panorama was exhibited in a rotunda-shaped tower, usually a temporary structure which had been developed some decades earlier, coincidentally by an Irishman, Robert Barker, from Kells, County Meath, whose two sons went on to corner the market for the representation of such major 'national' events as the Battle of Waterloo and the Coronation of George IV.[20] Dramatic lighting through a skylight, a contemporary theme – in Porter's case a recent imperial victory in India – and the availability of souvenirs, such as the accompanying booklet and the engravings, all combined to make a visit to the panorama a memorable experience. In fostering the illusion of an 'other' space, in particular of an exotic far-away location, the spectators inside the rotunda were encouraged to realize their total control over what was visible. As Bernard Comment has suggested in his recent book on panoramas, what you got was a sort of 'encyclopaedism on the cheap'.[21]

Various commentators on panoramas – Comment and Stephan Oettermann; more critically Alan Wallach in his analysis of subsequent American variations on the theme; and, most famously, Michel Foucault in *Discipline and Punish* – have linked the development of the panorama to Jeremy Bentham's almost contemporaneous invention of the panopticon, that 'all-seeing' prison design which allows for the constant surveillance of inmates.[22] As Wallach has pointed out, in the panorama the world is presented as 'a form of totality' which the spectator views from the central tower, what Foucault called 'the eye of power'. As our anonymous Dublin diarist looked out from his vantage point, 'in the middle of the battle', as he wrote, 'before the ramparts and without the danger', he was presented with the totality of his relationship with the imperial victory that lay before him. Indeed, the diarist takes on what Foucault called the 'sovereign gaze', an authoritative eye which allows him – and by extension an Irish audience – a participatory role in Baird's victory over Tipú Sultán. As Wallach has observed, having ascended the central tower of the panorama, 'the visitor had the opportunity to identify, at least momentarily, with a dominant view'.[23]

In the same year that Porter was touring his dramatic panorama around the cities of the United Kingdom, a compatriot of the anonymous diarist was also affirming his authority on the now-strengthened empire in India. In 1801, the govenor-general of Bengal, the Irish Marquess Wellesley, had his portrait painted by Richard Home.[24] In the painting, Wellesley places his right hand on the various treaties that concluded the fourth Mysore War while wearing the full regalia of the Order of St Patrick, of which he had been a founding member back in the 1780s. The prominently displayed collar of the Order is held together on Wellesley's chest by a crowned harp out of which hangs a large jewel-encrusted oval with a shamrock in the centre. Legend has it that Wellesley's regalia had been made from the plundered jewels of the defeated Tipú Sultán, found after the capture of the fortress at Seringapatam.[25]

In time, the third of Vendramini's engravings after Porter's panorama would be dedicated to Wellesley as the overall planner of the attack on Seringapatam. The central engraving (Figure 12) was suitably dedicated to the king while the first one was dedicated to directors of the East India Company. This latter dedication met with the approval of our anonymous diarist, who praised their 'liberal patronage'. This local support for the East India Company is worth noting because the company was a not unimportant source of employment in Ireland in the early years of the nineteenth century: 5,000 Irishmen joined the East India Company's army between 1802 and 1814, with almost 900 coming from Dublin alone.[26] India, it may surprise us to learn, probably loomed large in the Irish consciousness in the early years of the union. As recent historians of empire, such as Chris Bayly, Edward Spiers and others, have pointed out, by 1830 Irishmen accounted for perhaps more than 42 per cent of the British crown's

[117]

forces, while in Bengal itself, where Wellesley ruled, the Irish made up about 48 per cent of the army.[27] It is thus fair to speculate that many of those recruits, from both sides of the religious divide, would have had relatives and friends back home who would have paid the shilling entrance fee to see Porter's panorama in Dublin's College Green in 1801 and, the following year, in Cork and Belfast.[28]

Irish involvement in colonial expansion also should not be under-estimated: we might call to mind the numbers actually involved in military affairs or in passive support at home. As V. G. Kiernan has written: 'Irishmen might resent being under the British yoke, but they had little objection to other peoples being brought.'[29] A literary example from later in the century will illustrate this point. George Meredith opens *Diana of the Crossways*, published in 1885, with the return to Ireland of a 'British hero of Irish blood [who] after his victo-rious Indian campaign' is fêted at a ball in Dublin at which he meets Diana Merion, the heroine of the novel.

> [T]ruly could it be said, that all Erin danced to meet him . . . For 'tis Ireland gives England her soldiers, her generals too. Farther away, over field and bogland, the whiskies did their excellent ancient service of watering the dry and drying the damp, to the toast of 'Lord Larrian, God bless him! He's an honour to the old country!'[30]

A 'nationalistic' art

The popularity and preponderance of imperial imagery offers us an alternative visual tradition to the concern of recent re-examinations of Irish visual material from the nineteenth century, which has focused mainly on nationalist imagery. Jeanne Sheehy's *The Rediscovery of Ireland's Past* (1980) and studies of individual artists such as Daniel Maclise and Frederick William Burton have highlighted artistic careers and key images which, as Sheehy puts it, display a sensibility 'more sympathetic to Ireland than to England'.[31] Maclise's large painting of 1854, *The Marriage of Strongbow and Eva*, now in the National Gallery of Ireland, has over the past decade or so attracted a number of what one can only call 'nationalist' interpretations.[32] Following on from Sheehy, some see the painting as an exercise in the rediscovery of a lost culture, while others view it as a cultural lamentation. The prominence of the gold torcs, erroneously placed on the wrists and upper arms of the defeated Irishmen in the right foreground, and the old bard and his broken harp on the far left of the painting, do indeed suggest an effort by Maclise to explore his nation's past. But, given that the painting was originally planned as part of the redecoration of the Palace of Westminster and that it neatly fitted into a deeply colonial schema of moments from the ancient history of the various nations that made up the United Kingdom, its 'Irishness' is in need of serious questioning. Maclise's painting shows a defeated Ireland about to enter a marriage of convenience. Indeed the London *Art Journal* of 1854 recognized this only too well. Its critic praised the painting as displayed at the Royal Academy 'as one of the best productions of the modern schools', adding that it is 'the duty of government to secure' it, given that it is 'so well suited for a national property'.[33] That nation is not Ireland alone but the United Kingdom; Irish history to the mid-nineteenth-century writer in the *Art Journal* is also imperial history.

The establishment of an identifiable group of Irish nineteenth-century artists together with a body of recognized masterworks is an inevitable outcome of years of canonical indifference; but in formulating our gallery of Irish genius have we ignored a historical reality? In attempting to identify an Irish *school* in painting one cannot, by default, ignore the dominance of a British – primarily English, at that – visual presence in the experience of art in or about Ireland in the nineteenth century. Although art institutions in Ireland slowly developed and expanded throughout the century, and despite the fact that an Academy was formed and a National Gallery created in Dublin, with public collections also growing in Belfast and Cork, the story of the visual arts in the first century of union is not one of confidence in a national visualization.[34] Despite the attractions of tracing the development of national art, we should also focus on the art that was actually available in large quantities, be it the interminable Italianate altarpieces imported by the Irish clergy to decorate their new churches after Emancipation[35] or imperial imagery such as Robert Ker Porter's panorama.

Imperial imagery in Dublin was not difficult to find. A very public example was and is the Wellington Testimonial in the Phoenix Park. Designed by Robert Smirke, who went on to build the British Museum, the great obelisk in honour of the duke of Wellington was completed in 1820, while the bronze reliefs which decorate the four sides did not appear, due to money problems, until about 1860.[36] Three of the bas-reliefs represent scenes from Wellington's career, the earliest illustrating his formative years in India and, conveniently, in the light of our earlier discussion, his involvement in the victory at Seringapatam, where he is shown directing the storming of the walls of Tipú's fortress. The others celebrate further aspects of Wellington's long career: the military strategist at Waterloo and the successful politician. The latter relief, the work of Ireland's leading neo-classical sculptor John Hogan (1800–1858), commemorates the passing of the Catholic Emancipation Bill in 1829. Wellington as prime minister, is flanked by

Daniel O'Connell, Richard Lalor Sheil, Robert Peel and Lord Palmerston, while he hands 'Religious Liberty' to Hibernia and 'Civil Reform' to Britannia.[37]

In the half-century that separates the imperialist imagery of Porter's panorama and the Wellington reliefs in the Phoenix Park, Thomas Davis, writing in *The Nation* in 1843, could point out: 'Our portrait and landscape painters paint foreign men and scenes; and, at all events, the Irish people do not see, possess, nor receive knowledge from their works. Irish history has supplied no subjects for our great artists.'[38] One could argue that Davis had forgotten that Wellington had been born in Ireland, 'the stated impulse', as Judith Hill has pointed out, behind the erection of the Wellington Testimonial. In 1813, *Faulkner's Dublin Journal* reported: 'This tribute [was due to] a nation's admiration of the transcendent exploits of her son and hero . . .'.[39]

Cyril Barrett has claimed that there was no tradition of what he called 'nationalistic' art in Ireland in the nineteenth century.[40] Despite the fact that portraits of O'Connell, in both oils and engravings, as well as the many statues, were to be seen throughout Ireland from the 1840s onwards, 'the failure', Barrett says, 'to produce a body of extreme nationalistic art was . . . because there was no public demand for it'.[41] A trawl through the exhibition lists of the Royal Hibernian Academy, the one major venue for the annual display of art in Ireland from 1826, reveals many Irish subjects, but they are by no means in the majority.[42] Another institution, the Royal Irish Art Union (RIAU), founded in 1839, did valiant work in buying Irish paintings and distributing engravings to its members. Among the prints produced in the early years of the RIAU's activities were 'The Blind Girl at the Holy Well' and the better known, 'Aran Fisherman's Drowned Child', both taken from watercolours by the Irish artist Frederick William Burton (1816–1900). Set in a remote rural Ireland, the scenes represent common peasant practices, with a focus on religious devotion in the former and public keening at the death of a child in the latter. But, by the mid-1840s, interest in such indigenous subject matter in engraved form had so declined that the RIAU was offering engravings after Raphael and Correggio as well as plates after such contemporary British artists as Wilkie and Turner.[43]

David Lloyd's more recent discussion of the crisis of representation for the Irish novel in the early- to mid-nineteenth century offers us a solution to this reluctance to engage in Irish subject matter and the absence of a 'national art'.[44] Ireland's unstable middle class, he claims, did not 'furnish representative figures', a vital ingredient of so many realistic novels in the century, resulting in a 'struggle for hegemony' among the people who would otherwise buy and read novels, just as they might buy or view art in either oils or engraved form. Lloyd's def-inition of the 'complex and shifting affiliations' of this class allows us to see parallels with the art-viewing public.

Discussing the Irish nineteenth-century novel, Joep Leerssen has remarked how 'the narrative of romantic Anglo-Irish fiction . . . tend[s] to marginalize its most Irish characters . . . [they] exist only in the furthest corners of the country'. The middle classes do not feature; instead we fluctuate between peasants and feudal masters, what Leerssen calls 'real Irish characters', who live in 'spots that are inac-cessible and somehow separate from the normal world'.[45] The engrav-ings after Burton distributed by the RIAU in the early 1840s show such characters, inhabitors of remote glens and off-shore islands. The failure of mid-nineteenth-century Irish art was that unlike the novel, which depended on an English audience, paintings and fine engravings pro-duced in Ireland did not enjoy the same clientele.

Greatly annoyed by this lack of commitment to national subject matter, Thomas Davis published a list of themes to be taken up by Ireland's fledgling history and genre painters, but, due to what Lloyd has called the lack of a 'common story', such an idea was a non-starter.[46] Indeed Davis had been told as much by his friend Burton:

> I fear certain hundreds of pounds will never produce either art or nation-ality . . . You should give Ireland first a decided national school of poetry – that is song – and the other phases will soon show themselves. This I must allow is being done – but the effect is not complete. You know as well as I do, but you have lurking hopes that things can be forced. Ah, my friend, free, spiritual, high-aiming art cannot be forced . . . when Ireland can rub her eyes clear of short-sighted, mean, and petty, and too often selfish, ends, then shall the irresistible influence, the welcomed law of art, proceed also from them as from new centres.[47]

Instead of exhibiting a wealth of Irish material, institutions such as the Royal Hibernian Academy lined their walls with images of impe-rial drama, some of them painted by native artists, or with whatever England sent over.

The sovereign as intermediary

One such native artist was the grandly named Michelangelo Hayes, a prominent member of the Royal Hibernian Academy, who exhibited regularly in Dublin from the 1830s to the 1870s and in 1853 showed his spirited watercolour *The 16th Lancers Breaking the Square of Sikh Infantry at the Battle of Aliwal, January 1846*.[48] As Barrett has pointed out in his analysis of the contents of various mid-nineteenth-century exhibitions, the numerous images of Ireland exhibited in Dublin and Cork in the 1850s and 1860s were always 'more than balanced by scenes from Britain, France, Italy and other places'. The Dublin exhibition of 1865, for example, devoted a whole gallery to 'soldiers who had won the Victoria Cross in the Crimea, India and elsewhere'.[49] A year earlier, a painting by the English artist Thomas Jones Barker (1815–82), *The Secret of England's Greatness* or *Queen Victoria Presenting a Bible in the Audience Chamber at Windsor* (Figure 13), was displayed in Belfast shortly after the queen's highly popular visit to Ireland in 1861.[50] In the previous decade, Barker had shown a number of imperial images at the Royal Hibernian Academy exhibitions, mainly representing cavalry charges at Balaklava.[51] In 1860 he achieved national recognition for *The Relief of Lucknow*, a painting relating to the recent Indian Mutiny, but in *The Secret of England's Greatness* Barker turned from dramatic military incident to focus on the civilizing benefits of imperialism.[52] In Belfast, *The Secret* was displayed in Donegall Place Buildings with only one other painting, a now untraceable New Testament scene, *Jesus Journeying to Emmaus*, by James Sant. With an admission price of only sixpence, the exhibition of paintings met with great popular success leading to a four-day extension to the originally planned two-week schedule.[53] In Barker's painting, the queen hands a Bible to a suppliant African while the prince consort looks on. No record of a comparable event is known and, as at least one contemporary suggested, the whole scene may well be apocryphal.[54] Albert had died in 1861, thus implying that the supposed meeting between the queen and an African dignitary had occurred some years earlier, possibly during the first premiership of Lord John Russell (1846–52) who stands to the right with Foreign Secretary Lord Palmerston. Also observing the scene, on the extreme left, is the duchess of Wellington, a lady-in-waiting.

In 1801, as noted earlier, the Irish viewer of Robert Ker Porter's panorama was invited to participate in the controlling mechanism of the 'sovereign gaze'. Developing on from that, in attending the public exhibition of Barker's painting, a mid-nineteenth-century Irish audience was asked to acquiesce to the furtherance of the Christian Empire, the actual sovereign, Victoria, acting as intermediary. Through her, the citizens of the United Kingdom sanction this scene of African submissiveness. Indeed, the *Belfast News-Letter* attested:

> It is a picture that will engrave beautifully, and many a home in the North of Ireland, if we mistake not, will be decorated with this drawing representation of an incident in the life of the Queen which at once illustrates the virtues of the Court, the religious tone of her Majesty's mind, and in a certain sense, the very spirit of the age.[55]

[122]

Victoria's attachment to the Bible was much commented on during her lifetime. A pamphlet written by the Reverend J. H. Wilson entitled *The Late Prince Consort, Reminiscences of His Life and Character*, which may have appeared in 1862, tells of how a 'love of the Bible [was] peculiar to the [royal] family'. Wilson tells of an incident that is supposed to have occurred some years earlier:

> We know that when the Queen was requested by an African prince to say what was the secret of England's greatness and England's glory, Her Majesty presented a Bible to the Ambassador for his Court, and said, 'Tell the Prince that this is the secret of England's greatness.'[56]

It is not possible to prove that it is Wilson's retelling of this supposed incident that sparked Barker's painting, but the publication of the tract and the creation of the painting were within a year or so of each other. In the painting, the relationship between religion and imperial domination is all too clear, but by setting the scene, as Adrienne Munich has suggested, in the Throne Room at Windsor, 'the empire's representatives become domesticated as part of a symbolic nuclear family'.[57] This visualized domesticizing of Empire is given an added dimension by the showing of the painting in Ireland, by then a part of the United Kingdom and England's closest and oldest colony. Just as the 1801–2 display of Porter's panorama can be read as an acknowledgement of Ireland's involvement in the imperial military process, so the underlying message of the exhibition and the ensuing popularity of Barker's painting in Belfast indicates the superiority of Protestant Christianity and its implied alignment with the civilizing power of Empire. In the context of Belfast's growing industrial wealth, the specific relationship between business and Christianity had a particular relevance. Exhibited at the time of Belfast's great linen boom, created by cotton shortages due to the American Civil War, the *Belfast News-Letter* recommended 'the merchants and manufacturers of Belfast to spare a few moments from their avocations' and view Barker's *The Secret of England's Greatness*.[58] Indeed, the frame of Barker's painting, which we know dates from about 1862, carries two lines from a psalm, one of which specifically refers to the rejection of wealth: 'I love thy commandments above gold, yea above fine gold.'[59]

The visual focus of the painting is, of course, the Bible being offered to the kneeling African. The potency of this privileging of the King James Version on the walls of an exhibition gallery in Belfast in the 1860s is strengthened when we consider various contemporary events in nineteenth-century Irish Protestantism. In 1859, only five years before the arrival of Barker's painting in Ireland, Antrim and Belfast had witnessed one of the most remarkable evangelical revivals of the century: 35,000 had attended a meeting in the Botanic Gardens, while 'a total of 100,000 persons', as Sean Connolly has observed, 'was reported to have been converted, including Protestants of all denominations and also, it was claimed, numbers of Catholics'.[60] Such a popular Protestant revival urged on by blatantly sectarian street-preaching had occasioned serious urban riots in 1857 and, most spectacularly, in August 1864. In the earlier riots, a Catholic mill girl had been shot dead, while in 1864, only two months after the exhibition of Barker's painting, Belfast was overwhelmed by two weeks of street fighting. Under the Party Processions Act of 1832, the Orange Order was banned from indulging in processions but, angered by nationalist ceremonies in Dublin, they took to the streets.[61]

Ironically, in the light of what I said earlier regarding the dearth of 'nationalistic' art in Ireland in the middle of the nineteenth century, it was the laying of the foundation stone on 8 August 1864 for what was to become John Henry Foley's monument to Daniel O'Connell in the centre of Dublin that sparked off the Belfast riots. Later that same day, an effigy of O'Connell 'clothed in garments like those in which the Irish agitator, when in the flesh, was wont to enclose himself', as an Orange pamphleteer put it, was burnt on the appropriately named Boyne Bridge in the centre of Belfast.[62] Equally, Protestant anger at the importation of Catholic navvies into the city to extend the docks' area has also been suggested as a reason for the riots; but resentment at seeming Catholic gains, both political and economic, lay behind the riots. In the event, destruction was wrought by both sides: a Catholic church was attacked, as was a Presbyterian school, and families were terrified out of their homes while street-fighting resulted in the deaths of at least twelve.

Although the showing of the painting at Magill's galleries in Donegall Place proved popular, it is not known whether the working-class rioters from the Shankill Road and Sandy Row, who had burnt the effigy of O'Connell a couple of months later, visited the exhibition of Barker's painting in what was one of Belfast's most fashionable streets. The only recorded relationship between the rioters and Donegall Place is that 'a huge procession of Protestants openly carrying arms' followed the coffin of one of the slain inhabitants of Sandy Row through the city down Donegall Place and High Street to the cemetery at Knock.[63] And yet one cannot dismiss a connection between the display of Barker's painting and the religious tensions that ran through the streets of Belfast in 1864. We do have some contemporary responses to the painting, albeit not Irish, which prove its undeniable working-class Protestant allure. Remembering the exhibition of the picture in Newcastle-upon-Tyne in the early 1860s, the journalist and social reformer William Thomas Stead (1849–1912), the child of a strongly nonconformist family, wrote of how the painting caught

> the imagination of the common people, this tribute of earthly Majesty to God's word. Rude coalheavers, with but an imperfect grasp even of the vigorous vernacular of Tyneside, used to tell over and over again how the Queen had given the Book of Books, the Book of our Salvation, to the heathen from afar who sought to know what it was made England great. And so, dimly and half consciously, I began to gain a glimmering of the uses of the Sovereign as Grand Certificator for the truth and excellence of that which is best worth holding by in Church and in State. In the delight of the uncultured artizans and labourers of my native village over the Queen's act in giving the Bible to the savage lay the germ of the sentiment which in its full development proclaims the queen *Fidei Defensor*, and regards even the Christian Church itself as somewhat wanting in the necessary credentials until it is surmounted by the royal arms, and certified to be the Church of England as by law established under the sign manual of the Queen.[64]

The showing of *The Secret* in Belfast in 1864 was not a unique instance of the display of English paintings in Ireland in the mid–late nineteenth century. Art works frequently toured the United Kingdom either in group exhibitions or in small shows such as that enjoyed by the Barker canvas. Added to that, *The Secret of England's Greatness* was but one of many images shown in Belfast and other Irish cities that advanced what Tim Barringer has called 'nationalistic Protestantism'.[65] In 1875, for example, William Holman Hunt's highly acclaimed *The Shadow of Death* (1870–3, Manchester City Art Galleries) went on show in Dublin and Belfast.[66] Hunt's painting shows Jesus the carpenter, stretching his limbs after a day's labour. His uplifted arms cast on the wall behind a cross-like shadow which is viewed by his mother as a premonition of his death. Following Hunt's own comment that the painting is about the need to 'persevere' despite 'the [burden] of toil', recent discussion of *The Shadow of Death* has alerted us to its espousal of a firm belief in the Protestant work ethic.[67]

Returning to *The Secret of England's Greatness*, it needs to be pointed out that, unlike the international success enjoyed by William Holman Hunt, Barker's painting had a peculiarly low-key exhibition history – an 1863 display in London's Cheapside in a printseller's shop and then a tour that we know included Newcastle-upon-Tyne and Scarborough, as well as Belfast.[68] Yet engravings after the painting appeared within the same year of its exhibition in Belfast, and were still in circulation well into the twentieth century.[69] The not infrequent and varied recurrence in Ireland, and particularly in Ulster, of

Barker's image and its title is worth highlighting. Belinda Loftus has shown that by at least the 1930s Barker's painting was being used as the visual source for Ulster Orange banners, the central motif of the Bible being a major attraction.[70] On the other side of the political divide, the artist Jack Morrow (1872–1926) used the phrase 'The Secret of England's Greatness' as the title of a satirical cartoon published in a Belfast nationalist newspaper in 1907. Morrow's image shows *Seaghan buide* (sic), or *Seán Buí*, literally 'Yellow John', a standard Gaelic equivalent of John Bull, striding over colonized territory carrying 'the secrets' under his arms. Those secrets are Christianity and industry, in the shape of the Bible and a Belfast-built ship.[71] Yet another Irish appearance of this nineteenth-century imperialist image may lie behind James Joyce's well-known moment in the 'Cyclops' chapter of *Ulysses*, where the Citizen reads a newspaper report of an African delegation's visit to the cotton mills of Manchester. The Citizen informs his audience of an African chief's 'dearest possessions ... an illuminated bible, the volume of the word of God and the secret of England's greatness, graciously presented to him by the white chief woman, the great squaw Victoria'.[72] In terms of sources for this episode, scholars have long been aware that an actual African delegation which had visited London in 1904 was well known to Joyce. More recently, Emer Nolan has convincingly argued that Joyce uses this scene as 'a *protest* against the African's subjection to the protocols of British manners'.[73] But, given the longevity of Barker's image in Ireland, could it not also be that a lingering memory of *The Secret of England's Greatness* perhaps viewed in print form more than twenty years earlier in Dublin, reasserted itself in Joyce's consciousness?

Conclusion

This examination of the relationship between the condition of political union and artistic display in the Ireland of the nineteenth century has focused on two English works due to the fact that they, ironically, offer more insight into the role of the visual in Irish society than do home-produced works. Use was made earlier of David Lloyd's argument that the unstable and fissured nature of Irish society under union prevented the emergence of a stable middle class consensus needed to provide the necessary audience for the production of an indigenous Irish novel. As was suggested, we can easily substitute 'visual imagery' for 'novel' and come to the same conclusion. Later in the same essay, Lloyd discusses the 'crucial regulative function of the novel', that 'of belonging, of identity with the nation'. He goes on to say that, in 'certain contexts, like that of colonial Ireland, that process of identification breaks down, . . . because no cultural space is offered for representations which are not already apparently partisan'.[74]

The two images that have been the focus of this paper, Porter's panorama of the 'Storming of Seringapatam' (Figure 12) and Barker's *Secret of England's Greatness* (Figure 13), are distinctly partisan, that is, they create a false sense of cultural homogeneity. Through their displays in Ireland, in 1801 and 1864 respectively, these paintings, with their imperialist subject matter, reflect what Ashis Nandy has described as 'the cultural damage' that colonialism had on the internal cultures of Britain and Ireland.[75] Using Nandy's analysis, Porter's vigorous panorama displayed the development of a self-consciously violent, masculine and authoritarian attitude to the imperial other. In the central engraving (Figure 12) derived from the huge canvas, we see General Baird calling on his men to storm Tipú's fortress while below him British soldiers actively push their way up the incline. One particularly gruesome detail from this assault was chosen as the frontispiece to *Narrative Sketches of the Conquest of the Mysore*, sold for a modest 1s 6d in 'pocket 8vo size' to those viewing the panorama. Here a grenadier of the 74th regiment was shown defiantly slaying one of Tipú's guards (in the central engraving the scene appears to the lower left of where Baird is standing, directly below the figure of Sergeant Graham, who shouts 'the huzza of victory' from the ramparts). It can thus be said that many an Irish visitor to Porter's panorama, along with the large numbers attending in Britain, came away with not only a vivid memory of victory but tangible – visual – proof of imperial domination.

Equally, in accordance with Nandy's analysis of the psychology of colonialism, Barker's painting of sixty years later can be interpreted as representing 'the flowering of the middle-class British [and, by extension, Irish] evangelical spirit', and the beginning of a clear ascription of cultural rather than merely military or authoritarian meaning to British domination.[76] Nandy has identified the 'magical feelings of omnipotence and permanence',[77] that the United Kingdom imputed to itself regarding its missionary aims. Indeed, one of Victoria's several prime ministers, Lord John Russell, who conveniently appears on the right-hand side of Barker's painting (Figure 13), defined the aims of colonization as being

> to encourage religious instruction, let them partake of the blessings of Christianity, preserve order and internal peace, induce the African race to feel that wherever the British flag flies they have a friend and protector, check all oppression, and watch over the impartial administration of the law.[78]

In reading this and substituting 'Irish' for 'African' while at the same time looking at Thomas Jones Barker's *The Secret of England's Greatness*, we arrive at the conclusion that Union and display in nineteenth-century Ireland had become one.

Notes

I am grateful to Terry McDonagh, Alan Ford and Anthea Callen for offering useful criticism and to Jan Marsh and Peter Funnell for information.

1 See Cyril Barrett, 'Irish nationalism and art 1880–1921', *Studies*, winter 1975, pp. 393–409, and his two chapters written with Jeanne Sheehy in W. E. Vaughan (ed.) *A New History of Ireland*, vol. 6: *Ireland Under the Union, II, 1870–1921*, Oxford, Clarendon Press, 1996, pp. 436–99. Also John Turpin, 'Exhibitions of arts and industries in Victorian Ireland', *Dublin Historical Record*, vol. 25, 1981–82, pp. 2–13, 42–51, and Leon Litvack, 'Exhibiting Ireland, 1851–3: colonial mimicry in London, Cork and Dublin', in Glenn Hooper and Leon Litvack (eds) *Ireland in the Nineteenth Century: Regional Identity*, Dublin, Four Courts Press, 2000, pp. 15–57.

2 Pat Wallace, Foreword to Elizabeth Crooke, *Politics, Archaeology and the Creation of a National Museum in Ireland. An Expression of National Life*, Dublin and Portland, OR, Irish Academic Press, 2000, p. vi. An 1890s' photograph showing the Sikh guns in the rotunda of the Dublin Museum of Science and Art is in the Lawrence Collection, National Photographic Archive, National Library of Ireland, Dublin.

3 For Wheatley's paintings see Fintan Cullen, *Visual Politics. The Representation of Ireland 1750–1930*, Cork, Cork University Press, 1997, ch. 2. A mid-1790s' example of a satirical print with a College Green setting is 'The Irish Janus on His Way to the House of Peers Conducted by the Dublin Populace', *c.*1796, possibly a Dublin print. There is a version in the former collection of Nicholas Robinson, now in Trinity College Dublin Library. This print shows a two-faced Grattan being heralded through Dublin, one side of him supports Irish freedoms, the other supports the Insurrection Act.

4 Royal Irish Academy (RIA), Dublin, MS 24K14, f.249; for Hamilton's portrait, see Cullen, *Visual Politics*, pp. 104–15.

5 RIA, MS 24K14, f.273; discussion of the panorama goes on to f.278. Excerpts from the diary are included in Fintan Cullen, *Sources in Irish Art: A Reader*, Cork, Cork University Press, 2000, pp. 237–43.

6 *The Freeman's Journal*, 14 July 1801; the panorama was on display for six months from 15 July to the end of December.

7 See Denys M. Forrest, *Tiger of Mysore. The Life and Death of Tipú Sultán*, London, Chatto & Windus, 1970; for pictorial imagery see Mildred Archer, *India and British Portraiture, 1770–1825*, London and New York, Sotheby Parke Bernet, 1979; Fintan Cullen, 'The art of assimilation: Scotland and its heroes', *Art History*, vol. 16, no. 4, December 1993, pp. 600–18; and Anne Buddle, *The Tiger and the Thistle: Tipu Sultan and the Scots in India, 1760–1800*, Edinburgh, National Gallery of Scotland, 1999.

8 P. J. Marshall, '"Cornwallis Triumphant": War in India and the British public in the late eighteenth century', in Lawrence Freeedman, Paul Hayes and Robert O'Neill (eds) *War, Strategy, and International Politics. Essays in Honour of Sir Michael Howard*, Oxford, Clarendon Press, 1992, pp. 72–3.

9 For Porter see Stephan Oettermann, *The Panorama: History of a Mass Medium*, New York, Zone Books, 1997, pp. 115–18; Ralph Hyde, *Panoromania! The Art and Entertainment of the 'All Embracing' View*, London, Trefoil Press, 1988, p. 65, where the three engravings are reproduced in correct sequence; see also Archer, *India and British Portraiture*, pp. 427–9. Buddle, *Tiger and Thistle*, pp. 52–3, repro-

duces in colour a reduced oil painting by Porter of the *Storming of Seringapatam* which was possibly made for the engraver.

10 *Narrative Sketches of the Conquest of the Mysore, effected by the British Troops and their Allies, in the Capture of Seringapatam, and the Death of Tippoo Sultaun, May 4, 1799 with Notes, Descriptive and Explanatory, Collected from Authentic Materials*, 3rd edn, Edinburgh, 1801, p. 131.

11 *Narrative Sketches of the Conquest of the Mysore*, pp. 129–30.

12 RIA, MS 24K14, fos 276–7.

13 Thomas F. Dibdin, *Reminiscences of a Literary Life*, London, 1836, Part 1, pp. 146–7.

14 My thanks to Anne Buddle and Elizabeth Guest for information on Porter's panorama. The panorama in Cork was printed by J. Connor, Grand Parade, Cork, 1801. For the Belfast exhibition, see Eileen Black, 'The development of Belfast as a centre of art 1760–1888', unpublished PhD dissertation, Queen's University, Belfast, 1998, p. 11. See also Oettermann, *The Panorama*, pp. 115–17, 360.

15 *The Siege of Acre* was in Belfast in late 1802, see Black, 'The development of Belfast as a centre of art', p. 11; Oettermann illustrates the orientation plan for the Acre panorama, *The Panorama*, p. 116. Hyde, *Panoromania!* p. 22, gives a list of English venues for the *Seringapatam* panorama.

16 *Narrative Sketches of the Conquest of the Mysore*.

17 See C. A. Bayly, *Imperial Meridian. The British Empire and the World, 1780–1830*, London and New York, Longman, 1989, p. 114.

18 *Hibernian Magazine*, January 1792, facing p. 1; 'An account of his resources; by a European officer in his service' had appeared earlier, in May 1791, pp. 390–1. I am grateful to Lyn Innes for this reference. A plate showing Tipú's sons taken as hostages by Lord Cornwallis accompanied by a two-page account of the affair appears in the *Hibernian Magazine*, 1792, pp. 356–8.

19 From the *World*, 23 August 1792, quoted by P. J. Marshall in 'Cornwallis Triumphant', pp. 62–3.

20 Oettermann, *The Panorama*, pp. 99–112.

21 Bernard Comment, *The Panorama*, London, Reaktion Books, 1999, p. 19. Another Irish connection with Porter's display of the *Seringapatam* panorama in Dublin was the fact that in painting it he was assisted by a 14-year-old apprentice named William Mulready (1786–1863) who, with his family, ten years earlier had left County Clare for London and was soon recognized as a child prodigy. Porter and Mulready worked all out on the panorama, finishing it in a mere six weeks. In time, Mulready would become a leading genre painter and prominent Royal Academician: see Kathryn Moore Heleniak, *William Mulready*, New Haven, CT, and London, Yale University Press, 1980, pp. 29, 237n–8n; and Pauline Rohatgi, 'From pencil to panorama: Tipú in pictorial perspective', in Buddle (ed.) *Tiger and Thistle*, p. 52.

22 Oettermann, *The Panorama*, pp. 40–4, and Alan Wallach, 'Making a picture of the view from Mount Holyoke', in David C. Miller (ed.) *American Iconology*, New Haven, CT, and London, Yale University Press, 1993, pp. 80–91; also Michel Foucault, *Discipline and Punish. The Birth of the Prison*, trans. Alan Sheridan, Harmonsworth, Penguin Books, 1977, pp. 195–228, 317 note 4. For further discussion of the phenomenon, see William H. Galperin, *The Return of the Visible in British Romanticism*, Baltimore, MD, and London, Johns Hopkins University Press, 1993, ch. 2: 'The panorama and the diorama: aids to distraction'; for Porter, see pp. 50–1; see also Angela Miller, 'The panorama, the cinema, and the emergence of the spectacular', *Wide Angle*, vol. 18, no. 2, 1996, pp. 34–69.

23 Wallach, 'Making a picture', p. 83. See Michel Foucault, 'The eye of power', in Colin Gordon (ed.) *Power/Knowledge. Selected Interviews and Other Writings 1972–1977*, New York and London, Harvester Wheatsheaf, 1980, pp. 146–65.

24 See Cullen, *Visual Politics*, pp. 101–4, Plate 47.

25 For Wellesley's jewels, see Historical Manuscripts Commission, *Report on the Manuscripts of J. B. Fortesque, Esq., Preserved at Dropmore*, 10 vols, London,

1892–1927, vol. 6, p. 50; and Robert R. Pearce, *Memoirs and Correspondence of the Noble Richard Marquess Wellesley*, 3 vols, London, 1846, vol. 1, pp. 336–7.

26 RIA MS 24K14, fo. 278. For the East India Company's recruiting in Ireland, see Cormac Ó Gráda, *Ireland. A New Economic History 1780–1939*, Oxford, Clarendon Press, 1994, pp. 19–21.

27 Bayly, *Imperial Meridian*, p. 127; Edward M. Spiers, *The Army and Society, 1815–1914*, London and New York, Longmans, 1980, p. 48, and table, p. 50. See also Thomas Bartlett, ' "A weapon of war yet untried": Irish Catholics and the armed forces of the crown, 1760–1830', in T. G. Fraser and Keith Jeffery (eds) *Men, Women and War*, Dublin, Lilliput Press, 1993, pp. 66–85; J. E. Cookson, *The British Armed Nation 1793–1815*, Oxford, Clarendon Press, 1997, ch. 6; and T. G. Fraser, 'Ireland and India', in Keith Jeffery (ed.) *'An Irish Empire'? Aspects of Ireland and the British Empire*, Manchester University Press, 1996, pp. 77–93. My thanks to Frank O'Gorman for directing me to Cookson's work.

28 Entrance fee advertised in Dublin's *Freeman's Journal*, 11 July, 1801. The entrance fee was higher in Cork: see *The Grand Historical Picture of the Storming of Seringapatam*, Cork, 1801: 'Open every day from nine o'clock till dusk – admittance one shilling and eight-pence'.

29 V. G. Kiernan, 'The emergence of a nation', in C. H. E. Philpin (ed.) *Nationalism and Popular Protest in Ireland*, Cambridge, Cambridge University Press, 1987, p. 40.

30 George Meredith, *Diana of the Crossways*, London, 1906, pp. 17–18. I am grateful to Kiernan, 'The emergence of a nation', for this example from Meredith.

31 Jeanne Sheehy, *The Rediscovery of Ireland's Past: The Celtic Revival, 1830–1920*, London, Thames & Hudson, 1980, p. 45; for Maclise, see Arts Council of Great Britain, *Daniel Maclise, 1806–1870*, London, 1972, and Nancy Weston, *Daniel Maclise. Irish Artist in Victorian London*, Dublin, Four Courts Press, 2001; for Burton, see Mairie Burke, 'Rural life in pre-famine Connacht: a visual document', in Raymond Gillespie and Brian P. Kennedy (eds) *Ireland: Art Into History*, Dublin, Town House, 1994, pp. 61–74.

32 See Arts Council, *Maclise*, pp. 99–100, and Weston, *Daniel Maclise*, pp. 210–17; Anne Crookshank and the Knight of Glin, *Ireland's Painters 1660–1940*, New Haven, CT, and London, Yale University Press, 2002, p. 241; Catherine Marshall, 'Painting Irish history: the famine', *New History of Ireland*, vol. 4, no. 3, 1996, p. 50; also Pamela Berger, 'The historical, the sacred, the romantic: medieval texts into Irish watercolors', in Adele M. Dalsimer (ed.) *Visualizing Ireland. National Identity and the Pictorial Tradition*, Boston, MA, and London, Faber & Faber, 1993, pp. 71–80. A pro-union reading is suggested by Barrett, 'Irish nationalism and art 1880–1921', p. 408, and discussed by Cullen, *Visual Politics*, pp. 47–9.

33 *Art Journal*, 1854, p. 166; for other reviews, see Weston, *Daniel Maclise*, pp. 214–15.

34 For art institutions in Ireland in the nineteenth century, see Walter Strickland, *A Dictionary of Irish Artists*, 2 vols, Dublin, 1913, vol. 1, pp. 579–664; Catherine de Courcy, *The Foundation of the National Gallery of Ireland*, Dublin, National Gallery of Ireland, 1985; see also Black, 'The development of Belfast as a centre of art', and Peter Murray, *Illustrated Summary Catalogue of the Crawford Municipal Art Gallery*, Cork, City of Cork Vocational Education Committee, 1991.

35 An example is the painting *St Francis-Xavier Preaching in Japan*, by Bernardo Celantano (1860), in the Jesuit church, Gardiner Street, Dublin, illustrated in Maureen Ryan, 'Roman opulence in a Dublin church. The high altar of St Francis Xavier's', *Irish Art Review Yearbook*, vol. 14, 1998, p. 38.

36 See Judith Hill, *Irish Public Sculpture. A History*, Dublin, Four Courts Press, 1998, pp. 65–9; also John Turpin, *John Hogan. Irish Neoclassical Sculptor in Rome 1800–1858*, Dublin, Irish Academic Press, 1982, pp. 110–13, 149.

37 Turpin, *Hogan*, p. 149. The other reliefs were by Joseph R. Kirk (*Seringapatam*) and Thomas Farrell (*Waterloo*).

38 'National Art', in D. J. O'Donoghue (ed.) *Essays Literary and Historical by Thomas Davis*, Dundalk, Dundalgan Press, 1914, p. 121; see also Cullen, *Sources in Irish Art*, p. 67.

39 Hill, *Irish Public Sculpture*, p. 67.

40 Barrett, 'Irish nationalism and art 1880–1921'; an edited version of Barrett's article appears in Cullen, *Sources in Irish Art*, pp. 273–81.

41 Barrett, 'Irish nationalism and art 1880–1921', p. 408. For imagery of O'Connell, see Cullen, *Visual Politics*, pp. 90–101, and Fergus O'Ferrall, 'Daniel O'Connell, the "liberator", 1775–1847: changing images', in Gillespie and Kennedy (eds) *Ireland: Art into History*, pp. 91–102.

42 See Ann M. Stewart, *Royal Hibernian Academy of Arts. Index of Exhibitors and Their Works, 1826–1979*, 3 vols, Dublin, Manton Publishing, 1990, and Sheehy, *Rediscovery*, chs 3 and 4.

43 See Eileen Black, 'Practical patriots and the true Irishmen. The Royal Irish Art Union 1839–1859', *Irish Arts Review Yearbook*, vol. 14, 1998, pp. 140–6, and Sheehy, *Rediscovery*, pp. 41–3.

44 David Lloyd, *Anomalous States. Irish Writing and the Post-Colonial Moment*, Dublin, Lilliput Press, 1993, pp. 136–44, *passim*.

45 Joep Leerssen, *Remembrance and Imagination. Patterns in the Historical and Literary Representation of Ireland in the Nineteenth Centruy*, Cork, Cork University Press, 1996, p. 37.

46 'Irish historical paintings', in *Essays Literary and Historical by Thomas Davis*, pp. 112–15; see also Cullen, *Sources in Irish Art*, pp. 70–4.

47 Quoted by Barrett, 'Irish nationalism and art 1880–1921', p. 406; see also Charles Gavan Duffy, *Young Ireland. A Fragment of Irish History 1840–45*, 2 vols, London, Fisher & Unwin, 1896, vol. 2, p. 154.

48 For Hayes, see Anne Crookshank and the Knight of Glin, *The Watercolours of Ireland: Works on Paper in Pencil, Pastel and Paint, c.1660–1914*, London, Barrie & Jenkins, 1994, pp. 150–1, Plate 196. Like Robert Ker Porter, half a century earlier, Hayes accompanied the exhibition of his watercolour with a lengthy account of the battle and the individuals involved. See also Stewart, *Royal Hibernian Academy*, vol. 2, p. 73.

49 Barrett, 'Irish nationalism and art 1880–1921', pp. 401–2; also in Cullen, *Sources in Irish Art*, p. 278.

50 *Belfast News-Letter*, 29 April 1864, and *Northern Whig*, 30 April 1864; see also Black, 'The development of Belfast as a centre of art', p. 144.

51 Stewart, *Royal Hibernian Academy*, vol. 1, p. 36.

52 See J. M. W. Hichberger, *Images of the Army. The Military in British Art, 1815–1914*, Manchester, Manchester University Press, 1988, pp. 61–2.

53 *Belfast News-Letter*, 29 April 1864, and Black, 'The development of Belfast as a centre of art', pp. 144 and 160 note 126; the background of the Sant painting was executed by David Roberts.

54 W. M. Rossetti, *Fine Art Quarterly Review*, vol. 1, May–October 1863, p. 344. One plausible suggestion is that the African is an ambassador from the Kingdom of Dahomey. In 1848, Saguba and other chiefs of Abeokuta had presented on their behalf a petition to Victoria against slavery: see Walter Walsh, *The Religious Life and Influence of Queen Victoria*, London, Swan Sonnenschein, 1902, pp. 54–5. I am grateful to Jan Marsh for this information; for a fuller account of the painting, see her article in the *Guardian*, 27 January 2001, p. 3.

55 *Belfast News-Letter*, 30 April 1864. See note 70, below, for a reference to the appearance of a print after Barker's painting in the stage set of a 1912 Ulster play.

56 Reverend James Hall Wilson, *The Late Prince Consort: Reminiscences of His Life and Character*, London, c.1862, p. 22. Peter Funnell is of the opinion that Wilson's book was a shilling improving tract aimed at the popular market and its publication may have prompted Barker's picture. The *Belfast News-Letter*, 29 April 1864, carried an advertisement for the exhibition of the Barker painting with a reference to Wilson's explanation of the scene. Contemporary newspapers suggested differ-

ent dates for the event depicted: 1846, according to *Northern Whig*, 30 April 1864, and 1851, during the Great Exhibition in London, according to *Scarborough Gazette*, 10 August 1865.

57 Adrienne Munich, *Queen Victoria's Secrets*, New York, Columbia University Press, 1996, p. 144. Benjamin West's large canvas *The Institution of the Order of the Garter* (1787), still at Windsor, can be seen in the background of the Barker painting.

58 *Belfast News-Letter*, 6 May 1864.

59   Psalm 119:127; the other quotation on the frame, Psalm 119:105, reads: 'Thy word is a lamp unto my feet, and a light unto my path.' For the frame see Marsh, *Guardian*.

60 Sean Connolly, *Religion and Society in Nineteenth-Century Ireland*, Dundalk, Dundalgan Press, 1985, p. 45; Jonathan Bardon, *A History of Ulster*, Belfast, Blasckstaff Press, 1992, pp. 340–4; also Jonathan Bardon, *Belfast. An Illustrated History*, Belfast, Blackstaff Press, 1982, p. 116.

61 Bardon, *Belfast*, p. 111 and Bardon, *Ulster*, pp. 350–2, see also Sybil E. Baker, 'Orange and green. Belfast, 1832–1912', in H. J. Dyos and M. Wolff (eds) *The Victorian City: Images and Realities*, 2 vols, London, Routledge and Kegan Paul, 1973, vol. 2, pp. 797–8 and Andrew Boyd, *Holy War in Belfast*, Tralee, Anvil Books,1969, pp. 44–89.

62 Boyd, *Holy War*, p. 47, quoting from Thomas Henry's pamphlet, 'History of the Belfast riots of 1864'. See also, Paula Murphy, 'The O'Connell monument in Dublin. The political and artistic context of a public sculpture', *Apollo*, March, 1996, pp. 22–6.

63 Bardon, *Belfast*, p. 114.

64 W. T. Stead, *Her Majesty The Queen. Studies of the Sovereign and the Reign. A Memorial Volume of the Great Jubilee, June 22 1897*, London, Review of Reviews, 1897, pp. 18–19. Adrienne Munich discusses Stead's reactions to Barker's painting in *Queen Victoria's Secrets*, pp. 145–6 as does Antony Taylor in *'Down with the Crown'. British Anti-Monarchism and Debates about Royalty since 1790*, London, Reaktion Books, 1999, p. 23. For a discussion of working-class reactions to high art in the mid-nineteenth century, see Dianne Sachko Macleod, *Art and the Victorian Middle Class. Money and the Making of Cultural Identity*, Cambridge, Cambridge University Press, 1996, pp. 103–6.

65 Tim Barringer, *The Pre-Raphaelites: Reading the Image*, London, Weidenfeld & Nicolson, 1998, p. 127.

66 See Black, 'The development of Belfast as a centre of art', p. 146 and *passim* for a comprehensive account of paintings shown in Belfast during the period. Another notable 'Protestant' painting displayed in Belfast was Noel Paton's *The Man of Sorrow* (Laing Art Gallery, Newcastle-upon-Tyne), which went on tour in 1882 and inspired a sermon by a local Presbyterian clergyman, see Black, 'The development of Belfast as a centre of art', pp. 141 and 159 note 111. For Dublin exhibitions see Ann M. Stewart, *Irish Art Loan Exhibitions 1765–1927*, 3 vols, Dublin, Manton Publishing, 1990, and Stewart, *Royal Hibernian Academy*.

67 See Barringer, *The Pre-Raphaelites*, pp. 132–3, who quotes from Hunt's pamphlet, *Mr. Holman Hunt's Picture, 'The Shadow of Death'*, London, Thomas Agnew & Sons, 1873.

68 Marsh, *Guardian*; for a London review of the painting see *Illustrated London News*, 6 June 1863, p. 611.

69 Stead (1897) reproduces W. H. Simmons's engraving (1864) after Barker's painting in *Her Majesty The Queen*, p. 17.

70 Belinda Loftus, *Mirrors. Orange and Green*, Dundrum, County Down, Picture Press, 1994, p. 27 and Plate 10 which shows its continued use in the 1970s. The poet Richard Murphy has made reference to this motif on Unionist banners in the poem *Orange March*, see *New Selected Poems*, London, Faber & Faber, 1989, p. 49. In the stage directions to his 1912 plays, *The Magnanimous Lover* and *The Orange-man*, St John Ervine specifies Barker's image as hanging on the walls of the two homes described, their role being to indicate Protestant sectarianism: see St John

G. Ervine, *Four Irish Plays*, London and Dublin, Maunsel & Co., 1914, pp. 59 and 102. See also Norman Vance, *Irish Literature: A Social History. Tradition, Identity and Difference*, Oxford, Blackwell, 1990, pp. 180–1.The *Secret* was also used as an emblem on Orange banners in Manchester in the 1870s, see Antony Taylor, *'Down with the Crown'*, p. 22. My thanks to Jan Marsh for this reference.

71 See John Killen, *John Bull's Famous Circus: Ulster History Through the Postcard*, Dublin, O'Brien's Press, 1985, pp. 20, 25, 28, 152. Morrow's cartoon first appeared as a full page in *The Republic* on 17 January 1907 and was then produced as a post-card in April 1907. I am grateful to Terry McBride and Keith Jeffery for information on Morrow's image. My thanks also to Caoimhín MacGiolla Léith for clarification of the meanings of *Seaghan Buidhe*.

72 James Joyce, *Ulysses*, Harmondsworth, Penguin, 1960, p. 332.

73 Emer Nolan, *James Joyce and Nationalism*, London and New York, Routledge, 1995, p. 103 (original emphasis). For an alternative reading to Nolan, see Declan Kiberd, *Inventing Ireland. The Literature of the Modern Nation*, London, Vintage, 1996, p. 352. For discussion of Joyce's use of an the African delegation to London, see Robert Martin Adams, *Surface and Symbol. The Consistency of James Joyce's 'Ulysses'*, New York, Oxford University Press, 1967, p. 202; and Phillip F. Herring (ed.) *Joyce's Notes and Early Drafts for* Ulysses. *Selections from the Buffalo Collection*, Charlottesville, University Press of Virginia Press, 1977, pp. 138–41. I am grateful to Luke Gibbons for discussing with me this section of *Ulysses*.

74 Lloyd, *Anomalous States*: 'Violence and the constitution of the novel', p. 154.

75 I have borrowed this use of Nandy's ideas from the Introduction to Julie F. Codell and Dianne Sachko Macleod (eds) *Orientalism Transposed: The Impact of the Colonies on British Culture*, Aldershot, Ashgate, 1998, p. 2. See Ashis Nandy, *The Intimate Enemy. Loss and Recovery of Self under Colonialism*, Delhi, Oxford University Press, 1983, pp. 32–5.

76 Nandy, *The Intimate Enemy*, p. 6.

77 Nandy, *The Intimate Enemy*, p. 35.

78 Quoted in James Morris, *Heaven's Command. An Imperial Progress*, London, Faber & Faber, 1973, pp. 37–8.

CHAPTER EIGHT

Gentlemen connoisseurs and capitalists: modern British imperial identity in the 1903 Delhi durbar's exhibition of Indian art

Julie F. Codell

In 1877 Lord Lytton, Viceroy of India, held a coronation in Delhi to commemorate Victoria as Empress of India. Lytton's extravagant event was intended to retain and strengthen the loyalty of Indian princes: its medieval theme and decorations reminded them of their vassalage to the queen and of India's subordination to Britain. Coronation events included speeches and a long procession through Delhi over battle sites of the 1857 'Mutiny', the ghostly presence of which haunted the spectacle.[1] The event's pageantry was concocted from diverse British and Indian rituals, especially the Indian durbar, a ceremonial meeting of the rajah and his subjects.

In the traditional durbar gift exchanges embodied the incorporation of the recipient within the body of the ruler to express continuity and the incarnation of the system through the king's body.[2] Following the British victory in 1858, a flurry of British durbars was carried out, with invented titles, monetary rewards and gifts of land to those loyal to the British during the conflict. But, as Bernard Cohn argues, the Indian durbar ritual of incorporation was appropriated to become a British ritual of subordination, 'in which the presentation of a silk banner made the Indian princes the legal subjects of Queen Victoria'.[3] The durbar also maintained a spatial order in which status was expressed by proximity to the ruler.[4] Fearing status conflicts, Lytton did not call the event a durbar, but a more levelling 'assemblage'. Subsequent coronation ceremonies were called durbars.[5]

Lytton also held an exhibition of Indian art that had its own peculiar trajectory. The 1877 durbar exhibition, initially a haphazard affair consisting of gifts given by Indian princes to the Prince of Wales during his 1875–76 tour of India, became at the Paris International Exhibition in 1878 representative of Indian art, according to the catalogue's author George C. M. Birdwood. The collection then toured Britain with a revised catalogue (1880–81).[6]

Lytton's extravaganza was a template for later durbars, in 1903 and 1911.[7] In 1903 Viceroy George Curzon attempted both to outdo his predecessor and to substitute the theme of the modern for the 1877 theme of medievalism. According to the event's official recorder, Stephen Wheeler, the 1903 coronation durbar 'closed the page of the India of the past – the India of ancient chivalry and romance, of barbaric finery and mediaeval pomp – and appropriately opened the new chapter more prosaic, but also more progressive, of the Twentieth Century',[8] though Curzon also wanted his durbar to be 'Oriental or barbaric'.[9] Curzon believed his exhibition would be the most important contribution to the durbar.

In this chapter, I analyse the exhibition of Indian art as a 'thick' cultural experience, to use Clifford Geertz's word, to explore its multiple and contradictory representations of British imperial identity.[10] Curzon insisted on distinct boundaries between Indian and British cultural identities.[11] However, the extensive catalogue text by George Watt, exhibition curator, interjected inconsistencies that revealed permeable boundaries and undermined Curzon's purist cultural partitions, giving the exhibition multiple 'webs of significance', even among the British. Watt further tied his catalogue to the existing art knowledge/power base, the British art schools in India and their organ the *Journal of Indian Art*, what might be called the cultural arm of the Raj.[12] Out of these institutional forces and conflicts between stated ideals and actual practices – the ethnography of the exhibition – emerged unintended meanings for this dual display of Indian culture and Raj management. Furthermore, Curzon's own pose as gentlemanly capitalist combined with the exhibition's purpose to exonerate Britain of its role in the decline of Indian art production made it impossible to seal off Indian culture from global market demands and modern technologies. Indian press reception of the exhibition recognized inherent contradictions within the constructions of an ideal Raj administration of empire and of an essentialized 'Indianness', both inscribed by global markets which the exhibition was required to satisfy to demonstrate the well-intentioned paternalism and efficiency of British imperial management. Indian nationalists chose the exhibition as a flashpoint for their own political programme and even their own competing exhibitions, further thickening the exhibition's meanings.

[135]

Gentlemanly capitalists: economics of the raw and the cooked[13]

After leaving his position as Viceroy and returning to England, Curzon articulated a highly affective narrative about India that defined aristocratic cultural roles for both British imperialists and Indian princes: 'without her [India] the Empire could not continue to exist'; India is 'the only part of the British Empire which is an empire' – the 'strategic centre of the defensive position of the British Empire'.[14] His claims for Indians – fighting in the Boer War, living in Africa and the West Indies, building the Ugandan railway, and incorporating British institutions such as a free press, legal codes and a 'settled life' – made India a miniature empire, mirroring or mimicking Britain, each 'indispensable to the other', India being 'the great touchstone of British character and achievement'.[15] An independent India would no longer provide a field for the exercise of aristocratic duty and sacrifice, as it was 'essential to a nation's welfare that aristocracy should not be divorced from its public life', rank being a call to work, not a dispensation from work.[16]

Gentleman capitalists were centered in London's financial motivations and possessed most of the political clout in Britain and the empire. The notion of gentleman capitalists, introduced by P. J. Cain and A. G. Hopkins, defines them by shared patterns and ideals in their biographies, social circles, and political positions and clout. These capitalists looked down upon industrialists and manufacturers and pursued service professions requiring social status and Oxbridge educations – the law, finance, insurance, banking, communications, transport, public service, politics, the upper echelons of the Church and the military. Service professions, dynamic, innovative and accommodating of change, 'interposed an appropriately wide distance between the mundane world of producing commodities and the higher calling of directing others', aligned more with ideals 'fostered by the landed class ... than [with] the mores of manufacturing'.[17] Applying these ideals to Indian cultural management, Curzon, an aristocrat with an Etonian–Oxford education and a career in politics and the civil service, harkened back to eighteenth-century gentlemanly patronage of artists of lower rank by aristocrats who believed themselves, not the artists, to be the rightful bearers of aesthetic taste. While Victorian artists had become educated professionals, even gentlemen, Indian artists could be framed as subordinates, unable to maintain aesthetic standards and serve global markets without their Raj keepers. Patronage was a service that required knowledge, taste and wealth, aristocratic virtues displayed in Curzon's 1903 exhibition of Indian art, making it a showcase for British imperial management.[18] One of the socially elitist 'Souls' group of the 1880s, whose members loved art, Curzon restored Indian monuments (later, he spent his own funds to restore several castles in England) and planned the Victoria Memorial Hall in Calcutta.[19] He considered art the 'Olympic torch of civilization'.[20]

Curzon was also a modern businessman whose policies, especially on free trade, were determined largely by financial matters, not industrial concerns. He insisted that India's debt be repaid.[21] Adamant about promoting industry to improve the Indian economy, he began 'state incentives to the Indian iron and steel industry', and chastised British businessmen along with Indian aristocrats for not doing their share to help local manufacturers economize on imports, balance the budget and service India's debt.[22]

Curzon also sought to redeem the Raj from claims that its policies ruined Indian craft manufacture. Sankar Ghose comments that Britain treated India as if it were a country house and Indians its menial servants, and quotes Romesh Dutt's remark that British policy made 'India subservient to the industries of Great Britain' and reduced India to a maker of 'raw produce only,' so that Indians could work in company factories. These policies were carried out through prohibitive tariffs excluding Indian silk and cotton goods from England, while English goods were admitted to India duty-free or with nominal duty until 'millions of Indian artisans lost their earnings'.[23]

But British exhibition catalogues and government reports painted a rosy picture of Britain's administration of economics in India. The 1886 exhibition *Report* to which George Watt, Curzon's 1903 curator, contributed, argued for 'an enormous trade in Indian manufactured goods', including a potentially new industry using silk cotton fibre.[24] In his 1894 *Report on Economic Products* Watt spin-doctored India's vital statistics: 699 million acres with 222.5 million people produced 57,215,000 tons of food and India's non-food exports jumped in 1891–92.[25] He insisted that in famine 'vast communities' survived on wild foods and that India was 'in the foremost rank of producing-countries', needing only scientific improvement of native crops:[26] 'The contentment of the people, the growth of luxurious demands, and the expansion of foreign trade, must be admitted as prognostications of prosperity' which, through European 'principles and methods', would guarantee the 'growth of artisan industries' to become 'a feature of India's moral and material progress ... with such intrinsic wealth ... making immense advances in the arts and industries irrespective' of monetary exchange rates or foreign trade.[27] Yet Watt also lamented Western influences 'inimical' to ' India's most highly prized art manufactures', leaving them 'unimportant commercially'.[28] In 1894 Watt felt that handicrafts could not be revived and hoped new objects for European markets would replace crafts. By 1903 he favoured a revival of crafts through government patronage. In Wheeler's text, too, India was not a 'burden of empire' but rather fulfilled 'the dynamic force that it must exercise in the future history of the world', not as 'an alien yoke' but through 'the blessings' of British rule, 'felt by all its classes'. The durbar brought to Indians 'the Knowledge of the world' and 'the sympathy and regard of the British race'.[29]

Durbar exhibition: discovering pure Indianness

The 1903 exhibition had special importance for Curzon:

> We shall get together at Delhi such a collection as has never before been seen in India, and with the enormous crowd that will be there assembled, and from whom purchases and orders may be expected, I hope that I may give a real stimulus to the perishing industries of India. A single exhibition like this at such a time and such a place will do more towards that end than a score of Government resolutions or sporadic efforts in this or that locality.[30]

He even claimed to have drawn up the plans himself for the art exhibition's building.[31]

In his speeches before, during and after the durbar, Curzon, severely criticized for holding the durbar during a time of famine and the plague, argued for the importance of symbolic displays: the sovereign was the 'life and vigour of a nation' who 'symbolises its unity, and speaks for it', among many differences 'of race and class and custom and creed'. Indian loyalty and unity required a palpable display to reveal the 'political force and the moral grandeur of the nation'. The durbar paralleled the Greek Olympic games and the European community of exchange that has so improved 'the cause of peace' (a curious remark in 1902, following the Boer War!).[32]

But Curzon's primary concerns were commercial. Calling finances 'a sordid test', he nevertheless assured his Legislative Council that the durbar's costs would not be taken from funds set aside for famine relief and that its expenses rested on 'commercial principles': things produced for the durbar would be re-sold to recover 60–80 per cent of the costs or provided to the military. The durbar would generate profits from railway tickets, postal and telegraphic services to enhance the Government's paternal promotion of Indian self-sufficiency and economic prosperity by providing for 'hundreds of thousands of Indian workmen and artisans . . . full employment and good wages in preparing for the Durbar . . . one of the greatest opportunities that he [the

Indian artisan] has enjoyed for generations'. The durbar would prove 'to the world that India is not sunk in torpor or stagnation, but is alive with an ever-expanding force and energy', creating new markets for, and increased production of, Indian handicrafts.[33]

Curzon addressed the central issue of whether Indian art declined due to 'European competition', 'apathy', or a 'world-wide law' of progress and change. He presented these causes as agent-less – ineffable forces of 'nature' or the 'market' – rather than as outcomes of Raj policies. For Curzon, this decline was

> inevitable . . . in an age which wants things cheap and does not mind their being ugly, which cares a good deal for comfort, and not much for beauty, and which is never happy unless it is deserting its own models and traditions, and running about in quest of something foreign and strange.[34]

Despite modern 'commercial ideals and debauched taste', the exhibition could 'revive and stimulate . . . dormant and abashed' Indian traditions and improve English taste, to 'advertise to the world what we are capable of turning out, and also – which is much more important – encourage the aptitudes and educate the taste of our own people'.[35] The art exhibition would 'resuscitate these threatened handicrafts', and 'arrest the process of decay'.[36] That the 'decay' might be the consequence of Britain's stripping India of manufacturing to make it merely a source of raw materials was never addressed.

The exhibition site was Kudsia Bagh, a Muslim garden, in a building 'in careful accordance with the canons of Indo-Saracenic architecture'.[37] At the opening of the exhibition, on 30 December 1902, two days before the coronation, Curzon described the site – barren except for trees eight months earlier – as now filled with a 'great building . . . terraces . . . amenities', a 'mise-en-scène' that would disappear at the durbar's end. Creating beauty from barrenness was metonymic of empire-building itself, as it was also prophetic of the Raj's new patronage of Indian art in order to save 'barren' art traditions from 'their progressive deterioration and decline'.[38]

The task of supplying the exhibition was also a replay of imperial exploration. Curator George Watt and his assistant Percy Brown 'proceeded, travelling thousands of miles, everywhere interviewing the artisans, selecting specimens, giving orders, where necessary supplying models, and advancing money to those who needed it'.[39] Such travels to remote villages turned exhibition preparations into adventure, ethnology and archaeology to save the 'ruins' of handicrafts, just as Curzon had earlier embarked on restoring Indian architectural ruins, his pet project being the Taj Mahal.[40]

Insisting that this exhibition was the 'natural' outcome of empire, Curzon likens his three criteria to the 'laws of the Medes and Persians'. First, this exhibition would include only art, unlike international exhibitions which included raw materials and manufacturing technology. Second, nothing 'European or quasi-European' would appear in the exhibition, but 'only the work that represented the ideas, the traditions, the instincts, and the beliefs of the people', untouched by 'the process of Europeanisation'. However, this essential 'Indianness' was to be determined by British curators and bureaucrats 'selecting specimens, giving orders' and 'where necessary supplying models', making many of these allegedly Indian traditions as invented as coronation durbars.[41] Finally, '*I* would only have the best' (my emphasis), no 'vulgar lacquer, trinkets and tinsel', to ensure

> an exhibition of all that is rare, characteristic, or beautiful in Indian art, our gold and silver ware, our metal work, and enamels, and jewellery, our carving in wood and ivory, and stone, our best pottery and tiles, our carpets of old Oriental patterns, our muslins and silks and embroideries and the incomparable Indian brocades.

The rhetorical 'our' is curiously hybrid: British in ownership and control, Indian in artistic production.[42]

Because of declining taste and 'debased' modern models, Curzon 'endeavoured to set up, alongside the products of the present, the standards and samples of the past through a Loan Collection of objects' from Indian and British collections: private collections of Indian chiefs and connoisseurs, 'our own' Indian museums, and 'the unrivalled collection in the South Kensington Museum'. Curzon admonished Indian princes that their patronage must not be 'an adaptation of Eastern prescription to the Western standard' but must 'remain true to [the Indian's] religion, his traditions, and his people'.[43] They must work 'for the expurgation, or at any rate the purification, of modern tastes, and for a reversion for the old-fashioned but exquisite styles and patterns of their own country'. Indians must purify by reversing. The loan collection would inspire Indian workmen with 'fresh or rather resuscitated ideas'. Thus the keepers of Indian traditions were either Indian aristocrats (nonetheless condemned for their taste for European goods) or British connoisseurs and museums which had taken so many fine art works. The emphasis on resuscitation, rather than technological 'progress', industry and invention, maintained India at a distance from British 'modern' identity. But Curzon's 'modern' was also a time of debased taste, debased by the same British moderns now encouraged to set aesthetic standards for India, a contradiction that did not escape the attention of the Indian press.

[140]

Curzon's 'purity', based on his 'truism, that Indian art will never be revived by borrowing foreign ideals, but only by fidelity to its own', meant that every nation should produce and consume within its 'traditions'. But these parameters ignored realities of imperial trade and economics – Britain's world power was not the result of producing only for local markets. Such economic provincialism defined an essential 'Indianness' that now required protection by a cultural elite.[44] Curzon admitted that the British 'are just as bad in our pursuit of anything that takes our fancy in foreign lands', but limiting production to unspoiled internal markets was not a solution for British bad taste. The exhibition was to be 'an object-lesson' in British imperial management of Indian culture, and 48,000 people paid admission and often purchased works for sums greater than the prices, to net over 3.5 *lakhs* of rupees in sales.[45]

Classification, contradictions, connoisseurship

The exhibition was meant to redefine the Raj as a connoisseuring patron of Indian culture, not as a debased purchaser of Indian goods. Curzon insisted the exhibition was 'not a bazaar, but an exhibition . . . to encourage and revive good work, not to satisfy the requirements of the thinly lined purse'.[46] The 1903 durbar exhibition built upon the classification systems, economic intentions and imperial ideologies of prior international exhibitions, especially the 1886 Colonial and Indian Exhibition in which objects were arranged by locality to create 'the complete illustration of Indian Art industries in the Art Ware Courts . . . a complete Art-survey of India'.

Curzon's curator, George Watt, a botanist in the Revenue and Agricultural Department of the Raj, had organized earlier exhibitions in Calcutta in 1883–84 and the Colonial and Indian Exhibition.[47] His 1889 six-volume totalizing *Dictionary of the Economic Products of India* was written to 'form a nucleus of an extended and systematic enquiry into the productive resources of the Indian Empire', to help readers understand 'Indian economics . . . to advance the material interests of India, and to bring the trade and capital of the West into more direct contact with the resources of the Empire', presenting this knowledge as a benign master narrative.[48]

The 1886 exhibition anticipated another theme of the 1903 exhibition, that the British must promote Indian art because Indians were deemed incapable of modern economic behaviour: 'No artisans in the world are more dilatory, or less anxious to advertise their wares than the artisans of India. Except in the case of a few large dealers who have acquired the habit of dealing with English firms, liberal advances and

[141]

constant supervision.'[49] Indian artisans needed British tutelage in art, as well as in economics:

> Under European careful supervision the native Indian works beautifully. He cares more for patient manual labour and real handicraft traditional work than he does for progressive thought or invention, and it is not to be wondered at that it had been left to the quicker brain and the desire for development that characterises the people of the West, to produce results which find a readier market than his own unaided and unguided efforts can secure.[50]

In 1903 such intentions led to the arranging of crafts by their raw materials in Watt's supposedly unifying classification system. Watt's system has been attributed to T. N. Mukharji, a member of the Department of Revenue and Agriculture, in charge of the raw materials' collections and author of several exhibition catalogues praised by Anglo-Indians and British authorities.[51] Watt's detailed catalogue ran to more than 500 pages, with 90 plates and two indices, hardly the 'simple and practical account of the more noteworthy art industries of India' it claimed to be. Its classification system was 'a systematic sequence' to 'simplify inspection and facilitate future research' by offering 'descriptions by which the articles might be severally identified, rather than to furnish traditions and historic details regarding them'. Watt admitted his system deprived 'the subject of much of the beauty and poetry', but this ground was already covered, he claimed, by Birdwood's books on Indian art.[52]

Display was a *déraciné* affair that served the consumption of goods:

> [E]xhibits are arranged according to their kind and not their places of origin. It is thus made possible for visitors to compare, almost at a glance, productions of one kind from all parts of India both near and remote, and to make purchases in the Sale Gallery without being harassed by the importunities of competing traders.[53]

Thus European consumers were kept at a distance from Indian sellers. Raw materials, and sometimes techniques, defined categories, such as metal, stone, glass, wood, animal products, lac and lacquer. Textiles were described by fibre and embroidery by stitch technique. Categories existed within categories: metal wares, for example, were classified by material (iron, lead, tin, gold, silver, etc.) and technique (enamelled, encrusted, niello, damascened, etc.).[54]

Within each category, objects were described and arranged by province and by city, reclassified in the text by geography and historical explanations 'to admit of identification of each style of Indian work in association with the names of the centres of production and of the chief producers'.[55] Watt's overlay, however, contradicted consumption 'at a glance', with exhaustive scholarly details of geography and history.

This scholastic system was physically displayed within the European hierarchy of crafts and fine arts. Objects deemed higher in aesthetic value were closer to the great transept which housed the fine arts (sculpture, painting, book illumination).[56] Modifying Birdwood's argument that Indians excelled in crafts and Britons in the 'higher 'arts, Watt believed nonetheless that a 'Fine Arts class, which is to be strictly Indian, cannot itself be a very large one', since Indian art does not incorporate 'perspective, shadow and atmosphere', and 'oil-painting and sculpture . . . owe their existence almost exclusively to the Government Schools of Art'. So, the fine arts were treated as 'the highest utilisation of industrial materials', i.e. as crafts, because they were assumed to be 'little known and still less practised by the natives of India'.[57] Percy Brown, fine arts curator, classified objects as two- and three-dimensional – physically, not conceptually – and ignored iconography. Sculpture, which he called 'statuary', was 'crude and child-like in the extreme', not really 'Fine Arts', and he doubted that 'superior' European modelling 'will ever become really understood by the art student of India'.[58]

Brown divided painting into three styles based on external forces and conquest – Buddhist; Muslim portraits and 'book illustration' (referring to illuminations!) – and the 'modern style of oil and water-colour painting as practised in the Schools of Art'.[59] Praising the patronage of 'the broad minded Akbar', he reiterated the popular homology between Britons and Moghuls who the British felt were their direct antecedent. Without such external patrons, Brown implied, Indians could not produce fine art on their own.[60]

But crafts, not fine arts, were the exhibition's focus, and to encompass this vast topic, Watt created a closed intertextual field of knowledge. His 'art experts of India' included heads of the British art schools in India and museum directors, who selected exhibition pieces;[61] Sir Purdon Clarke of the South Kensington Museum (Victoria and Albert Museum), who loaned items;[62] and authors of articles from the *Indian Art Journal*, the periodical of the British art schools. These bureaucrat–experts were there to educate Indian artists and ensure the quality of the objects: 'when Kashmir thinks of reviving its former beautiful art of papier mâché, it will have to go to the Museums of Europe and America for the most desirable models'.[63]

British art patronage appeared metonymic of the Raj's roles of 'civilizing' and 'knowing' India as India's tutor and patron, presuming to have more knowledge of Indian art than did Indian artists. Such

[143]

patronage was even given a lineage and history. Watt credited the East India Company with introducing mixed fabrics, mulberry silk industry, and export trade in silks;[64] missionaries, with promoting lace and introducing some forms of knitting;[65] the Bombay School of Art, with improving enamelling techniques;[66] and European firms, with improving furniture-making skills.[67] Thus, Indian art embraced those European influences which Curzon hoped to weed out.

Yet much was made of Watt's and Brown's 'discoveries' (their word), such as a Pattan gold sari, 'discovered by Mr. Percy Brown while *exploiting* the resources of Aurangabad' (italics mine).[68] Their adventures were facilitated by the existing bureaucratic infrastructure: 'the task of encouraging the craftsmen to undertake the work required of them, of supervising and checking the special preparations, and of fixing the price, devolved primarily on the District Officers, and through them on the Magistrates or Tahsildars of the Towns of India'.[69]

Along with their 'discoveries', Watt and Brown commissioned replicas, reproductions, hybrid inventions of their own, and 'copies' made ostensibly to conserve old designs and methods. Brown commissioned a bowl from designs in the Taj, a synthesis all his own.[70] Watt commissioned the Bellary Door (Figure 14) from 'a carpenter whose ancestors had made nearly all the beautiful doors of Bellary city', and who needed only 'to devote a little more care and attention to it than he had originally intended' to make it good.[71] The paternal Briton infantilizing the artisans (whose families had been in the craft for generations!) was a model of Raj patronage, as administrators had claimed to 'improve' these Indian 'children' in so many other areas.

Artisans were not even the only art producers. Students from British art schools revived art to satisfy emerging markets, as they 'trained' Indian artists in Western conventions.[72] The Madras School 'tried to re-establish the trade in Nellore and Rajamundri handkerchiefs, by manufacturing these in the required shape, colour and perfume and sending out experimental consignments', showing 'that the weavers required only a helping hand to re-assert the old export trade'.[73] Schools introduced art forms, as in the case of some glazed pottery in Bombay.[75] Even Yeroda jail prisoners' rug production in Poona, inspired by old carpets in the Jamai Musjid of Bijapur, 'has absolutely conservated what might otherwise have been lost'.[76]

Thus, exhibition objects were not produced solely by Indian artisans who were displaced by and levelled with students and prisoners. Perhaps because of this displacement, there was an 'Artificers' Gallery of Workshops', where techniques 'may be studied' as craftsmen plied their trades as exhibition objects themselves.[77] The catalogue included drawings of craftsmen at work by Brown and by Munshi Sher

14 Bellary Door – Dravidian Style, in George Watt, *Indian Art Exhibition, Delhi, 1903. Being the Official Catalogue of the Delhi Exhibition, 1902–1903*, Calcutta, Government Printer, 1904, Plate 30, pp. 132–3

Mohamed, painting master of the Lahore School of Art, showing craftsmen working in 'primitive' conditions with simple tools, presumably
producing art in the same way artisans had done thousands of years
ago (Figure 15).

Given the variety of producers, categories were not impermeable,
discrete or even Indian.[78] When 'the classification of Indian Arts . . .
was being framed, it was not known how far some of the Divisions
then entertained might be represented by the collections'. Craftsmen's
transfer of painted wood-works to *papier mâché*, necessitated a hybrid
category of both.[79] Sometimes materials crossed boundaries: lac-ware
crossed over into ivory and metal crafts, as well as wood.[80] Some bro-
caded silks in the silk section also fitted into the 'mixed fabrics'
section. Such 'inconsistencies' emerged as production constantly
changed to meet new markets.[81] Even machine-made objects were
admitted, and sometimes praised.[82] Furthermore, Indians never
produced work intended for Watt's classifications: 'It thus becomes
hopeless to arbitrarily restrict the names given to textiles, the more
so since the same name or a derivative from it may, in the Provinces
of India, have different meanings attributed to it.'[83] Textiles exemplified classification problems in Watt's divisions into pre-and post-loom
manufacture:

> The difficulty that besets every attempt at a scientific classification of
> artificial (that is to say manufactured) articles is exceedingly great and
> overlappings are unavoidable . . . Such goods might, therefore, be either
> treated as illustrative of the use of certain materials or as methods of
> textile manipulation . . . done before and the remainder after being
> woven.

Kashmir shawls, the most highly prized textiles, could not readily be
categorized as loom work or subsequent to the loom.[84] In the end he
'raised' embroidery to a separate category because its 'individualities
and characteristics of the greatest beauty and interest . . . largely lost
sight of when merged . . . with certain corresponding forms of loom
work'. Expressing 'more individuality and less restraint' than weaving,
embroidery fitted European notions of artistic creativity.[85]

Watt's classification system was a quintessentially Victorian imperial project – to systematize all knowledge in every field, as Metcalf
argues, 'in ways that could sustain a system of colonial authority,
and through categories that made it fundamentally different from
Europe'.[86] Watt's catalogue upholds Metcalf's claims that the 'unequal
power relationship of imperialism helped shape the categories within
which that knowledge was constructed'.[87] Watt's admitted inconsistencies revealed how imposed that system was and how unreflective

THE MULTAN POTTER.

15 'The Multan Potter', by Sher Mohamad, Frontispiece to Watt, *Indian Art Exhibition, Delhi*

of Indian ways of organizing craft knowledge and relationships among objects, designs, patterns and traditions. The British scientized and classified what they knew or presumed of India, and fixed their invented categories of craft, tribe, caste and village community in an imaginary, originary and explanatory pastness.[88] This mechanical view of India as a static and fixed entity, making art by caste and repetition, allowed dynamic personae to remain British revivers, creators, entrepreneurs, classifiers and taste-makers.[89]

Inconsistencies between Curzon's criteria, the catalogue's ill-fitted systems and Indian art production problematized concepts of 'authenticity', 'Indian' and 'traditional'. Travelling to remote villages to 'unearth' traditional techniques and designs was undercut by the exhibition's entrepreneurial purposes to generate new markets, pay for the durbar, repay India's debt to Britain and attract future revenue. The attempt to 'purify' Indian art by 'the exclusion of all trace of the modern foreign influences which have tended to debase the ancient indigenous arts of India' could not be sustained despite frequent attacks on European influences.[90] And change was not necessarily degraded. Watt commended 'production of small tea-table cloths, table centres and such like articles on white cotton or linen in darn stitch', which, though 'too elaborate in the design to be regarded as art productions', might 'settle into more artistic forms and become of the greatest value to the shawl embroiderers of Kashmir', then losing their market.[91] Ivory-carving in Delhi, 'the result of the great influx of sight-seers', could still produce goods to 'meet the requirements of the European demand'.[92] New, simpler, cheaper methods, when applied 'skilfully', could be 'more pleasing than the overelaboration of the older method'.[92] Styles were homogenized and circulated, as in the widespread imitation of Calcutta's rural scenes on silverware.[93] Many works combined Oriental designs and European techniques or manufacture.[94] Even factory-produced objects, like the 'beautiful silk goods' of Sassoon and the Alliance Silk Mills Company, Bombay, were exhibited, though barred from receiving awards.[95]

European ideas and production modes intervened to 'save' or 'revive' Indian 'traditions', as they had earlier 'degraded' them. Goods circulating through global trade invariably altered local practices and added or erased raw materials.[96] Some things 'hardly worthy of a place in an Art Exhibition' were admitted nonetheless.[97] The adaptability required to meet future markets undermined the exhibition's 'pure' criteria and its policing of difference.

My focus on the exhibition's ethnography is on the British 'experts' who vetted Indian art production for both its authenticity and its marketability. Elaborate balconies and small rooms (Figure 16), 'exempli-

[148]

16 Bombay Room – Gujerat Art – furnishing, in Watt, *Indian Art Exhibition, Delhi*, Plate 2, pp. 4–5

fying the adaptability of the various better known styles of Indian Art, to modern household furnishing and architectural decoration', clearly exposed these practices' inconsistences. Watt claimed that the Madras Room, produced by art school students, could 'exemplify the accumulative and realistic Dravidian style of South India'.[98] The Mayo School of Art, Lahore, 'guided not only the workers in Lahore city, but . . . has striven to conserve and develop all that is beautiful in the various styles'.[99] The Fatehpur Archway by Lockwood Kipling, head of the Mayo School, was a copy of the school's doorway, itself a copy of a door from the town of Fatehpur Sikri.[100] The Bhavnagar House, commissioned by the Maharajah of Bhavnagar, was supervised by Proctor Sims, state engineer, to ensure that 'it is true in every detail to the architecture and household furnishing that prevailed a century ago'.[101]

British bureaucrat connoisseurs were part of a nexus of imperial cultural institutions in a closed circuit of disciplinary validation.

Watt's catalogue had a symbiotic relation to the *Indian Art Journal*, the mouthpiece of the British art schools, whose scholars also defined Indian art by materials and technique. Knowledge of Indian art circulated intertextuality among a select number of Raj bureaucrats, sharing imperial views of Indian art production and artists.[102] Pieces purchased for Indian museums subsequently transformed exhibition simulacra into 'evidence' of a historical 'tradition' that further validated the exhibition's display and textual ideologies. The Mysore carved wooden door, based 'on the model of a door in a portion of the old palace of Mysore . . . constructed under the orders of the Executive Engineer in charge of the new palace works . . . a faithful reproduction', later moved to the Madras Central Museum. Two wooden reproductions of stone architraves in the Chalukyan Temple of Hullabid were purchased by the Calcutta and Panjab Museums.[103]

These purchases institutionalized and authorized commissioned replicas and hybrid works as 'pure' 'Indian' art, and they were also fiercely marketed in the exhibition and catalogue:[104] 'Perhaps one of the most surprising features of the Exhibition may be said to have been the avidity with which every bit of this modern Kashmir work was purchased.'[105] Prices were cited and replicas blatantly advertised.[106] Embroidery's discrete classification was intended to generate markets.[107] The Jewellery Court was for sales pure and simple; its estimated value was about £1 million.[108]

Copies and hybrids, commissioned to preserve traditional styles and to accommodate modern European market demand, permeated boundaries between 'modern' and 'traditional'. Modern techniques and patterns through this British imperial connoisseurship could be incorporated into 'traditions' that were far from 'fixed' or 'past'. Schools of art, entrepreneurs and the Government's infrastructure were all points of permeability that contradicted Curzon's insistence on distinct national and cultural boundaries. Watt, not entirely convinced of the inevitability of decline, did not agree with the much-repeated argument that prisoners' carpets ruined that industry. To Watt, British jail carpets revived the Muslim introduction of carpet weaving, making British and Mughal again homologous in their patronage.[109] Praising aniline dyes, often disparaged as degradations of vegetable dyes, he argued:

> To bolster up the effete methods and appliances of bygone times would of necessity involve the suppression of national profession and the exposure of India to an even fiercer foreign competition . . . the endeavour should be to aid rather than obstruct the progress of India's manufacturing enterprise.[110]

Inscribing 'tradition' as 'effete' and 'progress' as manly, Watt himself advocated for change, as in his promotion of woodworking as a field for 'European ideas of comfort . . . creeping into the every-day life of the people', so that 'by careful guidance . . . the carpenters and cabinet-makers' can match demand with quality.[111] Presumably his and Brown's commissions exemplified such guidance, as did purchases by Viceroy and Lady Curzon; Lady Curzon, admiring a casket from the Calcutta Museum, inspired three 'chief craftsmen' to produce 'six exceedingly beautiful and carefully finished caskets'.[112] Lady Curzon's 'extensive orders for robes and gowns' called 'into existence a purified and refined style of embroidery that bids fair to considerable expansion in the future'.[113]

Curiously for Watt, the market forces condemned for undermining Indian art production became its salvation, cleansed through an ideology of the village caste system central to Birdwood's earlier praise of simple artisanal life. (Watt, to his credit, was skeptical, recognizing that many industries had already moved into cities.) Facing a growing urbanized educated resistance, the British nostalgia for rural Indian artisanal life became a self-deluding reaction against Indians educated in the West who, as Peter Robb points out, presented 'a special challenge', desiring self-government and political participation. In reaction, the Raj reasserted an 'essential' communal character of Indian society needing protection from 'outsiders'.[114] As Metcalf argues, 'crafts enthusiasts in no way emancipated themselves from the fundamental assumptions that sustained the imperial enterprise . . . the artisan craftsman alone, safely contained within the village order, posed no threat to the supremacy of the Raj', safe from urban modernization and subject to Raj control.[115] Heads of the art schools, 'new saviours of India's artistic heritage', became 'the most committed opponents of industrial development in India', according to Clive Dewey.[116]

Curzon's application of such British 'protection' to cultural production maintained 'separated and often artificial categories', and distances between cultural identities, perhaps not as distinct from Lytton's medieval paternalism as Curzon would have liked them to appear.[117] M. N. Das notes that Curzon de-politicized Indian masses, claiming that the 'people of India' were millions of illiterate peasants, without political aspiration and untouched by the Indian National Congress.[118]

Curzon's ideal also implied class distinctions between aristocratic connoisseurs, patrons with taste and deep pockets, and middle-class philistines, consumers of cheap goods. Indians had educated themselves to the 'cheapening' market, but now needed British guidance to be educated back to their own 'traditions' and to aristocratic patronage.[119] Watt even created a lineage for this patronage: Moghul patronage was continued by the East India Company, missionaries, connoisseuring bureaucrats and British art schools.[120] Education for Indians had been a cornerstone of liberalism, but it was to educate them for the future, in English ways, modern life and 'progress'.[121] The exhibition and catalogue suggested an education *back* to the past to maintain and reconstruct distinctions between 'Indian' and 'British', in line with Curzon's other plans to restrict maharajahs' European travel, eliminate Indian political participation and free university education, and eradicate the Indian National Congress.

As Metcalf notes, 'the more fully non-European peoples were accorded the prospect of future equality, the more necessary it become to devalue and depreciate their contemporary cultures'.[122] Indians – presumably separated spatially among scattered villages, socially among castes and Hindus and Muslims, and temporally from the present – could not 'claim to represent any "people" other than those constituting their own community', in Metcalf's analysis. Denying a public space for Indian political and cultural representation 'apart from the classificatory system of the Raj', the 'colonial state itself could alone overcome particular ties to create a rationalized whole concerned with 'general' interests'.[123] Watt, Brown and British civil servants constituted the only link among the villages' artisans, who represented only their locale or caste, but not 'India.'[124]

Curzon's classified and purified Indian artisans could then embody British imperial identity: raw material themselves, they would emerge authenticiated by the patronage of gentlemanly Raj administrators. As Britain's much-condemned mercantilism now redeemed and improved India's goods, so India could symbolize a well-run British empire.[125] Unable to choose between aesthetics and economics, Watt suggested that they transform one another. As co-creator of Indian culture, the Raj could continue to validate itself, in Metcalf's words, as 'an indigenous Indian ruler, necessary to India's economic and intellectual success, tied to India's past by its knowledge and creation of that past, rightfully maintaining order by its systematic classifications and geographical inspections'. Through craft production India would be made in the image of Britain's image of India.[126]

But for Indian economic viability, revivals also required attending to the future, as Watt recognized. His system, neither comprehensive nor universal, was infiltrated by economic, bureaucratic and modernizing forces that required hybrids, copies and production by a range of Indians (artisans, students, prisoners) deprived of their authority.[127]

The exhibition defined British and Indian imperial identities as complementary and oppositional: Indians, artisanal and local; British, technologically advanced and global.[128] Curzon shifted Lytton's medievalized India to an essentialized and fantasized India, and called the event a durbar, a term Lytton strenuously avoided. Curzon employed 'Saracenic' stylistic features, while Lytton had excluded Indian styles.[129] By 1903 Curzon was confident that the British could appropriate and represent the 'Asiatic' (his word) as a sign of British knowledge, duty and benevolence. However, the exhibition, intended to idealize, purify and amplify differences between 'Indian' and 'British', produced and hawked hybrids and 'inauthenticities' for modern markets.[130]

New imperialism and the press in India

In Charles O'Donnell's anonymously written book *The Failure of Lord Curzon* (1903), Curzon was identified with the new imperialism which O'Donnell characterized as militaristic, war-mongering, commercially motivated, greedy, autocratic, undemocratic and indifferent to Indians' suffering.[131] O'Donnell frequently quoted the conservative British and Anglo-Indian criticism of Curzon in the Tory papers,[132] middle-class Indian periodicals[133] and London papers.[134]

The press in India was a vociferous critic of Curzon's policies, the durbar, and the exhibition, identifying Curzon with an intention to push India backwards rather than forwards. The press called him 'Curzonation Durbar'. *Amrit Bazar Patrika* described Curzon's speech as 'full of the usual platitudes' and blamed Curzon for India's failure to prosper.[135] The *Bombay Gazette* complained about the durbar's excessive costs,[136] noting: 'the Art Exhibition is the only serious attempt to utilise the opportunity in a practical spirit, and that, according to some critics, has not been entirely successful'.[137] The *Friend of India* liked the exhibition but insisted that enlarging the sphere of rights and justice would 'convert what has been so confidently predicted would be a mere pageant into a great historical event'.[138] The *Friend of India*, citing the *Statesman*, called the exhibition the one durbar event 'which contains within itself the principles of permanence and the seeds of progressive development . . . a revelation not only of the inherent wealth of India as a country in which fine art has been produced, but also of the resources, still unrealised and unexploited, lying within the range of the ordinary craftsman in the bazaars'.[139] But it criticized the exhibition as 'a glorified bazaar' with 'no surprises'. The Punjab Room was an eighteenth-century British version of Sikh style by a Punjabi artist who visited Windsor Castle;

the Madras Room's furniture was 'Western in structure and aim', with only the decoration being Dravidian, as if Indian art were inspired only 'by the superstitions or atrophied conception of a religion and social order from which all reality has passed away'.[140]

The *Bengalee* complained that Curzon's refusal to protect Indian art against foreign goods failed to 'revive the Indian arts and industries and usher in an era of peace and prosperity to the people'.[141] The paper also criticized Watt's exhibition arrangement as unsatisfactory.[142] The *Hindoo Patriot* declared: 'If the Delhi Durbar is an extravagant waste, the Delhi Exhibition may with some degree of assurance be considered capable of economic recuperation.'[143] But the paper belittled Curzon's taste and his earlier description of Watt's Calcutta exhibition as ugly: 'An artistic and hungry people would be an anomaly and has been ever so in the world's economy. Inconsiderate indulgence in a dilettante spirit like [Curzon's] has been the loss of opportunities . . . Life has some ugly aspects we are afraid that the highest art will not cover or do away with.'[144] The *Indian Social Reformer* described Curzon as a 'whole-hearted and somewhat indiscriminate admirer of Indian art', whose taste would warm the 'soul of the most pronounced advocates of swadeshi movements', an ironic comment tying Curzon to a movement he loathed.[145]

The most interesting press strategy was to run information on the durbar and exhibition alongside reports of its competing event, the opening of the 18th Indian National Congress and its exhibition in Ahmedabad.[146] The Indian art scholar E. B. Havell noted that the INC's exhibitions provoked government fears that the Congress would 'temper the fervour of their political propaganda with rather more practical interest in the industrial development of the country'.[147] The opening speaker for the INC's exhibition was the maharaja of Baroda, Sayaji Rao Gaekwar III, who was Curzon's nemesis.[148] The *Bombay Gazette* praised the Maharaja's progressiveness and patriotism.[149] The *Friend of India* described him as one

> whose enlightenment and culture, whose broad and statesmanlike views and deep sympathy with all high endeavours for the public good have not only placed him in the forefront among the Sovereign Princes of India, but have won for him the unstinting homage and admiration of the educated community of India who are proud to reckon him as one of themselves.[150]

The *Hindoo Patriot* described his 'rousing speech the thread of which will be taken up to-day by the Viceroy, with no doubt greater force and effect but hardly with greater earnestness and zeal . . . Tawdry, gaudy, cheap and evanescent imitation on the model of European utilitarianism, now take the place of high class art and that is why Indian art-ware suffers on the European market.' The paper called the maharaja's speech 'revolutionary' and the INC's exhibition 'a marvellous demonstration' of the 'adaptability of various Indian art styles to modern domestic needs' vital to India's economic prosperity.[151] The durbar exhibition remained a ghostly 'symbol of Britain's power and glory in the East', not the substance.[152] The *Bengalee* described Baroda's durbar camp, with its steam and electric pumps arranged by 'his native assistants without the help of European officers', as a site of resistance to European assumptions about Indian incapacity for technological 'progress'.[153]

Real and imaginary identities

The Indian press recognized the gap between Curzon's fantasies of the East and the realities of policies harmful to India. The durbar exhibition symbolized very different things to Indians and to Britons. Curzon encouraged industry in the arts, as he had in iron and steel – promoted not for the sake of industrial interests or even India's future, but for financial gains through debt payment. In art manufacturing this was to be done through the wealth of those with taste who would encourage Indian crafts as a servile production. The multiple functions of the exhibition and catalogue – to display and assert knowledge as power and to recuperate durbar costs and India's debts – disguised imperial domination with a kinder, gentler blend of gentlemanly capitalism with aristocratic patronage. The exhibition became 'at once the sign and the proof of reality', to borrow Roland Barthes's critique of nineteenth-century historical narrative.[154] Curzon's ideals, which even his curator Watt sceptically treated as unrealized, constituted a modern British imperial identity in which Indian culture became a sign and proof of an imperial synthesis of 'modern' management and 'traditional' gentility within 'a utopian space of comprehensive knowledge', in Thomas Richards's felicitous phrase.[155] The ambitions of gentlemen capitalists were subsumed and melded with other 'imagined communities' – maharajahs, Moghuls, and eighteenth-century British gentry. This imagined genealogy formed an unstable cultural ideal that both disguised and fostered economic motives, as it distilled a pure 'Indianness' to feed fantasies of a genteel Raj readily unmasked by rising Indian nationalism and determination, symbolized, in turn, by the INC's competing exhibitions of Indian art.

Notes

1 Once called the Sepoy Mutiny, or 'the Mutiny', it is now also known as the War of Independence.

2 Bernard Cohn, 'Representing authority in Victorian India', in E. Hobsbawn and T. Ranger (eds) *The Invention of Tradition*, Cambridge, Cambridge University Press, 1983, p. 168.

3 Cohn, 'Representing authority in Victorian India', p. 191.

4 Cohn, 'Representing authority in Victorian India', p. 169.

5 For a study of how the British appropriated and misunderstood the Indian durbar, see Joanne Punzo Waghorne, *The Raja's Magic Clothes*, Philadelphia, University of Pennsylvania Press, 1994; and Cohn, 'Representing authority in Victorian India', pp. 165–209.

6 Birdwood popularized a taste for Indian crafts and was admired by members of the British arts and crafts movement. His 1878 catalogue also became a book: *The Industrial Arts of India*, London, 1880, repeatedly cited by later scholars.

7 Coming twenty years after the War of Independence/Sepoy Mutiny, Lytton's 1877 spectacle was intended to redefine British-Indian relations to forget and displace – *and* to recall the 1857 war.

8 Stephen Wheeler, *History of the Delhi Coronation* Durbar *Held on the First of January 1903 to Celebrate the Coronation of His Majesty King Edward VII Emperor of India from Official Papers*, London, John Murray, 1904, Preface, p. v. Wheeler's father, J. Talboys Wheeler, had written the official book of the 1877 durbar. In a letter to Arthur Godley, 22 July 1903 (British Library, Office of Indian Office Collection [OIOC], F111), Curzon describes Wheeler's 'official history of our Durbar' as 'a most inferior performance. How well the old school wrote, and how badly their degenerate successors.'

9 Curzon wrote to Earl Robert, 'I hope that our Durbar will be an even finer affair than Lord Lytton's . . . I think that the display will not be less Oriental or barbaric, since I shall invite all the Chiefs, even if they travel personally by train, to send their camps and elephants by road': British Library MS OIOC, no. 55, letter from Curzon to Earl Roberts, 17 March 1902. Curzon had 35,000 troops, Lytton, 15,000; spent twice Lytton's budget; had seating for 10,000–12,000 people instead of 5,000. See Thomas R. Metcalf, *Ideologies of the Raj*, Cambridge, Cambridge University Press, 1997, pp. 75–80; Alan Trevithick, 'Some structural and sequential aspects of the British imperial assemblages at Delhi, 1877–1911', *Modern Asian Studies*, vol. 24, 1990, pp. 561–78.

10 Clifford Geertz, *The Interpretation of Culture*, New York, Basic Books, 1973, p. 6. Geertz borrows the notion of 'thick description' from Gilbert Ryle's theory of language and includes in this description an event's unintended meanings and its parodies, a conglomerate fitting the durbar's diverse and parodic receptions among Britons and Indians (p. 7).

11 The economic domination of 'gentlemanly capitalism' over industrialization is developed in J. Cain and A. G. Hopkins, *British Imperialism, Innovation and Expansion, 1688–1914*, London and New York, Longman, 1993, and modified and challenged in R. E. Dumett (ed.) *Gentlemanly Capitalism and British Imperialism*, London and New York, Longman, 1999.

12 'Webs of significance', in Geertz, *Interpretation of Culture* (p. 5), is a phrase borrowed from Max Weber.

13 My reference, of course, is to Claude Lévi-Strauss, *The Raw and the Cooked: Introduction to a Science of Mythology*, trans. John and Doreen Wightman, London, Penguin, 1964.

14 Curzon, 'The place of India in the empire', *Address before Philosophical Institute of Edinburgh*, London, John Murray, 1909, pp. 9–10, 13–16.

15 'Place of India', 16–46. Curzon insisted that the Indian National Congress and Indian self-government would be the 'ruin to India and treason to our trust', shaped by 'the sense of sacrifice and the idea of duty' in 'The true imperialism', address

at Birmingham Town Hall, 11 December 1907, pp. 20–1. Curzon was president for the year.

16 Quoted in John Oliver Hobbes (pseudonym for Pearl Craigie), *Imperial India: Letters from the East*, London, T. Fisher Unwin, 1903, p. 30. The epitaph he wrote for himself began, 'Explorer, Writer, Administrator and Ruler of Men': see Jane Abdy and Charlotte Gere, *The Souls: An Elite in English Society, 1885–1930*, London, Sidgwick & Jackson, 1984, p. 18. His friends and colleagues considered him exemplary of a man devoted to public duty.

17 This list and the definitions of service professions comes from Cain and Hopkins, *British Imperialism*, pp. 21–3, 26.

18 Cain and Hopkins, *British Imperialism*, p. 46, Like other gentlemanly activities, this one served ideologically 'to subdue republicanism and democracy by demonstrating the superiority of the liberal ideal of improvement . . . to ease the transition from expansion to imperialism by extending the ideology of mission and rendering it patriotic' through 'projected gentility rather than industry . . . the chivalry of empire' (p. 46). Curzon's activities followed a half-century of development. From the 1850s on, 'India became a notable outpost of the new service and financial order' and professional families from south-east England and, to a lesser extent, aristocrats dominated the civil service; see Cain and Hopkins, *British Imperialism*, pp. 329–31.

19 An album from one of his dinner parties listed F. Rothschild, Lord Ribblesdale, the duchess of Westminster, Lord and Lady Cowper, Lord Pembroke, Lord Elcho, the duchess of Sutherland; see Abdy and Gere, *The Souls*, p. 23.

20 Abdy and Gere, *The Souls*, citing Curzon's remark from a speech in Delhi (p. 27).

21 According to T. Lloyd, *The Theory of Distribution and Consumption*, London, James Nisbet & Co, 1911, p. 264, Curzon was 'one of the few' who 'did take a business-like view' of his responsibilities as viceroy. According to Cain and Hopkins, *British Imperialism*, 'Curzon's efforts to promote manufacturing in India after the turn of the century aroused renewed alarm in Lancashire. But the textile lobby's representations were again ineffective because the Viceroy's policy, though interventionist, was not protectionist and did not endanger budgetary stability' (see pp. 337–45, especially 343).

22 Maria Misra, 'Gentlemanly capitalism and the Raj: British policy in India between the world wars', in Dumett (ed.) *Gentlemanly Capitalism*, p. 164. For debates on the extent of the influence of gentlemanly capitalism, see the essays in Dumett's volume, including the reply by Cain and Hopkins: 'Afterword: the theory and practice of British imperialism', pp. 196–220, especially p. 216.

23 Sankar Ghose, *The Indian National Congress, its History and Heritage*, Delhi, V. N. Malhotra, 1975, p. 12; quotation of Dutt on p. 3.

24 C. F. Cross, E. J. Bevan and C. M. King, *Report on Indian Fibres and Fibrous Substances Exhibited at the Colonial and Indian Exhibition, 1886*, London, E. & F. N. Spon, 1887, pp. 21, 64.

25 George Watt, *Report on Economic Products to the Government of India; Memorandum on the Resources of British India*, Calcutta, Government Printing Office, 1894, pp. 1–2.

26 Watt, *Report*, pp. 3, 6–7, 10–13. Watt insisted that with 27.6 million irrigated acres and double-cropping, Indian agriculture could prosper and feed India's entire population. He also claimed that coal production doubled in ten years and rising salt consumption signalled 'increased material consumption' (pp. 9–22).

27 Watt, *Report*, pp. 26–32.

28 Watt, *Report*, pp. 48–9.

29 Wheeler, *History of the Delhi Coronation* Durbar, p. vi.

30 British Library, OIOC, F111, 161, no. 24, letter to Right Hon. Lord G. Hamilton, secretary of state for India, 20 March 1902.

31 British Library, OIOC, F111, 161, no. 42, letter to Sir Arthur Godley, Under Secretary of State for India, 28 May 1902. Lord Hamilton, Secretary of State of India. praised Curzon for his opening speech at the exhibition as 'excellent both in the

encouragement you gave to the revival of the older art and trades of India and the excellent business like advertisement you made on their behalf. The modern millionaire, and particularly those who come from the other side of the water, though they may be wholly ignorant and devoid of taste, yet will give any price for something which is unique in its design and manufacture; and it seems to me that, with a little encouragement, they might take the place, as patrons of Indian art, of the old Native courses and nobles. The two latter classes have become so demoralised by cheap wholesale European articles that I doubt your being able to get them to abandon their cheap and gaudy modern tastes': British Library, OIOC, no. 106, letter from Lord Hamilton, Secretary of State for India, 31 Dec 1902. Curzon even went so far as to repair the throne of Diwan-I-Am in the fort for the investiture ceremony for several hundred pounds: British Library, OIOC, no. 61, letter to Arthur Godley, 31 July 1902.

32 George Curzon. *Speeches by H. E. the Lord Curzon Kedleston, Viceroy and Governor General of India (1902–1904)*, 3 vols, Calcutta, Government Printing, 1904, vol. 3, pp. 18–21. He later claimed the durbar was an assignment and not something he initiated; see Curzon, 'The place of India', p. 16.

33 Curzon, *Speeches*, vol. 3, pp. 23–9. Curzon insisted on doing things as cheaply as possible, '"Everything must be as cheap as possible" was his order . . . the most original of money-saving ideas of construction were evolved from the fertile brain of the Chief Engineer, Rai Bahadur Gunga Ram, but some of them were the Viceroy's own invention.' Examples of cheapness were domes of bamboo at one shilling a piece and lined with gypsum and plaster of Paris; see Valentia Steer, *The Delhi Durbar, 1902–03*, London, Simpkins, Marshall & Co; Madras, Higginbotham & Co., 1903, p. 9.

34 Curzon, *Speeches*, vol. 3, p. 90.

35 Curzon, *Speeches*, vol. 3, pp. 22–3.

36 Curzon, *Speeches*, vol. 3, pp. 87–8.

37 Metcalf, *Ideologies of the Raj*, pp. 196–7.

38 Curzon, *Speeches*, vol. 3, pp. 87–8.

39 Sometimes finding objects was difficult. Mr E. Dawson, sub-divisional officer of Myingyan, personally accompanied Watt to 'the rather inaccessible village of Pagan and there acted as his interpreter in studying this industry [lac work] and in selecting the samples now shown in the Exhibition': Watt, *Indian Art Exhibition, Delhi, 1903. Being the Official Catalogue of the Delhi Exhibition, 1902–1903*, Calcutta, Government Printing, 1903, p. 221.

40 Metcalf, *Ideologies of the Raj*, p. 154, describes this as restoring within 'appropriate categories of the British discourse on India's past', and often without any test of historical accuracy, as in this case.

41 Britons codified Hindu 'beliefs' as fixed in the past, and then constructed a role for caste in village social life. See Metcalf, *Ideologies of the Raj*, and Cohn, 'Representing authority in Victorian India', for extensive analyses of subjects made 'traditional' by British classification and definition.

42 Curzon, *Speeches*, vol. 3, pp. 88–9.

43 Cited in Hobbes (Craigie), *Imperial India*, p. 31.

44 He argued that 'no national art is capable of continued existence unless it satisfies the ideals and expresses the wants, of the nation that has produced it . . .'. Curzon claimed, however, that he could find no Indian expertise: 'I find great difficulty, however, in finding any Native with any claims to knowledge of art whom I can ask to serve. In all my wanderings through India I do not think that I have come across a single Indian whom I could describe as a connoisseur': British Library, OIOC, E 233, 16, letter to Ampthill, 27 September 1902.

45 Wheeler, *History of the Delhi Coronation Durbar*, pp. 91–6.

46 Curzon, *Speeches*, vol. 3, p. 89.

47 See Peter Hoffenberg's extensive study of international exhibitions, *An Empire on Display: English, Indian, and Australian Exhibitions from the Crystal Palace to the Great War*, Berkeley, University of California Press, 2001.

48 *Dictionary of the Economic Products of India*, 6 vols in 9 parts, Calcutta, Government Printing, and London, W. H. Allen, 1889–93; see the Preface, by E. C. Buck, secretary to Governor of India, Department of Revenue and Agriculture, p. vii. The dream of an ultimate unifying classification system for Indian plants and products was expressed by Watt in his vision of his *Dictionary* as a scientific record of 'all existing information' in Indian agriculture, trade and commerce, including 'all the Indian and European vernacular names of the animal, vegetable and mineral products of the Empire': *Dictionary*, vol. 1, p. 46. He created a complex cross-numbering system to connect objects and their raw materials. Visitors to the Museum in Calcutta's Commercial Gallery would find that each sample of wood had a series of numbers 'that will refer him to the art objects or to the ethnological objects that are made of the wood in question'. And numbers on all carved objects in the Art Gallery or objects in the Ethnological Gallery (e.g. bows and arrows) refer to raw materials in the Commercial Gallery, 'In this way the whole series of Galleries of the Indian Museum, the Library, the Ledger and the Dictionary, are intimately linked together with the one dominant idea of developing the Industrial resources of the Empire': *Dictionary*, vol. 1, p. 48.

49 *Empire of India. Special Catalogue of Exhibition by the Government of India and Private Exhibitions*, London, William Clowes, 1886, p. 1. The 1886 exhibition was a complex matter – objects were in the Art Ware Courts by province or state, or in the Economic Courts if agricultural and ethnological, or in the Administrative Courts by government department, and all arranged by additional different criteria (pp. 1–3). In the Economic Courts 'a complete economic survey of the Indian Empire has been attempted . . . reached its penultimate if not its final stage . . . a scientifically arranged frame-work upon which to rest future investigation and enquiry'(p. 3). Thus, the exhibition became the 'final construction' of the economic survey of India. Administrative Courts provided series of records and reports 'to give some practical notion of the vast machinery required for the administration of the Indian Empire'. The 1886 exhibition recognized problems in Raj economics, but treated them as 'objective', agent-less, natural events: 'The creation of the English cotton industry in Lancashire was followed by a great restriction in the Indian cotton industry, and gradually India not only ceased to export cottons to England, but came to depend herself to a very large extent upon England for the supply of clothing to her own people' (p. 299).

50 These words are by Thomas Wardle writing on Indian silks in *Empire of India. Special Catalogue of Exhibition by the Government of India and Private Exhibitions*, London, William Clowes, 1886, p. 307.

51 Hoffenberg, *An Empire on Display*, on Mukharji: pp. 52–6, 60–2, 111–13, 255–6. See T. N. Mukharji, *A Visit to Europe*, London, Edward Stanford, 1889, and his catalogue for the 1888 Glasgow International Exhibition: *Art-Manufactures of India*, Calcutta, Superintendent of Government Printing, 1888. He believed that India's participation in international exhibitions would lead to increased consumption of Indian products beyond just luxuries. Considering his knowledge and experience, and Watt's respect for him, it is likely Mukharji had a hand in Watt's exhibition.

52 George Watt, *Indian Art Exhibition, Delhi, 1903. Being the Official Indian Art Exhibition, Delhi of the Delhi Exhibition, 1902–1903*, Calcutta, Government Printing, 1904., pp. vii–viii. Birdwood's books on Indian art were generated by the 1877 durbar exhibition he later wrote about when it appeared at the 1878 Paris International Exhibition and then toured Britain, 1880–81.

53 Watt, *Indian Art Exhibition, Delhi*, p. 2. Manufacturers and traders were forbidden to put up stalls as in previous exhibitions.

54 Watt, *Indian Art Exhibition, Delhi*, p. 3.

55 Watt, *Indian Art Exhibition, Delhi*, p. vii.

56 Watt, *Indian Art Exhibition, Delhi*, p. 3.

57 Watt, *Indian Art Exhibition, Delhi*, pp. 3–4.

58 Watt, *Indian Art Exhibition, Delhi*, pp. 449–51; see also p. 248.

59 Watt, *Indian Art Exhibition, Delhi*, p. 454.
60 Watt, *Indian Art Exhibition, Delhi*, pp. 454–5. In his catalogue for the Indian section of the Glasgow International Exhibition in 1888, T. N. Mukharji *began* with Fine Arts, a long section that included frescos, oil-painting, paintings on paper, glass, ivory, leather, cloth and wood and manuscript illumination, prints, photographs, sculpture, and even funeral pyres and masks. He also traces painting back to mythological origins, although he, too, denies the value of most Indian conventional painting and argues that India is 'on the threshold of a revival of pictorial science . . . as it is now understood in Europe', thanks to the British art schools. Still, this is a remarkable list for a category whose quality and even existence Birdwood denied in 1878, and which was reduced by Watt and Brown to a small section, and denigrated by Brown in his 1903 catalogue text. I suggest here that Mukharji resisted this British denial of Indian fine arts in a subtle and unobtrusive way. See his *Art-Manufactures of India*, pp. 9–13. In general, Indian participation in the 1903 exhibition was small, consisting of contributions by maharajahs, writings by T. N. Mukharji and the Hon. Madho Lall, Rais of Benares, 'a member of the Judging Committee': Watt, *Indian Art Exhibition, Delhi*, p. 322.
61 E.g. Watt, *Indian Art Exhibition, Delhi*, p. 327: C. L. Burns, principal of Bombay's School of Art, chose a *kinkháb* for the panelling of the Bombay Room.
62 Watt, *Indian Art Exhibition, Delhi*, pp. x, 442.
63 Watt, *Indian Art Exhibition, Delhi*, p. 164.
64 Watt, *Indian Art Exhibition, Delhi*, pp. 360, 290–2. The 'historic importance of Gujarat in the silk trade of India, is therefore, an important factor to be considered, and, seeing that mulberry silk-worm is not reared in that Province, the raw material must have always been imported by sea' by, among others, agents of Dutch and British trading companies (pp. 308–9).
65 Watt, *Indian Art Exhibition, Delhi*, pp. 409–11.
66 Watt, *Indian Art Exhibition, Delhi*, p. 464.
67 Watt, *Indian Art Exhibition, Delhi*, pp. 114–15.
68 Watt, *Indian Art Exhibition, Delhi*, p. 332.
69 Watt, *Indian Art Exhibition, Delhi*, p. xi. Mr R. Hughes Buller, census officer of Baluchistan, provided a 'splendid series of embroideries' (p. 281). Mr W. W. Drew, collector of the district of Bijapur, helped Watt find a series of old carpets (pp. 431–2).
70 Watt, *Indian Art Exhibition, Delhi*, p. 78.
71 Watt, *Indian Art Exhibition, Delhi*, p. 133. The *repoussé* copy of a tray from Travancore was copied by the Madras School of Art students (p. 59). Two companies sent copies of the Ardebil Mosque Carpet; the original is in the Victoria and Albert Museum (p. 431). Watt also commissioned spandrils copied from a monastery (p. 7) and copies of stone lintels from the 'famous Chalukyan temple of Hallabid' originals in Bangalore (p. 129).
72 This purpose was resisted by John Lockwood Kipling, head of the Lahore Art School, and E. B. Havell, but other school directors trained Indians in Western classical conventions.
73 Watt, *Indian Art Exhibition, Delhi*, p. 279. Others did revivals, too. The *kinkháb* made by Bhagwan Das Gopi Nath of Benares was a 'charming design found by the writer on an old garment in the possession of the Hon'ble Munshi Madho Lal of Benares, who kindly permitted it to be copied' (pp. 322–3).
74 Watt, *Indian Art Exhibition, Delhi*, p. 92.
75 Watt, *Indian Art Exhibition, Delhi*, pp. 440–3.
76 'Hara Prasad of Benares, who has contributed many good *kinkhábs* to the Main Gallery, has also set up looms and is ready and willing to show them and explain every detail to the visitor': Watt, *Indian Art Exhibition, Delhi*, p. 325.
77 Watt noted that stone and glass wares 'might be dealt with under numerous headings . . . materials used . . . purposes served . . . designs pursued': *Indian Art Exhi-*

bition, Delhi, p. 63. Some objects could be classified as either metals or turquoise (p. 75).

78 Watt, *Indian Art Exhibition, Delhi*, pp. 160–1.
79 Watt, *Indian Art Exhibition, Delhi*, p. 211.
80 Woolen embroidered tablecloths 'have induced some of the carpet manufacturers to open special branches to deal with this important new trade': Watt, *Indian Art Exhibition, Delhi*, p. 393.
81 Goods from the cotton mill in Nagpur were 'not only equal to the best of the hand loom *dhotis* of old but equal, if not superior, to the finest imported articles': Watt, *Indian Art Exhibition, Delhi*, p. 276.
82 Watt, *Indian Art Exhibition, Delhi*, p. 320.
83 Watt, *Indian Art Exhibition, Delhi*, pp. 236–7.
84 Watt, *Indian Art Exhibition, Delhi*, pp. 367–8.
85 Metcalf, *Ideologies of the Raj*, p. 113.
86 Metcalf, *Ideologies of the Raj*, p. 67; see also p. 26.
87 Metcalf, *Ideologies of the Raj*, p. 117.
88 Interestingly, craft production in England was treated in the art press like the 'high' arts, as displays of individuality, style and originality, and its producers named and praised as artists.
89 Watt, *Indian Art Exhibition, Delhi*, p. 1. Watt sometimes links the decline of art with other economic and social shifts to present a wider view of changes under the Raj. He refers to 'poorly paid calico-printers' of Jaipur (p. 247), to 'the subordination of the artificers to the money lenders and traders' (p. 23), and to workers 'who earn from two to three annas, after labouring for ten hours daily, on the most monotonous of all occupations and one that must after a very few years exercise a very depressing influence on the operators' (p. 256).
90 Watt, *Indian Art Exhibition, Delhi*, p. 379.
91 Watt, *Indian Art Exhibition, Delhi*, pp. 176–7.
92 Watt, *Indian Art Exhibition, Delhi*, p. 144. Two writing tables produced by pupils of the local industrial school are 'European in feeling both in construction and ornamentation', but still 'good examples of inlaying' (p. 144).
93 Watt, *Indian Art Exhibition, Delhi*, p. 37.
94 Examples are Bombay embossed book covers by Mr A. Leslie or embroidery by Faiz Mohammed of Karchi, combining European silk with 'Kashmir darn stitch': *Indian Art Exhibition, Delhi*, pp. 204 and 381.
95 Watt, *Indian Art Exhibition, Delhi*, p. 309.
96 Watt, *Indian Art Exhibition, Delhi*, pp. 325–6.
97 Poor-quality Gwalior painted wood and basket-work were exhibited: *Indian Art Exhibition, Delhi*, p. 162.
98 Watt, *Indian Art Exhibition, Delhi*, p. 4.
99 Watt, *Indian Art Exhibition, Delhi*, p. 107.
100 Watt, *Indian Art Exhibition, Delhi*, p. 10.
101 Watt, *Indian Art Exhibition, Delhi*, pp. 8, 124–5.
102 These scholars included Thomas Hendley, George Birdwood, William Griggs and E. B. Havell, and administrators, art schools heads and government scientists.
103 Watt, *Indian Art Exhibition, Delhi*, p. 11.
104 Purchasers were also cited, the Nizam of Hyderabad bought the Madras Room, the Bombay Room, which won a gold medal, the Panjab Room, and the Jodhpur Balcony, 4–7).
105 Watt, *Indian Art Exhibition, Delhi*, p. 109.
106 Examples of advertised prices in the catalogue, Agra House façade (p. 10) cost Rs 3,000; the catalogue included the price list for agate cups from Cambay (p. 74). Watt, *Indian Art Exhibition, Delhi*, p. 111: 'Should replicas of the Saharanpur Door be desired these could be obtained to order for about Rs 1,000 but could not be turned out in less than a year for each door.' The exhibition encouraged sales for rugs from Peshawar and Quetta (p. 434) and cotton jail carpets (pp. 406, 446).

107 Watt, *Indian Art Exhibition, Delhi*, p. 411, argued that embroidery 'when separately recognised . . . may be more highly appreciated'.
108 Watt, *Indian Art Exhibition, Delhi*, p. 489.
109 Watt, *Indian Art Exhibition, Delhi*, pp. 427–8. Lockwood Kipling also argues that the jail carpets have created an industry, especially in Panjab carpets exhibited in 1862 (p. 433). The Agra Central Jail won a gold medal for its carpets (p. 436).
110 Watt, *Indian Art Exhibition, Delhi*, p. 239.
111 Watt, *Indian Art Exhibition, Delhi*, p. 102. See also pp. 99–104, 123.
112 Watt, *Indian Art Exhibition, Delhi*, p. 155.
113 Watt, *Indian Art Exhibition, Delhi*, p. 380.
114 Peter Robb, 'Some aspects of British policy towards Indian nationalism, 1885–1920', in Mike Sheppardson and Colin Simmons (eds) *The Indian National Congress and the Political Economy of India, 1885–1985*, Aldershot, Avebury Press, 1988.
115 Metcalf, *Ideologies of the Raj*, pp. 91–2.
116 C. Dewey, 'The Government of India's "new industrial policy", 1900–1925: formation and failure', in K. N. Chaudhuri and C. Dewey (eds) *Economy and Society*, Delhi, Oxford University Press, 1979, pp. 229–30. Dewey considered Curzon 'perhaps the greatest administrator India has ever known' because of his desire to solve every problem he could and to be, above all, efficient (p. 219).
117 See Robb, 'Some aspects of British policy', pp. 63–4. Lytton refused to incorporate Indian designs in his durbar's decoration and architecture, while Curzon chose to combine British and Indian decoration.
118 M. N. Das, *Indian National Congress versus the British*, vol. 1: *1885–1918*, Delhi, Ajanta Press, 1978, pp. 127–8. See letter to Hamilton in 1900, cited in Das, *Indian National Congress*, p. 179. Curzon reduced the numbers of elected Indian members of the Calcutta Corporation from 75 to 50, provoking a protest from INC President Surendranath Banerjea; see Daniel Argov, *Moderates and Extremists in the Indian Nationalist Movement, 1883–1920*, New York, Asia Publishing House, 1967, p. 98.
119 This idea was first suggested by Macaulay; see Metcalf, *Ideologies of the Raj*, p. 34.
120 Birdwood in 1878 blamed sloppy workmanship and bad taste on uneducated working-class artisans who simply need self-help and mechanics' institutes.
121 Metcalf, *Ideologies of the Raj*, pp. 29–32.
122 Metcalf, *Ideologies of the Raj*, p. 34. Curzon expressed his desire for the 'peaceful demise' of the INC in a letter to Lord Hamilton, EUR MSS 510/6, 18 November 1900, quoted in Argov, *Moderates and Extremists*, p. 95. His application of the partition of Bengal as a means to do this was expressed in a letter he sent to John Broderick in 1905, cited in Argov, *Moderate and Extremists*, p. 109.
123 Metcalf, *Ideologies of the Raj*, p. 188.
124 Metcalf, *Ideologies of the Raj*, p. 191.
125 Metcalf, *Ideologies of the Raj*, p. 66.
126 Curzon was continuing the imperial project begun in 1871 with the archaeological survey of India, 'compiling a 'systematic record and description of all architectural and other remains that are remarkable either for their antiquity, or their beauty, or their historical interest', in the Government's words: quoted in Metcalf, *Ideologies of the Raj*, pp. 150–1.
127 See Metcalf, *Ideologies of the Raj*, p. 153, on Curzon's restoration of the Taj based on his fantasies, rather than on archaeological methods.
128 Curzon, *Speeches*, vol. 3, pp. 90–1.
129 Metcalf, *Ideologies of the Raj*, p. 197.
130 See Nicholas B. Dirks, 'Colonial histories and native informants', in Carol A. Breckenridge and Peter van der Veer (eds) *Orientalism and the Postcolonial Predicament*, Philadephia, University of Pennsylvania Press, 1993, p. 279; Anwar Abdel Malek, 'Orientalism in crisis', *Diogenes*, vol. 44, 1978, pp. 107–8.

131 *The Failure of Lord Curzon. A Study in 'Imperialism', an Open Letter to the Earl of Rosebery*, London, T. Fisher Unwin, 1903, pp. vi, vii, 4–5.

132 Including the *Englishman* (Calcutta), the *Pioneer* (Allahabad), the *Capital* (for Calcutta's commercial community): see O'Donnell, *The Failure of Lord Curzon*, pp. 22 and 50.

133 Including *New India* or the *Indian Mirror*, intended for European-educated Indians.

134 Including the *Morning Post* (p. 6), also critical of Curzon. *The Bengal Times*, 22 December, 1902, p. 5, printed a letter to editor attacking Curzon as honouring only himself, showing off to Americans (Curzon's wife was American and several Americans were invited to the durbar), all 'to add to his prestige as Viceroy'.

135 *Amrit Bazar Patrika*, 3 January 1903. The quoted statements are from Das, *Indian National Congress versus the British*, vol. 1, pp. 183–6.

136 *Bombay Gazette*, 6 January 1903, p. 5.

137 *Bombay Gazette*, 2 January 1903, p. 4.

138 *Friend of India*, 25 December 1902, p. 17.

139 *Statesman*, 1 January 1903, p. 4; citation is from *Friend of India*, 30 December 1902.

140 *Statesman*, 1 January 1903, p. 8.

141 *Bengalee*, 1 January 1903, p. 4.

142 *Bengalee*, 2 January, 1903, p. 5.

143 *Hindoo Patriot*, 30 December 1902, p. 2.

144 *Hindoo Patriot*, 1 January 1903, p. 2.

145 *Indian Social Reformer*, 11 January 1903, p. 176.

146 See Argov, *The Failure of Lord Curzon*, pp. 100–1, for a brief description of the 19th Congress in Madras in December 1903 and its views on the durbar and on Curzon's regime.

147 E. B. Havell, *Essays on Indian Art, Industry and Education*, Madras, G. A. Nateson & Co., 1907, p. 51.

148 Curzon and the Gaekwar, Maharaja Sayaji Rao III, were often in conflict. Curzon called him 'the churlish Baroda' (British Library, OIOC, no. 61, letter to Arthur Godley, 31 July 1902) and expressed his dislike in many of his letters. See Codell, 'Resistance and performance: native informant discourse in the biographies of Maharaja Sayaji Rao III, 1863–1939', in J. F. Codell and D. S. Macleod, *Orientalism Transposed: The Impact of the Colonies on British Culture*, Aldershot, Ashgate Press, 1998, pp. 13–45. The Maharaja, sometimes called the Gaekwar, of Baroda financed Dadabhai Naoroji, who was elected to Parliament in 1892, taking out over a *lakh* of rupees without consulting his financial officer to give Rs 1,000 to Naoroji. See Pram Nath Chopra, Ram Gopal and M. L. Bharga, *A Century of Indian National Congress, 1885–1985*, Delhi, Agam Prakashan, 1986, p. 93; Sayaji Rao 'was known for his progressive views' (p. 94).

149 *Bombay Gazette*, 17 December 1902, p. 6.

150 *Friend of India*, 15 December 1902, p. 17.

151 *Hindoo Patriot*, 30 December 1902, pp. 6, 8.

152 *Hindoo Patriot*, 30 December 1902, p. 2.

153 *Hindoo Patriot*, 10 December 1902, p. 5. Its condemnation of the durbar appears on pp. 1, 9–10.

154 Roland Barthes, 'The discourse of history', trans. Stephen Bann, *Comparative Criticism*, vol. 3, 1981, p. 20.

155 Thomas Richards, *The Imperial Archives: Knowledge and the Factasy of Empire*, London, Verso, 1993, p. 11.

CHAPTER NINE

Albion's legacy – myth, history and 'the Matter of Britain'

Sam Smiles

My purpose in this chapter is to examine the place of Arthurian myth in aspects of British culture c.1850–1940. The discussion focuses in particular on Edward Burne-Jones, not to offer new iconographic interpretations of particular images but to try to establish a critical appreciation of such work as part of much wider considerations relating to the place of myth in modern Britain. In looking at the complexities involved in refurbishing Arthurian material for modern usage, I argue that some of the procedural difficulties associated with that refurbishment, especially those surrounding the apprehension of mythical material, have wider implications. If the Arthur story invokes a sense of mysticism and timelessness, in an overtly de-historicized narrative, these same qualities can also be found applied to Britain itself. In the hands of some artists and writers Britain becomes a place which, properly understood, replaces a linear notion of time and history with another ordering of experience. The landscape itself is read as a palimpsest, where the traces of earlier cultural activities are simultaneous with the more assertive signs of the present. The Britain that emerges from this reading hovers between an imaginary and a historicist identity; the meaning and character of the country are to be found as much in its myths and ancient history as in its contemporary social, economic and political formation. Although we might want to characterize such beliefs as implicitly anti-modern, if the experience of modernity is defined as a sense of a break with the past, their presence in the mature work of some significant artists and writers working in the modern period points to an understanding of Britain's identity which is inherently opposed to any straightforward notion of historical progress. Artists and writers involved in this enterprise contest the possibility of the modern's displacement of tradition and insist, instead, on the importance of cultural continuity.

It is, of course, well known that Edward Burne-Jones was fascinated by Arthur, the Grail and the whole so-called 'Matter of Britain' from his student days at Oxford up until his death in 1898. In that same year he wrote:

> Lord! how that San Graal story is ever in my mind and thoughts continually. Was ever anything in the world beautiful as that is beautiful? If I might clear away all the work that I have begun, if I might live and clear it all away, and dedicate the last days to that tale – if only I might.[1]

Given such a declaration it seems reasonable to consider that Burne-Jones's use of the Arthur myth was crucial to his art, with paintings such as *The Sleep of King Arthur in Avalon*, the picture he was working on at his death, standing as some sort of definitive statement of his artistic ideals (Figure 17). If we accept the centrality of Arthur for Burne-Jones, there are two relevant questions that are worth posing with respect to his declaration. First, what does the painter's use of Arthurian material say about him? Second, by comparing Burne-Jones to others, can we detect similar creative responses to the Arthur myth in the modern period?

In attempting to sketch the beginnings of answers to these questions I approach Burne-Jones through the widest possible framework, looking back with the benefit of twentieth-century understandings of Arthur and forward from the position of Arthur within European culture up until the nineteenth century. It is legitimate to work at such a remove from Burne-Jones's historical context if only because the Arthur myth speaks through its interpreters; Burne-Jones in a sense needs to be positioned in a relay of texts such that his authorial primacy is surrendered to a tradition that uses him for its articulation. To say this is to recognize that Arthurian literature in its 1,000–year development cannot be considered a case of original and copy but instead is inflected by its every artistic reworking. Burne-Jones's contribution can be judged legitimately insofar as it is capable of refurbishing or renovating that tradition; but, equally, that tradition informs its own renovation. As Matthew Arnold noted in the 1860s with respect to *The Mabinogion*:

> The very first thing that strikes one . . . is how evidently the . . . story-teller is pillaging an antiquity of which he does not fully possess the secret; he is like a peasant building his hut on the site of Halicarnassus or Ephesus; he builds, but what he builds is full of materials of which he knows not the history, or knows by a glimmering tradition merely; – stones 'not of this building', but of an older architecture, greater, cunninger, more majestical.[2]

[165]

17 Edward Burne-Jones, *The Sleep of King Arthur in Avalon* (1881–98), oil on canvas, 282 × 645 cm. Museo de Arte de Ponce, Luis A. Ferré Foundation Inc. Ponce, Puerto Rico

Burne-Jones knew Arnold's text well; but, that he considered his own contribution to the Arthurian myth as peasant-like in his ignorance of the secret is debatable. In a period when Arthurian literature was available to the general public as never before, he took pains to read older texts, rather than simply relying on what Tennyson or even Malory had supplied. But Arnold's central insight is instructive, that all who work on the Arthurian material are working with elements of that 'older architecture'. And once that possibility is recognized, all artists handling the tradition must perforce see their interpretation as essentially exegetical, a further contribution to the necessarily unfinished business of explicating the import of the Arthur story and the mystery of the Grail. This is no mere episode of the late nineteenth century, either: the work of elaboration extends into the twentieth century. As I show, a mystical understanding of Britain, one associated with its ancient or mythological history, continued to make its presence felt long after Burne-Jones's death.

The period with which this chapter is concerned seems one of the least propitious times for a serious investment in myth to have taken place. Positivistic and materialist analyses of the world marked modern consciousness, while the established historiography of Britain brooked little dissent. Eighteenth- and nineteenth-century historians had confirmed the need for exacting method, documentary authority and the scrupulous avoidance of unsubstantiated evidence. Political, economic and constitutional histories outlined in considerable and

[166]

verifiable detail a rich and complicated picture of the past, from at least the Anglo-Saxon settlement to the present.[3] The Arthur legend, on the face of it, could have little to contribute to such a narrative and could influence modern cultural life only as an imaginative diversion from historical reality. To locate the identity of Britain with its founding myths and its ancestral landscape is surely to disregard its modern political character, and to substitute for it a more nebulous concept of cultural belonging. Yet, the tendency in much of the Arthurian revival is one of deliberately transcending political and economic frameworks in its invocation of another identity for Britain. In doing so, it attempts to offer a serious possibility for mythical understandings in the midst of modern consciousness. Beyond even that conservative notion of organic constitutional change, associated with eighteenth- and nineteenth-century historiography, lies a deeper sense of the land itself as witness and guardian of the soul of the nation. The survival of such thinking in the modern era is worthy of notice, especially insofar as it posits an alternative to empirical understandings of cultural development.

As a preliminary to the discussion it is worth considering the status of Arthurian literature, commonly referred to from the Middle Ages as 'the Matter of Britain'. The Arthurian mediaeval corpus was inescapably pluralist and contradictory. Different authors in different languages grafted on new material, enriching the literary tradition, and it was not until Malory's *Morte d'Arthur* (1485) that a more unified text was offered to the reading public. Malory made sense of a confused mass of mediaeval interpretations of Arthur, primarily written in England and France, and in harmonising his sources produced a narrative, which fused both traditions. From Geoffrey of Monmouth's 1136 *History of the Kings of Britain* (*Historia Regum Britanniae*), he inherited the imperial Arthur and the Roman war, a chronicle of military conquest and national glory; under the impress of twelfth- and thirteenth-century French material he gave increased prominence to the Knights of the Round Table, the quest for the Holy Grail, and the lovers Launcelot and Guinevere and Tristram and Isoud. But the text that Malory produced is necessarily marked by the difficulties involved in reconciling these different traditions, both internally, in its compressions and elisions, and externally, from the texts that it must suppress for coherence. To compare Malory to the material on which he drew is to realize that his (or his publisher and editor, Caxton's) redactions are every bit as partial and as influential as Tennyson's were to be four centuries later. They offer a comprehensive account of the Matter of Britain for those who have no need to inquire further; they make it intelligible in terms appropriate to their historical culture. Similarly, of course, notwithstanding fleeting mentions of Arthur in earlier chronicles, a full 600 years separate Arthur's possible existence from Geoffrey of Monmouth's account, the earliest substantial treatment of his activities. Given this, it is senseless to think of archaeological accuracy in attempting to depict Arthur, to kit out the Knights of the Round Table, itself a mediaeval interpolation, in authentic fifth- or sixth-century garb. There is no historical fixity for Arthur's existence, despite attempts to locate it within the material culture of Dark Age Britain, attempts which in our own era have seen excavations at South Cadbury and Tintagel in pursuit of a truth less elusive than the twelfth-century exhumation of his and Guinevere's supposed tombs at Glastonbury.[4]

The establishment of Arthur thus is and always has been entirely provisional. In the Middle Ages the choice of text indicates how literary devices were themselves used to legitimize different approaches, from sober Latin chronicles to prose narratives in the vernacular, to epic poetry and, finally, to prose romances, each retelling allying its story to the protocols and the authority of other narratives (historical, mythical or biblical) already established in that format. There is a sense that each text strives to fashion credibility for Arthur within a sophisticated understanding of its discursive realm and that it needs to do so because of Arthur's ambivalent position between history and myth. Burne-Jones's efforts to establish a credible artistic rendering of Arthur are caught up in that difficulty and his solution, effectively multi-temporal and meditative as opposed to historicist and narrative, immediately distinguishes his treatment of the theme from those of other Victorian artists.

Burne-Jones's involvement with Arthur started early. His first encounter with Malory, when a student at Oxford in the 1850s, led to a life-long preoccupation with the Matter of Britain, and a number of his most significant paintings have Arthurian subject matter.[5] His final painting, *The Sleep of King Arthur in Avalon*, had been worked on for seventeen years and went through numerous revisions, as Burne-Jones refined his design. What, then, can be said of his approach to this material? Most noteworthy, of course, is his eschewal of Tennyson, the publication of whose *Idylls of the King* had begun with sensational results in 1859. At first sight, Burne-Jones's decision to move beyond Tennyson and make use instead of Malory seems telling. His recourse to Malory might be understood, in effect, as a more resolute engagement with the Matter of Britain than Tennyson provided; it seems to be of a piece with that mediaevalizing tendency and avoidance of anachronism so typical of Victorian culture at its most historicizing. This historicist valorization of sources should give us pause, however, for it is arguable that historicism was the least of Malory's attractions for Burne-Jones, that his importance for the painter lay in the artistic completeness of what Malory had accomplished rather than any notion of his historical authority. Indeed, although Tennyson's *Idylls* helped concentrate attention on Malory rather than the sources from which Malory had himself drawn, those other sources were themselves in the process of being re-examined and were thus available for scrutiny alongside the new nineteenth-century editions of Malory.[6] An English translation of Geoffrey of Monmouth had been published as early as 1718[7] and was reissued in the middle of the nineteenth century.[8] For the genuine scholar of the Arthurian tradition, the Welsh texts were also commonly available: English translations of material from *The Mabinogion* had appeared as early as 1795,[9] and the first complete English edition was published by Lady Charlotte Guest in 1838–49.[10] In fact, Burne-Jones's development as an artist coincided with a surge of interest in the extant Arthurian texts, with over twenty English translations published from the 1850s to the 1890s. Burne-Jones himself began to seek out precisely such sources in the 1870s and 1880s, and felt impelled to research the roots of the Matter of Britain:

> I worked in all my leisure at Celtic Origins. Irish chiefly, Welsh of course, Breton French; everywhere that is Celt-land...Besides [Matthew Arnold's *Study of Celtic Literature*] there is not a line that I know of in English to hint that anyone knows or cares for it ... but you see all this was my home, and it was natural I should care so much for it. I wanted to track that blissful sweet song piteous into the thick of the forest, and I did it at last.[11]

Had historicism been Burne-Jones's motive, his own reading of earlier sources would have demonstrated that a reliance on Malory would itself have been simplistic, for Malory's *Morte d'Arthur* is not necessarily 'truer' to the Matter of Britain than is Tennyson's version. As I have said, Malory's task was to discipline the efflorescence of texts that had grown up in the three centuries following Geoffrey of Monmouth's *History of the Kings of Britain*. Tennyson's use of Malory is thus a further emphasizing of the French tradition and a moving away from the idea of Arthur in history that Geoffrey had attempted. Malory manipulated the two major Arthurian traditions to produce a coherent whole; Tennyson's version may have been more selective, but the redactive principle was essentially the same.

If Malory remained for Burne-Jones the mainstay of his artistic approach to the Matter of Britain, his use of Malory was as selective as was Tennyson's, ignoring Arthur's imperial conquests in Europe and the emphasis on battlefield carnage that went with it. Like Tennyson,

[169]

Burne-Jones concentrated particularly on the French tradition, combining chivalric romance with the mysticism of the Grail legend. There is little sign of the *realpolitik* and military expeditions associated with the imperial Arthur of Geoffrey of Monmouth. Given Burne-Jones's antipathy to contemporary British imperialism, his version of Arthur could hardly have been otherwise. His decision to abandon any possibility of an historicist Arthur makes sense, of course, in the context of his own aesthetic. As an artist regarded by some commentators as seeking to emulate the emotional conviction of early Italian art, Burne-Jones's emphasis on the French Arthurian tradition allowed him to minimize narrative detail. Had he been tempted to address Malory's or Geoffrey of Monmouth's account of imperial conquest, the required narrative detail would have rendered the subject unpaintable from the artist's point of view.

As is well attested, he cared little for the historicist project associated with the art of Alma-Tadema or Poynter, in which minutely detailed and archaeologically credible renderings of artefacts are presumed to authenticate the image of the ancient world. But Burne-Jones's mediaevalizing taste required him to make some accommodation to the past and the price of this aesthetic decision might be understood as negotiable. At its most extreme it propels Burne-Jones towards elegant but essentially empty decoration, where non-naturalistic pictorial devices produce effects of line and colour that supplant the ostensible subject matter of the image. But the reduction of narrative also provided the opportunity for Burne-Jones to paint pictures whose effects are fully iconic, even though the narrative is minimal. Just as a Christian artist might work with the narrative of the Passion to distil its spiritual essence, so Burne-Jones can pare down the narrative embellishments of the Arthurian corpus to produce images whose function is not to narrate but to embody the Matter of Britain.

The freedom of interpretation enjoyed by Burne-Jones needs further comment. Of course, there is no Ur-text, no literary place of departure for Arthur, which might become the measure of permissible artistic licence. Nor is there any historical fixity; Arthur wavers between history and myth. The implication of this uncertainty is profound, for Arthur is perhaps and paradoxically a sign without a referent, an image that grasped imaginatively can show a truth but never describe any reality. But for this to happen, for the image to embody a truth, the representation must *constitute* rather than illustrate its message. Its truth inheres in its formal structure and technical means, which alone have the power to keep the possibility of Arthur open. For the mediaeval reader this had resulted in a self-conscious approach to these texts, combining what Chrétien de Troyes called *matière* and *sens*, to distinguish the story proper from the meaning it contained. In the mediaeval text an object, scrupulously described in detail, is also a symbol, but any character who fails to understand that symbolic significance will also fail to see the organization and interrelationship of objects whose coherence results not from their actual presence in the world, but from this symbolic register. To rely purely on sense data and routine understandings of the world would be to lose forever the key to understanding. The spectator's universe, a mass of solely material unrelated objects, would be chaotic. Perceval is originally limited in just this way and, as a result, fails to ask the correct question when shown the Grail for the first time. Only when he learns to understand it at a higher level can he understand the value of what it represents, and so ask the right question and heal the Fisher King.[12]

We might liken the distinction between *sens* and *matière* with Burne-Jones's own *dicta* regarding the 'burden' of his art.[13] For, patently, what distinguishes his achievement from the majority of his contemporaries' approaches to Arthur is the positioning of his aesthetic of the Matter of Britain in a more spiritual context. The interrelationship of objects is palpably visible, and this coherence at the level of style allows Burne-Jones to elide the mediaeval world with Celtic mythology and the Christian mystery of the Passion. As with his mediaeval predecessors, the Matter of Britain clothes a transcendental understanding, allowing a glimpse of something mystical and immutable, an inward truth wrapped in a material garment. In this respect, Burne-Jones was perhaps truer to the intentions of Chrétien and other early mediaeval writers than were his own contemporaries, who, if they avoided the traps of mere illustrative narrative or historicist attempts at accuracy, were prone to clumsy one-to-one allegorical interpretations of the myth. It is significant in this respect that Burne-Jones resisted the attempt made by Sebastian Evans to allegorize the Grail quest when discussing his *High History of the Holy Graal*, which he read to the painter in the studio: 'his theory of the allegorical meaning of the story met with no sympathy or acceptance . . . To explain a story that to him was an explanation of life he felt intolerable.'[14] The problem with an allegorical reading of the Grail quest is that it reduces all incidents and characters to fixed and unitary meanings and, in so doing, renders the work of art superfluous. For if the allegory is already known, a painting's function could only be to illustrate an existing truth. Burne-Jones, on this evidence, resisted Evans's allegorical interpretation because of its closure of meaning and the implied threat to the work an image might undertake. If Burne-Jones's Arthurian designs resist easy interpretation it is because they function more like devotional images than as symbolic narratives.

To elaborate this point, it is worth dwelling a moment on the difficulties of making a convincing representation of Arthur – what, indeed, would 'convincing' mean with regard to such a representation? To think of the historicity of Arthur is to attempt an impossible understanding. Whether or not a Romanized commander of mobile forces actually used cavalry tactics to check Saxon advances in late fifth- and early sixth-century Britain is beside the point; at best a dim memory of such a commander may have been grit for the mediaeval oyster, at worst the elaboration of Arthur throughout the Middle Ages was an exclusively literary phenomenon. Historicity was not a major representational problem for the Middle Ages, nor was there any sustained vexation over Arthur's authenticity and how he should be depicted. In the Victorian era self-consciousness about history and historicity raised the stakes. Tennyson, despite some early investigation of Arthur's historical existence, had the good sense to follow Malory and his predecessors in presenting Arthur in an almost atemporal frame.[15] However, Tennyson's decision was not inevitable, especially at a time when historicist enthusiasm for the Middle Ages was at its height, and it is no surprise to note the emergence of attempts to provide Arthur with a historical legitimacy in the mid-nineteenth century.[16]

In the visual arts, this historicist tendency is much more rarely encountered. The Arthur customarily depicted lacks any indication of Celtic culture and most often inhabits a simulated mediaeval world.[17] On a few occasions, however, historicist thinking ruptures this willed fiction; and, immediately it does so, the vacuity of the gesture reveals itself. As a good example, we may take Frederick Sandys's *Morgan la Fay* (1862–63; see Figure 18). Sandys's evocation of Morgan la Fay as a dangerous, perhaps diabolical, woman is most successful in direct proportion to its lack of historical specificity, but two details in the image reveal his inability to let well alone. Perhaps influenced by renewed enquiries into the historicity of Arthur at mid-century and by his own work for the Norfolk antiquarian James Bulwer in the 1850s, Sandys seems to have been impelled to use illustrated source books when seeking to represent the Dark Ages.[18] Between the sketch for this picture and the finished result he added some 'authentic' elements, decorating the newly woven mantle with Celtic interlace ornamentation and the hem of Morgan la Fay's robe with devices filched from Pictish symbol stones.[19] Such additions can only confuse two registers of experience, confounding history with myth. In doing so, Sandys allows the genuine material culture of the sixth and seventh centuries CE to collide with a fictive world whose temporal frame is surely an

18 Frederick Sandys, *Morgan la Fay*, 1862–63, oil on panel, 62.9 × 44.5 cm

irrelevance.[20] The Celtic and Pictish devices, once seen for what they are, offer another context for the image and threaten to reduce it from a creative statement of ecstatic emotion to something more banal, merely an illustration of priesthood in the Dark Ages. Ironically, the greater the antiquarian precision used to banish anachronisms from the story of Arthur the more absurd his representations become.[21]

Burne-Jones might be said to have avoided such category mistakes in his Arthurian subjects, and is known to have felt that the *Holy Grail* tapestry series, commissioned from Morris and Co. in 1890 should not be set in a specific period. Nevertheless, while most of the costumes and ornamental details are non-specifically mediaeval, loosely twelfth century in origin, individual details are derived from genuine artefacts. Thus, in the tapestry design for *The Attainment* (woven 1895–96; see Figure 19), the figure of Sir Perceval, the kneeling knight on the far left, and the Holy Grail, seen on the right, are derived, respectively, from sketches Burne-Jones made of a fourteenth-century figure in the

19   Edward Burne-Jones, *The Attainment: The Vision of the Holy Grail to Sir Galahad, Sir Bors and Sir Percival* (1895–96), wool and silk tapestry, 245 × 693 cm

Westminster Psalter and the eighth-century Tassilo Chalice.[22] What distinguishes these details from Sandys's antiquarian elements is their wide separation in time. It is almost as though Burne-Jones is replicating the growth of the Arthurian tradition through history by bringing together objects from different cultural contexts. The Grail quest, on this reckoning, is simultaneously eighth, twelfth and fourteenth century and thus transcends time.

It takes but a moment's reflection to realize that the incorporation of historicist detail would, in fact, destroy Arthur, reducing him and his myth to a mundane episode with no possibility of return. Arthur, if he is to sleep in Avalon (Figure 17), demands a sedulous avoidance of history, and this is, largely, what Burne-Jones achieves. The architectural decoration is thus vaguely Byzantine and/or Romanesque, the figures' dress non-descript and the whole image could act as a pictorial demonstration of Malcolm Bell's critical understanding of Burne-Jones's art:

He cared not at all for minute archaeological accuracy . . . That the garments and accessories should be in themselves beautiful and susceptible of rich ornament and fine colouring; that they should be subordinate to, yet expressive of the spirit of the picture, outweighed in his eyes all such considerations as whether the person represented would really have worn such clothes in such surroundings. It was the soul that he strove after, and so long as the mantle that enwraps it is seemly and pleasing to the eye, he asked no more.[23]

What Bell describes here is an aesthetic predicated on the ability of pictures to make meanings without leaning on the crutch of history. It would be wrong, however, to conclude that such an aesthetic was wholly formalist, for Burne-Jones holds to the idea of communication through pictorial means. In the case of Arthur and the Grail, what could be communicated pictorially would be the authority necessary for the myth to function. A comprehensive achievement at the sensual level of design, form and colour would produce rhetorical effects powerful enough to command attention. As I have said with reference to Sandys, in pictorial art the isolated or isolatable historicist fragment is ruinously disruptive of the myth, threatening the wholeness of the presentation with the possibility of different frames of reference, with details that seek their authenticity in material fact rather than rhetorical effect. Far from buttressing the Arthur story, the inclusion of presumed archaeological precision contaminates the image with a hostile virus. If any conventional representation of Arthur is to succeed, if the Matter of Britain is not to fragment, archaeological and historicist understandings must be kept at bay. The truth of Arthur lies in emotional or spiritual coherence, not historicist understanding.[24]

What remains of history in Burne-Jones's encounter with Arthur is his desire to 'track that blissful sweet song piteous into the thick of the forest'. His remarks about researches into Celtic texts demonstrate his awareness of the Matter of Britain as a process, a literature developing over a millennium, with a proliferation of accretions and redactions. Inevitably, an awareness of that tradition will prompt an understanding of history that emphasizes continuities and overlays as opposed to breaks and discontinuities. In the early twentieth century that same lineage has been deployed, on occasion, within modernism as a guarantor of national consciousness. The two best-known examples of the tendency are the Arthurian references in the works of David Jones and Charles Williams. For both of them, the route back through Tennyson to Malory, Geoffrey of Monmouth, *The Mabinogion* and the Celtic tradition offers a profound understanding of the Matter of Britain as a deep sediment underlying all honest attempts to create authentic art in this country. The writing and rewriting of Arthur on the body of these islands becomes an apt symbol for the lived reality of shared culture, for continuities at the level of the national myth.[25] As Charles Williams understood it, Britain, seen under Arthurian aspect, is poised at the western limits of the intelligible world. To the east, Europe, history and doctrine, birthplace of classical civilization and the *logos*; to the west, ocean, myth and mysticism, limitless and transcendental.[26] The importance of the Arthurian tradition is its reconciliation of these understandings of the world.

For David Jones, deploying the Arthurian tradition was one response to a cultural situation in which the creation and display of true signs had become exceptionally difficult. For Jones, the nineteenth century witnessed – what he christened – 'the Break', a shift in consciousness that divides modern man from a pre-modern understanding of the world. The transition from a world of myths to a world of formulae has far-reaching implications for the possibility of sacrament and sign as vehicles of meaning.[27] As he concluded with regard to his own hermetic masterpiece *The Anathemata*: 'My intention has not been to edify . . . nor, I think, to persuade, but there is indeed an intention to "uncover"; which is what a mystery does, for though at root "mystery" implies a closing, all "mysteries" are meant to disclose, to show forth something'.[28]

What marks this recourse to the past in the Arthurian myth is thus usefully envisaged as a mystical rather than a historical celebration of the tradition. And with that tradition comes a developed comprehension of the landscape as invested with the same truths. Those whose art allows them to 'uncover' may also see beneath the surface appearance of the modern nation to find layer upon layer of traces from earlier epochs. These fragments of earlier inscriptions on the body of the land complicate and perhaps confound the authority of modern experience. The sense of communion with that layered history can be characterized as mystical, for it suggests that the true nation can be understood only by its initiates. From the Arthurian revival, with its invocation of a mystical comprehension of reality, to the investment of the landscape with a mystical sense of history is but a small step. Kipling's *Puck of Pook's Hill*, first published in 1906, might stand as the epitome of that particular tendency in British culture. The book's conceit is that Puck, who was old enough to have accepted food offerings when Stonehenge was new, is the last survivor of a whole band of erstwhile gods and goddesses now absent from modern Britain. Under his tutelage two Sussex children are 'seized and possessed of all Old England', from the Roman occupation to the Middle Ages.[29] Puck, in Kipling's narrative, is the ultimate *genius loci*, and the privilege he affords his charges is to render transparent the normally opaque overlayering of British history. Their ownership of 'Old England' is more than a history lesson: it is rooted in a particular location, providing a deep comprehension in place of more superficial understanding, and the implication is that they – and the book's readers – will now engage in a different kind of relationship with 'their' land. What links such different texts, produced for very different purposes and at such a remove from one another, is the idea of coming to terms with the nation through a deep understanding of its past. Modern developments contribute to, but are contained by, a landscape still bearing the traces of its previous incarnations. The modern does not cancel the old, but finds itself making an accommodation to the past.

As I have argued, there is something in the Arthurian tradition which promoted this sort of thinking, whether it be the invitation to respond through *sens* as well as *matière* or Burne-Jones's seventeen years' pondering of the mystery of Arthur in Avalon. The presence of the Arthurian tradition suggests a cultural orientation that is rooted in myth, that sees intellectual development not as a linear progression but as an accretion of knowledge around a spiritual core, that reads the very landscape as a mystical palimpsest. It is a quietist, meditative and essentially conservative approach that stands in stark contradistinction to those modernizing and modernist tendencies which lie this side of David Jones's 'Break'. Equally, of course, it offers a secure haven from the vicissitudes of an uncertain world, if only because its temporal reach makes contemporary events less urgent. Burne-Jones's feelings about Morris and the socialist movement makes this particularly clear.

> When [Morris] went into it I thought he would have subdued the ignorant, conceited, mistaken rancour of it all – that he would teach them some humility and give them some sense of obedience, with his splendid bird's-eye view of all that has happened in the world and his genius for History in the abstract.[30]

For Burne-Jones, history in the abstract means taking the long view, understanding the course of historical events through the contemplation of epochs. The messy and uncomfortable reality of contemporary demands and the urgency of political action will diminish in proportion as the viewpoint lengthens. Georgiana Burne-Jones recorded that *The Sleep of King Arthur in Avalon* originally contained a raging battle in the background which had been painted over, with 'only the suggestion of it . . . given in a figure watching at a door, and others looking out and listening to the tumult of the world'.[31] It is an apt symbol, perhaps, of the uses of Arthur in the modern period, when the tumult of the world is subordinated to contemplation of the Matter of Britain and reworking the national myth becomes a self-sufficient activity. If the tumult of the world is necessarily outside the place of myth, then what the mystical understanding of Britain-as-palimpsest provides is not so much a record of historical change, the product of real transformations in political and material circumstances, as it is an atemporal register of cultural continuity and identity. 'Old England' as Kipling's Puck expresses it, can be only a refuge from modernity. The banishment of history and the modern, and in their place the celebration of myth and mystical continuity, allows Arthur to sleep on in Burne-Jones's picture. The artist himself seems to have well understood the implications of this. As he wrote to Georgiana in 1898, musing on recent events in southern Africa: 'There was a great deal of Rhodes talked – to my sickness – but it wasn't the time for angriness, and I let it pass. I shall let most things pass me by. I must, if ever I want to reach Avalon.'[32]

Notes

1   Georgiana Burne-Jones, *Memorials of Edward Burne-Jones*, London, Macmillan, 1906, vol. 2, p. 333.
2   Matthew Arnold, *On the Study of Celtic Literature*, London, Smith, Elder & Co., (1867) 1891, p. 51. The lectures on which this book is based were first delivered at Oxford in 1866.
3   See J. W. Burrow, *A Liberal Descent: Victorian Historians and the English Past*, Cambridge, Cambridge University Press, 1981.
4   The discovery of Arthur's supposed tomb was the subject of a study by the artist J. H. Mortimer in the 1760s. See John Sunderland, 'Mortimer, Pine and some political aspects of English history painting', *Burlington Magazine*, vol. 116, June 1974, pp. 317–26.
5   His early interest in the Arthur cycle resulted, among other works, in his painting *Merlin and Nimuë* for the Oxford Union murals (1858–59), his 1861 watercolour *The Enchantments of Nimuë* (now in the collection of the Victoria and Albert Museum) and his designs for stained glass at Walter Dunlop's home Harden Grange, on the theme of *Tristram and Isoude* (1862).
6   After the 1634 edition, Malory languished unpublished until the beginning of the nineteenth century. By the end of 1817 *Morte d'Arthur* had been reprinted in three separate editions.
7   Aaron Thompson, *The British History, Translated into English from the Latin of Jeffrey of Monmouth, with a Large Preface Concerning the Authority of the History*, London, J. Bowyer, 1718.
8   *The British History of Geoffrey of Monmouth, in Twelve Books, Translated from the Latin by A. Thompson, Esq., a New Edition, Revised and Corrected*, ed. J. A. Giles, London, Bohn, 1842. This translation was included in *Six Old English Chronicles*, ed. J. A. Giles, London, Bohn, 1848.
9   Owen Pughe published a version of the first part of the tale of Pwyll in *The Cambrian Register* for 1795 and again, modified, in *The Cambro-Briton*, February 1821. In 1829 he also published a complete translation of 'Math, son of Mathonwy' in *The Cambrian Quarterly*.
10 Lady Charlotte Guest, The Mabinogion *from the Llyfr Coch o Hergest, and Other Ancient Welsh Manuscripts, with an English Translation and Notes*, 3 vols, London

and Llandovery, 1838–49. This nineteenth-century interest in *The Mabinogion* culminated in Gwenogvryn Evans and Sir John Rhys, *The Text of* The Mabinogion *and Other Welsh Tales from the Red Book of Hergest*, Oxford and Pwllheli, 1887.

11 See Georgiana Burne-Jones, *Memorials of Edward Burne-Jones*, vol. 2, pp. 42–3. See also p. 40 for Burne-Jones's enquiries to the publisher F. S. Ellis in 1872 about translations of Welsh texts. It is reasonable to suppose that Matthew Arnold's *Study of Celtic Literature*, published five years earlier, provided Burne-Jones with the names of these texts.

12 See Norris J. Lacy, *The Craft of Chrétien de Troyes: An Essay in Narrative Art*, Leiden, E. J. Brill, 1980, especially pp. 16–23.

13 Georgiana Burne-Jones, *Memorials of Edward Burne-Jones*, vol. 2, pp. 261–2.

14 Georgiana Burne-Jones, *Memorials of Edward Burne-Jones*, vol. 2, p. 332; *The High History of the Holy Graal* was published by Evans in 1898.

15 In the 1830s Tennyson was investigating Arthur through historical and literary sources, for example Collinson's *History of Somersetshire*, whose notes he copied verbatim. When he published the first version of *The Lady of Shalott* in May 1832, however, he played down the topographical elements he had researched. In his *Poems* (1842), the poem reappeared, much revised, along with other Arthurian treatments and, like them, was marked by a lack of topographical and historical detail. This refusal to provide a historicist context is noteworthy. For information on Tennyson's early Arthurian explorations I am indebted to Roger Simpson, *Camelot Regained: The Arthurian Revival and Tennyson, 1800–1849*, Cambridge, D. S. Brewer, 1990, pp. 190–8.

16 A series of five articles on the historicity of Arthur was published in the *Gentleman's Magazine* between April and August 1842.

17 For comprehensive coverage of the Arthurian revival in pictorial terms, see especially Christine Poulson, *The Quest for the Grail: Arthurian Legend in British Art, 1840–1920*, Manchester, Manchester University Press, 1999; Debra N. Mancoff, *The Arthurian Revival in Victorian Art*, New York and London, Garland, 1990; Muriel Whitaker, *The Legends of King Arthur in Art*, Cambridge, D. S. Brewer, 1990. Simpson, *Camelot Regained*, provides a useful check-list of pictorial works produced in the first half of the nineteenth century, prior to the major upsurge of pictorial depictions of Arthur and the Grail cycle.

18 See *Frederick Sandys, 1829–1904*, Brighton, Brighton Museum and Art Gallery, 1974.

19 The sketch for the picture is now in the collection of Birmingham Museum and Art Gallery. The two likely illustrated works on which Sandys could have drawn are Patrick Chalmers (ed.) *The Ancient Sculptured Monuments of the County of Angus*, Edinburgh, Bannatyne Club, 1848, and John Stuart, *The Sculptured Stones of Scotland*, Aberdeen, Spalding Club, 1856.

20 J. D. Merriman, *The Flower of King: A Study of the Arthurian Legend in England Between 1485 and 1835*, Lawrence, Kansas University Press, 1973, p. 173, has made the same point in respect of literature: 'Such attempts to historicize or localize the Arthurian stories are inherently contradictory, and far from lending credibility to the legend, they are but disturbing and irrelevant reminders of another order of reality. The truth of the material is poetic or imagined truth, and Arthur ruled not in history but rather in the "long, long ago" over a kingdom that had never existed save in the minds of men, a realm that had little to offer to the impulse for historical reconstruction that delighted the age.'

21 Simpson has discussed the tension between the historicist and imaginative approaches to Arthur. In the romantic era, Warton and Scott had both argued for the separation of romance from irrelevant critical precepts. The marvellous cannot be judged by mundane standards of truth. Even so, some of the creative literature on Arthur was tainted by an antiquarian obsession with period detail and the avoidance of anachronism: for example Henry Hart Milman's *Samor, Lord of the Bright City* (1818), John Fitzgerald Pennie's *The Dragon–King* (1832)

and Baron Lytton's *King Arthur* (1848). See Simpson, *Camelot Regained*, pp. 32–3, 149–51.

22 The sketchbook, dated *c.*1890, is now in the collection of Birmingham City Museum and Art Gallery.

23 Malcolm Bell, *Sir Edward Burne-Jones: A Record and Review*, London, G. Bell & Sons, 1898, pp. 113–14.

24 For a particularly useful analysis of this point, see Julie F. Codell 'Decapitation and deconstruction: the body of the hero in Robert Bresson's *Lancelot du Lac*', in Debra N. Mancoff (ed.) *The Arthurian Revival. Essays on Form, Tradition, and Transformation*, New York and London, Garland, 1992, pp. 266–82.

25 David Jones, *In Parenthesis*, London, Faber & Faber, 1937; and *The Anathemata*, London, Faber & Faber, 1952. Charles Williams, *Taliessin Through Logres*, London, Oxford University Press, 1938; and *The Region of the Summer Stars*, London, Nicholson & Watson, 1944.

26 Charles Williams, *The Figure of Arthur*, in C. S. Lewis (ed.) *Arthurian Torso*, London, Oxford University Press, 1948, pp. 80–1.

27 Preface to Jones, *The Anathemata*, 1972 edn, pp. 15–25.

28 Preface to Jones, *The Anathemata*, p. 33.

29 Rudyard Kipling, *Puck of Pook's Hill*, London, Macmillan, 1922, p. 13.

30 Georgiana Burne-Jones, *Memorials of Edward Burne-Jones*, vol. 2, p. 97.

31 Georgiana Burne-Jones, *Memorials of Edward Burne-Jones*, vol. 2, p. 116.

32 Georgiana Burne-Jones, *Memorials of Edward Burne-Jones*, vol. 2, p. 340.

CHAPTER TEN

Architecture and 'national projection' between the wars

Mark Crinson

During the 1930s, and for some time after, the phrase 'national projection' became widely used to describe a particular form of official propaganda. National projection was a way of representing Britain, outside of the homeland, as a country of enlightened public institutions and modernized industries, a place of democratic freedoms and well-made products, an essentially peace-loving land whose empire was to be transformed, in the words of Leo Amery, secretary of state for the Dominions, into 'a co-operative venture...a society for mutual help'.[1] The propaganda was conveyed by several major enterprises, among them the newly created British Council (1934), the films produced under John Grierson at the Empire Marketing Board and the BBC foreign-language broadcasts.[2] Another area where national projection was particularly directed – and this is the subject of the present chapter – was in the architecture and the displays of the national pavilions designed for international exhibitions. This was a temporary architecture, intended to stand for a few months, but it was built for highly charged and prestigious events where the quality of national cultures, the power of national economies and even the character of national identities were all at stake.

Of course architecture and nationalism have often been understood as complementary. Whether the sources of some originary type have been claimed as belonging to the national landscape, or whether a building has been deemed to monumentalize some founding or pivotal moment in national memory – or indeed a host of other such connections – architecture since the German romantics has regularly been taken to embody what that abstract modern concept, the *nation*, most required: 'the outward shell of [its] being', as Jacob Burckhardt expressed it.[3] As Adrian Forty has pointed out, architecture has had a privileged place in national imaginings, where, following Goethe, it was presented as the built equivalent of what was understood as the nation's distinctive and most essential means of expression – its language.[4] When architecture had the same ubiquity and apparent inevitability as language then it too could reveal the national spirit. But while the romantics may have linked national identities reasonably directly with moments and monuments of the past, the forging of new understandings of the nation through new architecture became an enduring concern only with the Gothic revival.[5] However, Gothic revivalist approaches to architectural nationalism presented distinct problems both to the religious identity of the nation and to the nation's relation with the expanding empire beyond it.[6]

In the first two decades of the twentieth century, a firm weld between nation and empire seemed to have been established in architecture with the ubiquitous deployment of classical solutions. Lutyens's domes, colonnades and cenotaphs traced a common overriding culture and a universalism of ideals across the diverse landscapes of the empire. Arguably this same model can be detected in many of the practices and assumptions of imperial classicism's successor – modernism. Here too the notion of a deeply embedded language of architecture can be found, not as a style or a dialect but as a fundamental part of a culture. If the culture was universal, or globalized, so must the architecture be. But if architecture was to become language-like, in the romantic sense, in its integration with the larger culture, this brought with it at least two problems. The first concerned the shape of that larger culture and its unlikely homology with the shape of the nation or even the shape of the empire. The second concerned a latent confusion within the language analogy itself: if architecture was language-like in the romantic sense, this was not the same as saying that it had the ability to *signify* as does a language, to convey meaning as a system of signs.

What is most interesting in the inter-war idea of national projection is that the kind of architecture with which it became most identified had little or no associational value and, even more problematically for many of its contemporaries, little or no ability to mark itself as nationally particular, and thus to distinguish itself from the architecture of many other nations. If this architecture could be called a language, then it was, for its critics, an esperanto – both a rootless creation and something spoken by as yet too few people, a mere gesture towards collective understanding and a hoped-for internationalism.

This is the course to be mapped out in this chapter. First the constituents of the official project of national projection is analysed. Then the distinct architectural form of this project is traced in several national pavilions, culminating with the British Pavilion in the Paris International Exhibition of 1937. Finally, the often directly opposed critical reactions to the appearance of that pavilion are discussed. Architecture, it is argued, presented particular problems for the advocates of national projection. To some extent, because national projection was directed at publics outside of Britain, this official architecture came to outstrip its stay-at-home versions in its formal adventurousness; and when it was reproduced and reviewed in Britain it inspired aesthetic and political controversy. National projection in architecture was an enterprise marked by deep fault lines: it was neither the expression of a unanimous official will nor the product of some clear-cut political or social ideology. Despite – or even, perhaps, because of – its avoidance of the accepted rhetorics of imperialism, it was successful in the colonies; but the nearer it came to Britain, the more its fault-lines threatened to break open.

The projection of England

The example of architecture, and its potential, had been central to the earliest and most influential vision of national projection, the one sketched out by its main advocate Sir Stephen Tallents in *The Projection of England* (1932). Tallents, who was the first person to use the phrase 'national projection', was secretary of the Empire Marketing Board – the body set up by Baldwin's Government to promote imperial products and guide consumer choice – and a civil servant with great influence and many connections.[7] For Tallents, national projection was not propaganda but public relations – another term which Tallents may have invented – and therefore bound up with the processes of marketing, advertising and research. National projection was about the conveyance of a group of images of England and approved new subject matter: industry, tourism, universities, scientific research. These were linked with an older set of approved icons – the monarchy, London buses, the Boat Race, the English countryside – and the combination would evoke both tradition and modernity. In one of Tallents's most striking images, Britain's imperial responsibilities were to be dealt with through a set of new research stations and bureaux focused on agricultural problems: 'secluded guilds of young workers, dotted here and there about England, such as once were dotted the hospitalries of the Order of St John, and happily absorbed in the deft and keen-eyed study of the problems which belong unto our Imperial peace'.[8] Essentially philanthropic and staffed by devoted young researchers, these research stations in their pastoral settings were reassuringly traditional in their evocation of guilds and Oxbridge colleges; at the same time, however, they were dedicated to the most advanced techniques and the most contemporary of problems (they would be extended, for instance, to building science and, within that, to the problems of tropical architecture). Tallents also argued for a 'school of national projection', which was later to become the British Council.

But the particular example of architecture that Tallents settled on to exemplify national projection was neither British nor in any obvious way nationalistic; and it was certainly not a building much known in Britain at the time. This was the German Pavilion designed by Mies van der Rohe for the Barcelona International Exhibition of 1929. For Tallents, Mies's pavilion 'was a gesture rather than a building, deriving its effects from that sense of spacious and efficient simplicity more commonly associated with an up-to-date hospital or a modern powerhouse'.[9] The pavilion made no reference to Germany's past nor to any established attribute of German nationhood. Instead it identified Germany with a certain spiritual quality – 'lonely, powerful, forward-looking' – and its spaciousness, simplicity and absence of irrelevant detail seemed to embody efficiency and industrial modernity.[10] In a similar way England must spread throughout the world a newly renovated image of itself, 'of English industrial quality and ambition, an impression of English adaptability and modernity no less than of English craftsmanship and thoroughness and finish'.[11] What is notable about Tallents's idea of the place of architecture in national projection is that it combines generic aspirations towards 'industrial quality', 'modernity' and 'craftsmanship' with certain notional but highly abstract national characteristics – 'adaptability' and, perhaps, 'thoroughness' – which take the place of the 'lonely, powerful, forward-looking' German. Tallents was calling for a distinct move away from the conventional appurtenances of the 'heart of empire'. Furthermore, there is no sign in Tallents's writing of the association of British nationalism with political liberty that had marked the Gothic revivalists' approach; indeed, if anything, the example of Mies's Barcelona pavilion seems to indicate that Tallents imagined national projection as working within a pan-national style, a kind of language group of modern nations each with its own variations within it. Modernism, in this way of thinking, was similar to Enlightenment theories of language according to which individual languages shared general features. Modernism was thus not a way of rising above nationalism but a category capable of containing national forms within it.[12]

In the British context Tallents saw a particular form of modernism arising out of its association with native 'craftsmanship and thoroughness and finish'. He was not alone in such a view: indeed, one of his colleagues at the Empire Marketing Board was Frank Pick who, by the time of Tallents's book, had become the main creative presence behind the transformation of the London Underground. Pick also became the dominant creative presence behind the 1937 pavilion through his chairmanship of the Council for Art and Industry (under the Department of Overseas Trade), and Tallents served on three of the committees responsible for the pavilion. In Michael Saler's recent account, Pick's approach to aesthetics and industry has been identified by the term 'medieval modernism', meaning that Pick and his stable of artists, designers and architects, attempted a fusion between the arts and crafts movement of William Morris and his followers and the new forms of avant-garde modernism.[13] It was its Protestant moral rhetoric of 'fitness for purpose' rather than formalism, its attention to detailing, and its desire to conjoin traditional practices with what Pick called 'new materials and new circumstances'[14] that marked out this important but, until recently, neglected aspect of modernism in Britain.[15] 'Medieval modernism' also provided a framework in which modernism and culturally conservative tendencies could coexist – this would be the aim of the 1937 pavilion, for instance.[16] While Pick and Tallents certainly had differences,[17] they were united in the desire to find a form of modernism that could manifest national identity in twentieth-century conditions.

National pavilions

If there was one building in the 1930s that might be taken as a test case of what Tallents meant by 'national projection' it was the British Pavilion at the Paris International Exhibition of 1937. Equally, if there was a recent building of the same type that might have epitomized what national projection should *not* be then it could be found in the British Government Pavilion designed for the Empire Exhibition at Wembley in 1924 (Figure 20). The Wembley building was a squat concrete temple, its flight of entrance steps guarded by six lions. The main space within this grim edifice was a 'Court of Honour' where, lit by a stained-glass roof, a relief map of the world showed 'tiny ships ploughing their way through real water on all the trade routes of the empire'.[18] Looking down on this court was an open gallery that displayed the various activities of those government departments that administered imperial business; dotted around were figures in armour, weapons, trophies and pictures; and on the balustrades were banners representing the dominions and colonies, as well as the royal arms.[19]

This, then, was not a commercial space but a public space advertising government activities, as Tallents wanted national projection to do. But it was also a space of some portentousness, one whose piers and naked concrete walls, whose red-and-gold painted ceiling, with evocations of heraldry and global networks, evoked familiar symbols

[186]

20 British Government Pavilion, Empire Exhibition, Wembley, 1924; architects – J. W. Simpson and Maxwell Ayrton, *Architectural Review*, June 1924

of the continuity of tradition and the overarching reassurance of imperial power. Familiarity of identity was the point here, and identity was a matter of placement, hierarchically and geographically, within the spaces of the building and beyond it to the world of the empire. There was little or nothing here of the distinctly modern, probably because the distinctly modern, whether of industrial modernity or of a modernity of space and detail, might over-stretch the thinly layered webs of allusions of which the Government Pavilion was made up.

Most of all, the distinctly modern might compromise that key virtue in the lexicon of most contemporaries who commented on the pavilion – 'dignity'. Dignity was not a virtue associated with the commercial, the minor, the relativistic or the peripheral, and it was certainly neither youthful nor new.

Before turning to the Paris pavilion, I have something to say about what was at the time a much-praised transitional pavilion between Wembley and Paris; transitional in terms of its date as well as its synthesis of styles, its content and its modes of display. The United Kingdom Pavilion for the Empire Exhibition, Johannesburg, had been the tallest and one of the two most prominent buildings in this 1936 exhibition devoted to projecting South Africa as a modern and prosperous country (Figure 21). In the architect's sketch for it, the pavilion appeared as a somewhat visionary adumbration, a comic-book apparition with a set of halo-like clouds and radiating strokes of pencil around it.[20] The mismatched scales of figures, flagpoles and massive globes, set on plinths, accentuated the staginess of the image. The

21 United Kingdom Pavilion, Empire Exhibition, Johannesburg, 1936; architect – Howard Robertson. *Architects' Journal*, 6 August 1936

building itself was organized symmetrically using simple geometric units – spheres, cylinders and cuboids – painted white and left unornamented except for a coffered screen wall above the entrance and behind a curved colonnade of elongated pillars. The prominent royal arms on the rotunda was the only conventional attribute of British identity on the outside; in fact the pavilion was known by contemporaries as 'A Building Which Needs No Name',[21] presumably because the sheer bulk of its elementally grandiose presence was enough to indicate its symbolic centrality both to the exhibition and to the empire. This lack of a name, or rather the building's capacity to communicate its identity largely without conventional attributes or signs, relates in an interesting way to my earlier comments on architecture as a language of the nation. Laurens van der Post reviewed the building in those terms for the *Star*: 'The United Kingdom Pavilion has been well and significantly named in its namelessness for it expresses in the clear terms of its own design what it is and what it symbolizes with greater dignity than anything else could have done . . . [Here was] the reduction of a vast idea to one central and essential theme, and on a magnaminous modesty.'[22] For van der Post the design of the pavilion made its symbolism unmistakeable: it did not require the lions and the classical references of the Wembley pavilion. The link between British nationalism and the English-speaking empire was thematized in the very form of the pavilion; indeed, the absence of such references and titles – its 'namelesness' – gave it both dignity and modesty. In other words it signified *like* language rather than *as* language.

Inside, the pavilion was, if anything, even more theatrical. The Court of Honour housed another large world map in a sunken well with a royal niche and a bust of the king looking down from a dais in the concentric galleries that rose above it. The theme for all the displays was modern transport, given an imperial tilt by focusing on the prominence of the 'British peoples' in developing transport, as well as transport's role 'in welding together the peoples which constitute the British Empire'.[23] The pavilion and its displays imagined the empire as a modern global system, a network of links and nodal points, brought about through advanced transportation systems. Mobility and the interconnection of geographic space were the main themes, just as they were *leitmotivs* of modernism, and the circular design and dynamic planning of the pavilion attempted to give architectural form to that theme. There was, of course, nothing here about uneven economic relations, finance or governance, and the image of the king showed where the symbolic centre of empire still lay. The pavilion could be understood – and, in the extraordinary unanimity of commentary, it clearly was thus seen – as combining the necessary ele-

[189]

ments of both continuity and change. The *Rhodesia Herald* summed it up: 'somehow the United Kingdom pavilion, although as modern and up to date in design as any other building in the exhibition, has added more dignity in its line and looks on the pavilions of the Commonwealth around it with a wise, paternal, almost maternal air'.[24]

Democratic projection

For all its success with its South African critics, the United Kingdom Pavilion at Johannesburg was not the best test case of what Tallents had meant by national projection. That would have to wait for the realization of a pavilion already, in 1935, being planned for the Paris Exhibition of 1937, the first time that a pavilion was blatantly conceived as an exercise in national projection.[25] Yet there is no doubt that the Paris Exhibition, like previous exhibitions in that city, presented problems to the British in terms of how they might represent national and imperial identity.[26] It may have been from this that stemmed the half-hearted British engagement with the Paris Exhibition and thus, when it came to some of the critical decisions in the planning process, the flat-footed response of the British. There was considerable confusion and dispute over what kind of exhibition the French were going to have in 1937, and this was not helped by its title: Exposition internationale des Arts et des Techniques dans la Vie moderne. Although the Governments of India, Palestine, South Africa, New Zealand and Australia were all invited to participate in the mid-1930s, the message given by the British Government was that this was an exhibition 'in which the colonies would not be particularly interested'.[27] Perhaps this dismissive attitude towards the participation of the British empire was dictated by the fact that there was a substantial section given to France's colonial possessions on the Ile des Cygnes, a little way downstream from the main exhibition grounds, and so once more, following the 1931 'Exposition coloniale' in Paris, the representation of Britain's colonies could be only tokenistic in these circumstances (Britain had actually refused to participate in 1931). As a consequence, the representation of Britain's empire and of imperialism was minimal and the weld between nation and empire, so successfully achieved in Johannesburg, had, seemingly, simply disappeared. That this was not a permanent separation of British nation and British empire became quickly evident both in the Glasgow Empire Exhibition of 1938 and the combined United Kingdom and British Empire Pavilion at the New York World's Fair of 1939.

But what was most confusing was the category of exhibition planned for Paris in 1937. Certainly it was initially agreed that Paris

1937 would be a 'second category' exhibition and this meant, according to the 1928 International Convention, that it was neither industrial nor competitive (meaning no separate pavilions).[28] In the event Germany and the USSR, and many of the other participating countries, did not observe that distinction. The British felt a march had been stolen on them: suddenly, for example, late in 1936 the British Embassy in Paris discovered that Germany was putting £380,000 into its pavilion whereas they were budgeting for only £30,000.[29] The final result of these manoeuvres was the most memorable image of the exhibition: the face-off between 'worlds on exhibition' – between the German Pavilion and the Soviet Pavilion, with the German eagle atop its tower looking across at the colossal pair of sculpted Soviet workers.

The British Pavilion was located on the other side of the Seine, sited at the corner of the Place d'Honneur among a small group of foreign pavilions, opposite the Belgian Pavilion, beside the Canadian and Swedish Pavilions, and close to the Eiffel Tower and the French regional section (Figure 22). Responsibility for planning the pavilion

22 British Pavilion, International Exhibition, Paris, 1937; architect – Oliver Hill (perspective by J. D. M. Harvey)

was given by the Department of Overseas Trade to the Council for Art and Industry, newly formed in 1934 and chaired by Frank Pick.[30] The architect for the pavilion, Oliver Hill, was certainly not among the most advanced modernists in Britain at this time (he had no affiliation with the MARS Group, for instance) but he was keenly aware of contemporary developments, and skilled at eclectic compromises. Hill was also a member of Pick's stable of architects and artists, a group highly versed in the arts and crafts but keen to see them married with the machine and the machine aesthetic.[31] This attempted marriage can be seen in the main body of the pavilion, a rectangular volume painted predominantly white but with red details and a blue lower level, its length hardly enlivened by a long spray-painted frieze by John Skeaping. This combination of the arts was what Pick, in a clear reference to national projection, called 'a definite publicity value, based upon architectural or decorative treatment with a dramatic or pictorial quality to attract the attention of the public'.[32]

Although it had no Court of Honour and no imperial map, unlike both Wembley and Johannesburg, Hill's design did encompass several of the features found in previous British Pavilions, even if these features tended to be both more abstract in form and, despite the smooth white surfaces, somewhat piecemeal. Like the British Pavilion at the 1925 Exposition des Arts décoratifs, in Paris, which had a free-standing and distinctively designed restaurant between it and the river,[33] Hill's pavilion was linked by a bridge over the Quai d'Orsay to a buttery, also beside the river but presenting to it a windowless wall. Each of the three smaller units in this group – entrance cube, bridge and buttery – had strong circular features: a circular ceiling within the entrance cube; a drum over the bridging section, and the circular form of the buttery with its curved wall projecting under the bridge. Most interesting, perhaps, in relation to the issue of imperial representation was the circular drum that formed the bridge, with the royal arms hanging beneath and the *porte-cochère* below flanked by long pillars. Here was a reminiscence of the drums, domes and colonnades of the pavilions at Johannesburg and Wembley, but reduced to the simplest shapes and the most basic honorific role – converted effectively into the language of Le Corbusier's modernism.

In other respects Hill's design drew back from a thoroughgoing modernism, perhaps in accord with Pick's own growing antipathy towards it.[34] A narrow line was to be walked, treating the building as a shell expressive of simplicity and directness but not evocative of 'continental tricks', Pick's term for uncompromising modernism.[35] Inevitably the distinction was missed by many: 'the shell should have been in keeping with some suggestion of national tradition . . . Instead of which . . . it might have been designed by the foreign ultra-modernists'.[36] Nevertheless, it is tempting to see the pavilion as an attempt at conciliation or appeasement between tradition and modernity, between a feeling for the national independence of craft traditions and an international aesthetic: for instance, the use of various artists working in various mediums to decorate the inside and outside of the building evoked arts and crafts ideals, the tall vertical windows had enough of the neo-Georgian about them to offset some of the abstract modernist geometries elsewhere, and the traditional symbols of royalty (despite Pick's opposition) and nationality were still present.[37]

This appeasement continued inside. Pick's idea for the pavilion's contents, dating back to 1935,[38] was that they should be based around certain English words adopted in French and supposedly representative of British institutions: tennis, bridge, tea, sport, the week-end and so on. This provided the peg for a display of functional objects created in a British tradition of craftsmanship and linked by having accepted connotations of British culture: they would be 'comely and pleasant . . . a liberal conspectus of our English life'.[39] Objects like sports rackets and bats would demonstrate the fitness for purpose that Pick had learned to admire from writers like William Lethaby.[40] In Pick's words, these and other such objects 'represent a condensation and materialization of experience stretching over many years':[41] they were more culturally specific than the *objets-types* of Le Corbusier, in that they embodied a long experience of 'condensation' within a national tradition. In the display of 'week-end houses' British architecture was to be seen as an integral part of a European movement: 'it is alleged that the furnished rooms reveal an international rather than a British style, as though current movements in design were continental only and not European; as though Great Britain were not a part of Europe'.[42] To offset this, the week-end house was also regarded as manifesting a typically British institution, despite its class-specific nature.[43] Democracy was thought to have an important place here: 'to us [it] means more than a mode of government: it means a fashion of living which leaves men and women free to express themselves'.[44] In other words, 'freedom' meant the freedom to have 'happy and comfortable ways of living'.[45] If democracy was to be defined as a 'fashion of living', then it might easily seem class-specific, smug and insubstantial. Nevertheless, Charles Reilly supported this linkage: the pavilion 'has exactly the right attitude for a democratic country which still cultivates free and open discussion'.[46] These are obviously very different kinds of sentiments than might have been possible in a pavilion that sought to represent Britain as the 'heart of empire'; indeed Pick preferred to imagine Britain as merely 'an outlying island in the Atlantic off the coasts of Europe'.[47]

Within the pavilion, the most prominent architectural feature was a grand spiral ramp at the far end of the main hall from the entrance, which led down to a lower riverside hall. A large photomural was arranged in a semi-circular well around the ramp showing a regressive touristic vision of English landscape scenes, with giant pictures of traditional figures (a shepherd in a smock, a girl in Welsh national costume), including Prime Minister Neville Chamberlain as a fisherman, suspended in front of it. Meanwhile transport, the central and sometimes the exclusive subject of British Pavilions since 1924, was allotted merely a shallow window between textiles and weekend houses. Although nothing directly attested to Britain's imperial role,[48] Chamberlain's Tory mythology of class stability and pre-industrial yeoman traditions was given a newly revamped image through its association with the technique of photomontage and the *élan* of the modernist ramp.[49] Effectively, this spiral and its photomural had taken over the typological role of the Court of Honour of previous national pavilions.

A 'mere box'

Reactions to the British Pavilion were predominantly hostile. The main criticisms were that it was indecorous or undignified and insufficiently British. These aspects were commented upon even by French critics who were surprised by the light-hearted display and even more by the lack of clear national attributes in the building.[50] Attacks on the pavilion tended not to distinguish its exhibits from their container: 'dignity' was at stake in both. The *Daily Express* found the pavilion too commercial 'cheap, tawdry, inadequate, a shop display, a one-class exhibition', and for the *Southern Daily Echo* 'every Briton feels humiliated at the sorry figure cut by his own country'.[51] The point here is that where these commercial qualities were suitable for an exhibition devoted to the decorative arts, as in the Paris Exhibition of 1925, they were out of step with what had become an exhibition of national industrial and, by implication, military power in 1937. When questions were asked in Parliament – and even the prime minister was drawn into the controversy – the Council for Art and Industry was forced to conduct an inquest.[52] A number of points were made about perceptions of the pavilion. There was felt to be a problem deriving from the comparisons inevitably made at the exhibition: the pavilion was smaller than Belgium's, opposite it; contrasted with the German and Italian Pavilions, the British could hardly look other than insipid and indecisive; and, compared to the Soviet display, Britain appeared pampered and idle.[53]

Criticism of the British Pavilion from the Right was to be expected, but criticism from the liberal Left was often couched in similar terms. J. M. Richards, writing in the *Architectural Review*, explicitly contrasted the pavilion with the ideals of national projection and, echoing the *Daily Express*'s views, found it wanting – still essentially a trade show and lacking in the new kinds of subject-matter that Tallents had advocated.[54] For the *New Statesman*'s Raymond Mortimer, the British Pavilion in Paris was 'penurious ... a mere box [with] a bleak, windowless and boring wall to the river'.[55] Mortimer's editor was Kingsley Martin, who also wrote, retrospectively, in negative terms:

> Britain was modestly housed in something that looked like a white packing-case. When you went in, the first thing you saw was a cardboard Chamberlain fishing in rubber waders and, beyond, an elegant pattern of golf balls, a frieze of tennis rackets, polo sets, riding equipment, natty dinner jackets and, by a pleasant transition, agreeable pottery and textiles, books finely printed and photographs of the English countryside. I stared in bewilderment. Could this be England? If so, it was the England of the cultivated rich or perhaps of the England foreseen by Bernard Shaw when Britain's economy would depend on the export of chocolate creams. An entirely upper-class England.[56]

Two elements in Martin's commentary stand out: the image of a rural and artisanal but also sport-loving upper-class England; and the image of the 'white packing-case'. The first provided what had become a common retreat from the problems of modernity for national identity, and to seek national character in the land and pre-industrial history was also to avoid the conundrums of the links between national and imperial identities.[57] As for the second, many modernist architects in the late 1930s would not have been unhappy to have one of their buildings called a 'white packing-case', or indeed 'a mere box'. Perhaps for any of the young modernists who had read Le Corbusier such phrases might suggest a purposefulness and simplicity, a lack or pretension, even perhaps a purity of intent. For a few reviewers this simplicity spoke of modesty. *Country Life*'s reviewer, in a sometimes lukewarm commentary, felt relief on arriving at the British Pavilion with its 'friendly, unostentatious and even whimsical atmosphere'.[58] Howard Robertson, the architect of the pavilion in Johannesburg, even suggested that simplicity was a national characteristic, 'for the English tradition is always of external reticence.'[59]

For other observers, however, the 'mere box' or 'white packing-case' was mute – at least it spoke no language that they recognized. Boxes and packing-cases may be useful but they were not to be looked at:

they were not decorous, and they implied not just a cheap and tossed-off object but an attitude that was far too contingent and rough and ready. If it was daring to produce a building that had none of the conventional attributes of 'dignity', that key concept in these circumstances, and little reference to royalty or to the empire, it could also be regarded as foolhardy. The *Daily Express* described it as 'a grey-white, practically square structure. Its walls from the outside look like great advertisement hoardings . . . it is one of the ugliest buildings in the exhibition'.[60] *The Times*, which preferred the German Pavilion, printed a series of letters attacking Hill's construction as a building that 'might be anywhere, a riding school, an aerodrome, or a factory on or off the Great West Road'.[61] The *Journal of the RIBA* gained the impression 'of a stutterer saying nothing very important.'[62] The *Marseille libre* exclaimed: 'Pauvre Angleterre!' Even Pick confessed to finding the exterior of the building 'dull' and lacking in 'pictorial or dramatic quality'.[63]

There was undoubtedly, therefore, a huge risk in using architectural modernism, even of a diluted kind, for national projection in 1937. It might be said that, unlike the British Pavilion in Johannesburg, the semiotics of Hill's pavilion in Paris were both too internally contradictory and too unspecific in their referentiality to address and be significant to a sizeable language community. If architecture is, as Umberto Eco has described it, 'a system of rules for giving society what it expects in the way of architecture',[64] then the pavilion had simply failed to establish clear enough correspondences with previous buildings to connect with such expectations. And if the correspondences required were with non-architectural dispositions, then again the pavilion failed to make sufficient connection. By contrast, the modernist Spanish Pavilion, which deeply impressed many observers in 1937, was understood as standing for embattled anti-fascist democracy and internationalism because of that with which the Spanish Republic itself was identified. And that message was reinforced by what was inside the pavilion, from its photomontages of the new woman to its work by artists who had died in the defence of Madrid, and most of all its rapidly iconicized *Guernica*.[65] Modernism had no established linkage with Britain's national image and aspirations, and even the organizers of the British Pavilion were equivocal about the idea of it as a symbol of internationalism. On the one hand Pick was distrustful of 'continental tricks', while on the other Tallents would probably have approved of the internationalist links forged by other modernist national pavilions, like those of Finland, Czechoslovakia and Sweden. Furthermore modernism did not have ties at this time with Britain's imperial image, where the closest approximation was the pavilion at

[196]

the Johannesburg Exhibition the previous year, modernist perhaps only in its undecorated geometric volumes. At the heart of the disputes about the British Pavilion in Paris lay differences invested in defining British national identity: principally, those concerned with the durability of attributes and the dignity of the link between nation and empire, and those who felt a new alliance might be made with the emerging forms of modernism under the sign of 'national projection'. Ultimately, such interests proved irreconcilable.

Notes

Research for this article was supported by a Leverhulme Trust Fellowship.

1 Quoted in Philip M. Taylor, *The Projection of Britain: British Overseas Publicity and Propaganda 1919–1939*, Cambridge, Cambridge University Press, 1981, p. 104.
2 Taylor, *The Projection of Britain*, pp. 88, 192.
3 Quoted in Adrian Forty, ' "Europe is no more than a nation made up of several others . . .": thoughts on architecture and nationality, prompted by the Taylor Institute and the Martyrs Memorial in Oxford', *AA Files*, vol, 32, autumn 1996, p. 30.
4 Forty, ' "Europe is no more than . . ." ', p. 30.
5 Forty, ' "Europe is no more than . . ." ', pp. 30–1.
6 Some of these problems are explored in M. Crinson, *Empire Building: Orientalism and Victorian Architecture*, London, Routledge, 1996, ch. 5.
7 After his work at the EMB Tallents became the BBC's controller of public relations in 1935 and, later, from 1948 to 1949, the first president of the Institute of Public Relations. His influence on architecture and design was recognized by his Honorary ARIBA in 1946 and his presidency of the Design and Industries' Association in 1954: *Dictionary of National Biography*.
8 Stephen Tallents, *The Projection of England*, London, Faber & Faber, 1932, reprinted edn, London, Olen Press, 1955, p. 25.
9 Tallents, *The Projection of England*, p. 34.
10 Tallents, *The Projection of England*, pp. 34–5.
11 Tallents, *The Projection of England*, p. 38.
12 Cf. Forty, ' "Europe is no more than . . ." ', p. 31. Forty argues that 'because of the association of nationality with racism, the general view among modernists after 1945 was that architecture should *suppress* its nationality and concentrate on the development of a universal, non-national formal language' (p. 36).
13 Michael T. Saler, *The Avant-Garde in Interwar England: Medieval Modernism and the London Underground*, Oxford, Oxford University Press, 1999.
14 Saler, *The Avant-Garde in Interwar England*, pp. 75–6, 117.
15 Relations with certain discrepant forms of continental modernism, such as Adolf Loos's paradoxical attitude to technology and his admiration of English culture, might be pursued in relation to 'medieval modernism': see, for instance, Janet Stewart, *Fashioning Vienna – Adolf Loos's Cultural Criticism*, London, Routledge, 2000, pp. 51–5.
16 'Medieval modernism' also gives the lie to arguments that the arts in 1930s' Britain were largely characterized by divergent tendencies, either towards internationalism or towards landscape traditions and the picturesque: see Charles Harrison, 'England's climate', in Brian Allen (ed.) *Towards a Modern Art World*, New Haven, CT, Yale University Press, 1995.
17 One important difference was Pick's attitude to continental modernism, which he saw as negatively 'cosmopolitan' and severed from national traditions: Saler, *The Avant-Garde in Interwar England*, p. 116. This, as will be seen, was his eventual view of the British Pavilion in 1937.

18 Lawrence Weaver, *Exhibitions and the Arts of Display*, London, Country Life, 1925, p. 88.

19 This upper floor was rearranged as a 'Court of Heroes' and a bronze figure of St George was added when the exhibition was extended into 1925: *Guide to the Pavilion of His Majesty's Government*, London, British Empire Exhibition, 1925.

20 The pavilion was designed by Howard Robertson and in several features was a near copy of the same architect's British Pavilion at the International Exhibition in Brussels of the previous year. That pavilion had been attacked as unworthy of the aspiration to national projection because as a 'solely commercial trade show . . . [it was] too narrow and not very dignified': J. M. Richards, 'The problem of national projection', *Architectural Review*, vol. 82, September 1937, p. 104.

21 *South Africa*, 25 January 1936.

22 *Star*, 18 September 1936.

23 *Guide to the Pavilion of H. M. Government in the United Kingdom*, Johannesburg, Empire Exhibition South Africa, 1936, p. 3.

24 *Rhodesia Herald*, 18 September 1936. For other reactions to the pavilion see M. Crinson, *Modern Architecture and the End of Empire*, London, Ashgate, 2003, ch. 4.

25 This was recognized, beyond Britain, in the pages of the *New York Times*: see quotation in *Architectural Forum*, vol. 67, September 1937, p. 174.

26 See Crinson, *Modern Architecture*, ch. 4.

27 Public Record Office (PRO), BT 60/38/1. India did not participate, but Australia and South Africa both eventually contributed pavilions located some way down the Champ de Mars. There was also an unofficial pavilion from Palestine, the Pavilion of Israel in Palestine: PRO, CO 323/1500/13.

28 PRO, BT 60/38/1. The French had planned in mid-1935 to build a series of linked pavilions for the foreign displays, and this was what the British were working towards until spring 1936: PRO, BT 60/38/4.

29 PRO, BT 60/38/2.

30 PRO, BT 60/38/1.

31 See Saler, *The Avant-Garde in Interwar England*, pp. 141–2.

32 PRO, BT 57/22.

33 For the 1925 pavilion see *The Builder*, vol. 129, 24 July 1925, p. 134, and 22 May 1925, p. 788; *Architectural Review*, vol. 58, July 1925, p. 3; and *Building News*, vol. 128, 22 May 1925, p. 788.

34 Saler, *The Avant-Garde in Interwar England*, p. 158. A modernist critic like H.-R. Hitchcock would fault the design for its moderation: *Architectural Forum*, vol. 67, September 1937, p. 168.

35 The term was used by Pick to oppose the suggestion that Moholy-Nagy should be one of the designers: 'The pavilion is a British pavilion and Mr Moholy-Nagy has not got the British tradition, I fear. We must not be tempted to copy the latest continental tricks': RIBA Hi 0/63/1.

36 *Morning Post*, 16 January 1937.

37 PRO, BT 57/21. The window near the entrance was sandblasted with an image of Britannia.

38 PRO, BT 60/38/1.

39 RIBA Hi 0/61/4.

40 See Christian Barman, *The Man Who Built London Transport: A Biography of Frank Pick*, Newton Abbot: David & Charles, 1979, pp. 175–6. Michael Saler sees the pavilion as evidence of a sea-change in Pick's aesthetics, away from modernism: Saler, *The Avant-Garde in Interwar England*, pp. 158–9.

41 RIBA Hi 0/61/4 – anonymous CAI paper (probably by Pick) dated 9 October 1937.

42 RIBA Hi 0/61/4.

43 The RIBA was responsible for this. For their thinking behind the concept see *Journal of the RIBA*, vol. 44, 5 December 1936, p. 111.

44 Frank Pick, Foreword to Catalogue of the pavilion, in PRO BT 57/19. For Pick,

English life embraced Scotland, Wales and Northern Ireland, though Scotland had a separate section in the display.

45 Frank Pick in *The Listener*, 19 May 1937, p. 973.

46 C. H. Reilly, Letter to the editor, *The Times*, 19 July 1937.

47 *The Listener*, 19 May 1937, p. 973.

48 An absence very rarely commented on at the time, but see *The Listener*, 28 July 1937.

49 A similar mythology might be found in Stanley Baldwin's *On England and Other Addresses*, London, Philip Allen, 1926.

50 See *Revue mensuelle de l'association des anciens élèves de l'école des hautes études commerciales*, no. 54, October 1937, pp. 58–9.

51 *Daily Express*, 6 August 1937; *Southern Daily Echo*, 20 July 1937.

52 PRO, BT 61/62/8.

53 Weak arguments were presented against the notion that the displays were non-intellectual and upper class biased: PRO, BT 57/19.

54 J. M. Richards, 'The problem of national projection', *Architectural Review*, vol. 82, September 1937, pp. 104–5.

55 *New Statesman*, 31 July 1937.

56 Kingsley Martin, *Editor*, Harmondsworth: Penguin, 1969, p. 223.

57 See, for instance, both Stanley Baldwin's Introduction and the essays in Arthur Bryant (ed.) *The Man and the Hour. Studies of Six Great Men of Our Time*, London, Philip Allen, 1934. I am grateful to Andrew Causey for this reference.

58 *Country Life*, 24 July 1937, p. 93. The reviewer was Christopher Hussey, an ally of Pick, who wrote this review using much of Pick's publicity material and before he had even seen the pavilion: RIBA Hi 0/63/1 Pick–Hill, 9 August 1937.

59 *Architects' Journal*, 26 August 1937, p. 329.

60 *Daily Express*, 6 August 1937.

61 Quoted in Barman, *The Man Who Built London Transport*, p. 193.

62 *Journal of the RIBA*, vol. 44, 17 July 1937, p. 911.

63 *Marseille Libre*, 12 September 1937; PRO, BT 60/40/2.

64 Umberto Eco, 'Function and sign: the semiotics of architecture', in Neil Leach (ed.) *Rethinking Architecture*, London, Routledge, 1997, p. 194.

65 On the Spanish Pavilion see Marko Daniel, 'Spain: culture at war', in Hayward Gallery, *Art and Power: Europe Under the Dictators 1930–45*, London, South Bank Centre, 1996, pp. 63–8.

INDEX